A MYSTIC'S GUIDE TO 2023

NICOLE MARIE

BALBOA.PRESS

A DIVISION OF HAY HOUSE

Balboa Press books may be ordered through booksellers or by contacting:

Balboa Press
A Division of Hay House
1663 Liberty Drive
Bloomington, IN 47403
www.balboapress.com
844-682-1282

ISBN: 979-8-7652-3032-9 (sc)
ISBN: 979-8-7652-3031-2 (e)

Library of Congress Control Number: 2022911515

Print information available on the last page.

Balboa Press rev. date: 07/08/2022

TABLE OF CONTENTS

Section 1

Welcome to 2023 2

Your 2023 Mindset................... 5

Fixed vs Growth Mindset 6

Life Inventory 9

Wheel of Life 10

Limiting Beliefs....................... 12

Your Ideal Life........................ 14

Section 2

Finding Your Zen................16–24

Consult the Universe 25-27

2023 Year Ahead 28

2023 Astrological Dates............30

Section 3

JANUARY...........................32–71

FEBRUARY....................... 72–107

MARCH 108–147

APRIL 148–185

MAY 186–225

JUNE 226–263

JULY 264–303

AUGUST 304–343

SEPTEMBER 344–381

OCTOBER.......................382–421

NOVEMBER 422–459

DECEMBER 460–498

This Guidebook belongs to:

_____

We're back. I almost can't believe it, but here we are. It is my incredible, humbled pleasure to have created, **A Mystic's Guide to 2023**. Sometimes, I just sit back in amazement. Have you ever done that? Have you ever created something and then looked at it and thought, "Oh man, I did that?"

My ultimate goal for this project is to help people condense what they feel is necessary when planning their year, giving them more time to create, instead of being bogged down by the action of filling out an entire planner. For me personally, I previously had more planners and workbooks then I knew what to do with, which left me confused, overwhelmed and ultimately, immobile. I did nothing, created nothing. I stood still. Ever done that? *(I bet not because you had last year's planner, huh?)* Well, if you have felt that way, too, then I think you'll find this year's upgrades to be wildly helpful.

What I hope you will find in the pages of this planner, is a deeply woven love for creation and education. A place where you can connect with a primal version of yourself and feel the magic of creating something new. Where you can use the manifestation techniques Tesla discovered many years before us. A tool designed to help you align with the cosmos and move into the divine. This planner is an invitation to step into yourself, your true self.

Just as with the first edition, the purchase of this planner is in direct support of the Project Iris program. **Project Iris** is a local program aimed at teaching children the power of creation and sustainability. Focusing on plant education in early childhood teaches children how to develop environmentally conscious behaviors and the power of creation. When I was ill and battling for my life, I found solace in my garden, learning magic and hope. I learned healing remedies and how to craft intentions, but most of all, I learned what it felt like to grow something. By purchasing this planner, you have helped sponsor a child in our mission of bringing this same hope and learning to children across the Valley. Thank you, from the bottom of our hearts, for your contribution.

We have a huge dream. One that is focused on budget-friendly sustainability for American families, while cutting down on the harsh chemicals entering our homes through our **EcoWitch** initiative. For more information on Project Iris or how to convert your own home, please scan the QR code in the bottom corner.

Last, but not least, you'll probably notice this planner is a little lighter than last year - true, but we didn't skimp on content. **Our QR code will take you to a "Linktree" style web page, allowing you to reach all the supplemental content you may need. This includes chakra testing, mediations, and all other downloadables. Please do not skip this step.**

Now, let's go create!

Links

2023 AT A GLANCE

JANUARY

S	M	T	W	T	F	S
1	2	3	4	5	6	7
8	9	10	11	12	13	14
15	16	17	18	19	20	21
22	23	24	25	26	27	28
29	30	31				

FEBRUARY

S	M	T	W	T	F	S
			1	2	3	4
5	6	7	8	9	10	11
12	13	14	15	16	17	18
19	20	21	22	23	24	25
26	27	28				

MARCH

S	M	T	W	T	F	S
			1	2	3	4
5	6	7	8	9	10	11
12	13	14	15	16	17	18
19	20	21	22	23	24	25
26	27	28	29	30	31	

APRIL

S	M	T	W	T	F	S
						1
2	3	4	5	6	7	8
9	10	11	12	13	14	15
16	17	18	19	20	21	22
23	24	25	26	27	28	29
30						

MAY

S	M	T	W	T	F	S
	1	2	3	4	5	6
7	8	9	10	11	12	13
14	15	16	17	18	19	20
21	22	23	24	25	26	27
28	29	30	31			

JUNE

S	M	T	W	T	F	S
				1	2	3
4	5	6	7	8	9	10
11	12	13	14	15	16	17
18	19	20	21	22	23	24
25	26	27	28	29	30	

JULY

S	M	T	W	T	F	S
						1
2	3	4	5	6	7	8
9	10	11	12	13	14	15
16	17	18	19	20	21	22
23	24	25	26	27	28	29
30	31					

AUGUST

S	M	T	W	T	F	S
		1	2	3	4	5
6	7	8	9	10	11	12
13	14	15	16	17	18	19
20	21	22	23	24	25	26
27	28	29	30	31		

SEPTEMBER

S	M	T	W	T	F	S
					1	2
3	4	5	6	7	8	9
10	11	12	13	14	15	16
17	18	19	20	21	22	23
24	25	26	27	28	29	30

OCTOBER

S	M	T	W	T	F	S
1	2	3	4	5	6	7
8	9	10	11	12	13	14
15	16	17	18	19	20	21
22	23	24	25	26	27	28
29	30	31				

NOVEMBER

S	M	T	W	T	F	S
			1	2	3	4
5	6	7	8	9	10	11
12	13	14	15	16	17	18
19	20	21	22	23	24	25
26	27	28	29	30		

DECEMBER

S	M	T	W	T	F	S
					1	2
3	4	5	6	7	8	9
10	11	12	13	14	15	16
17	18	19	20	21	22	23
24	25	26	27	28	29	30
31						

JANUARY

S	M	T	W	T	F	S
	1	2	3	4	5	6
7	8	9	10	11	12	13
14	15	16	17	18	19	20
21	22	23	24	25	26	27
28	29	30	31			

FEBRUARY

S	M	T	W	T	F	S
				1	2	3
4	5	6	7	8	9	10
11	12	13	14	15	16	17
18	19	20	21	22	23	24
25	26	27	28	29		

MARCH

S	M	T	W	T	F	S
					1	2
3	4	5	6	7	8	9
10	11	12	13	14	15	16
17	18	19	20	21	22	23
24	25	26	27	28	29	30
31						

APRIL

S	M	T	W	T	F	S
	1	2	3	4	5	6
7	8	9	10	11	12	13
14	15	16	17	18	19	20
21	22	23	24	25	26	27
28	29	30				

MAY

S	M	T	W	T	F	S
			1	2	3	4
5	6	7	8	9	10	11
12	13	14	15	16	17	18
19	20	21	22	23	24	25
26	27	28	29	30	31	

JUNE

S	M	T	W	T	F	S
						1
2	3	4	5	6	7	8
9	10	11	12	13	14	15
16	17	18	19	20	21	22
23	24	25	26	27	28	29
30						

JULY

S	M	T	W	T	F	S
	1	2	3	4	5	6
7	8	9	10	11	12	13
14	15	16	17	18	19	20
21	22	23	24	25	26	27
28	29	30	31			

AUGUST

S	M	T	W	T	F	S
				1	2	3
4	5	6	7	8	9	10
11	12	13	14	15	16	17
18	19	20	21	22	23	24
25	26	27	28	29	30	31

SEPTEMBER

S	M	T	W	T	F	S
1	2	3	4	5	6	7
8	9	10	11	12	13	14
15	16	17	18	19	20	21
22	23	24	25	26	27	28
29	30					

OCTOBER

S	M	T	W	T	F	S
		1	2	3	4	5
6	7	8	9	10	11	12
13	14	15	16	17	18	19
20	21	22	23	24	25	26
27	28	29	30	31		

NOVEMBER

S	M	T	W	T	F	S
					1	2
3	4	5	6	7	8	9
10	11	12	13	14	15	16
17	18	19	20	21	22	23
24	25	26	27	28	29	30

DECEMBER

S	M	T	W	T	F	S
1	2	3	4	5	6	7
8	9	10	11	12	13	14
15	16	17	18	19	20	21
22	23	24	25	26	27	28
29	30	31				

YOUR 2023 MANTRAS

Mantras, or affirmations, are positive verbal statements we confirm with ourselves daily. These mantras are powerful tools we can use to support us in directing energy towards the visions we have for our lives. Starting your day with your own personal mantras is the first step in creating your best year yet.

Suggested Daily Mantras:

1. I am worthy of love; I am loved.
2. My capacity to achieve my goals is limitless.
3. I trust my intuition.
4. I am abundant, wealth flows easily to me.
5. The universe is always working for my highest good.

My Personal Daily Mantras:

1. _____

2. _____

3. _____

4. _____

5. _____

5 Goals I want to Achieve this Year:

1. _____

2. _____

3. _____

4. _____

5. _____

FIXED vs GROWTH MINDSET

Our mindset affects every area of our lives—they can keep us stuck or fuel our growth. A fixed mindset is the belief that certain traits are innate and cannot be changed or learned. A growth mindset means you can acquire and improve the traits you desire over time. Only a growth mindset will allow us to truly meet our highest potential.

Below are examples of how a fixed versus growth mindset may show up in our lives. This exercise will help you start to shift your fixed mindset into a growth mindset.

	Fixed Mindset	Growth Mindset
Challenges	I avoid challenges so I don't have to worry about failing.	Challenges are a way for me to improve.
Desires	I only stick to what I know.	I want to try new things.
Skills	I can only be good or bad at what I create.	There is always more for me to learn or improve.
Obstacles	I'm not any good and I cannot change it.	I can adapt my approach until I succeed.
Success of Others	It's not fair they are successful while I am not.	I am inspired by the success of others and am open to learning from them.
Criticism	I feel threatened and defensive when I am criticized.	I am able to learn and grow from the feedback I receive.

Two things I feel are a fixed mindset about myself:	Two things I want to shift into a growth mindset:

CHANGING YOUR MIND

In this exercise we will identify your mindset in a range of areas to discover where you can shift your mindset more productively. It's important to note that productive in this case means anything encouraging you to take action and work towards a solution. Take a moment to think about the prompt, consider how you could shift your fixed mindset into a growth mindset, and then write your adjustments in the blanks.

How do I react when I don't develop the skills I want quickly enough?

How do I react when obstacles occur? Do I give up or find a way?

How do I express my desires, gratitude, or successes?

How do I react to criticism? Do I feel threatened or get defensive?

SELF-ASSESSMENT

Use the following to gauge your well-being across multiple aspects of life, including physical, emotional, spiritual, and professional. At the end of the assessment, you'll create a plan to help you improve upon each of these areas in your life.

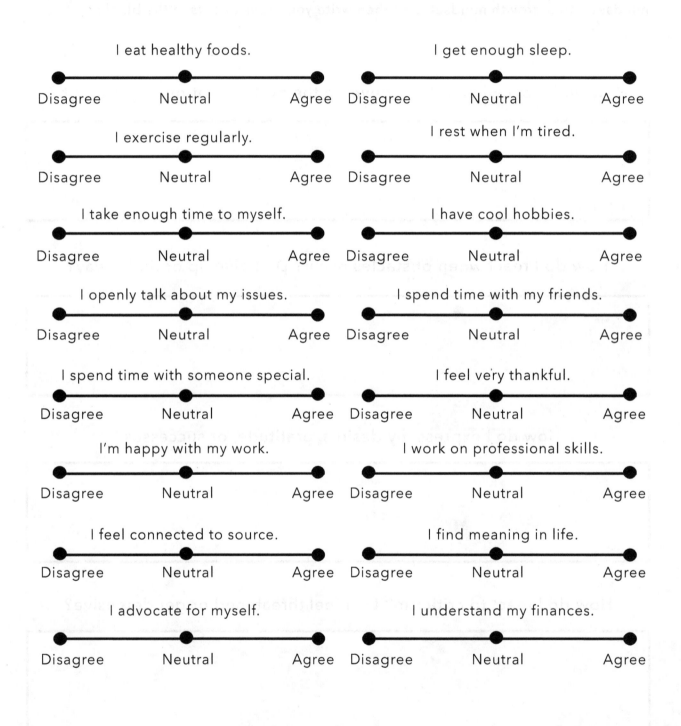

I eat healthy foods.

Disagree   Neutral   Agree

I get enough sleep.

Disagree   Neutral   Agree

I exercise regularly.

Disagree   Neutral   Agree

I rest when I'm tired.

Disagree   Neutral   Agree

I take enough time to myself.

Disagree   Neutral   Agree

I have cool hobbies.

Disagree   Neutral   Agree

I openly talk about my issues.

Disagree   Neutral   Agree

I spend time with my friends.

Disagree   Neutral   Agree

I spend time with someone special.

Disagree   Neutral   Agree

I feel very thankful.

Disagree   Neutral   Agree

I'm happy with my work.

Disagree   Neutral   Agree

I work on professional skills.

Disagree   Neutral   Agree

I feel connected to source.

Disagree   Neutral   Agree

I find meaning in life.

Disagree   Neutral   Agree

I advocate for myself.

Disagree   Neutral   Agree

I understand my finances.

Disagree   Neutral   Agree

LIFE INVENTORY

Using your self-assessment from the previous page, you'll now rank each category from one-to-ten, based on how fulfilled you feel about each. In the boxes provided, note what you are or are not satisfied with for each section. This exercise is a snapshot of where you're at currently and is good to do periodically (every six months, ideally).

Rank each category as follows: 1 being completely unsatisfied and 10 being completely satisfied.

RELATIONSHIPS

1	2	3	4	5	6	7	8	9	10

FINANCE

1	2	3	4	5	6	7	8	9	10

CAREER

1	2	3	4	5	6	7	8	9	10

HEALTH/WELLNESS

1	2	3	4	5	6	7	8	9	10

SPIRITUALITY

1	2	3	4	5	6	7	8	9	10

PERSONAL GROWTH

1	2	3	4	5	6	7	8	9	10

WHEEL OF LIFE

In the following pages, we'll begin to explore a technique called scripting. Scripting is a written manifestation exercise. It is ideal for those who struggle with visualization, or seeing imagery in their mind's eye. In this exercise, we are focusing on what we want to bring to life this year. Then, on the next page, you'll have space to write out what you're happy with in each category, where you need to put in work to improve, and what you desire for each section of your life.

Rate each slice from one-to-ten: 1 denoting very little attention is needed and 10 being a lot of attention is necessary.

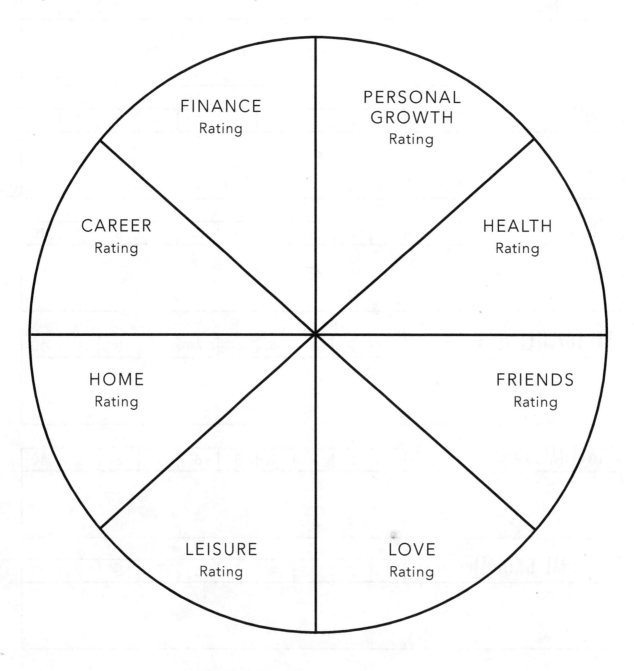

WHEEL OF LIFE

PERSONAL GROWTH

HEALTH

FRIENDS

LOVE

LEISURE

HOME

CAREER

FINANCE

LIMITING BELIEFS

The purpose of this section is to help identify any limiting beliefs preventing your growth. There is always a better narrative we can speak into existence and this practice will help with reframing your own beliefs in a more productive way. In the left column, list the limiting beliefs you feel are most prominent in your life currently, and then on the right, list how you can reframe the belief into an open-ended format.

Current Limiting Beliefs

New Limitless Beliefs

EXAMPLE	EXAMPLE
Money doesn't grow on trees.	The more I give, the more I will receive.

LIMITING BELIEFS

Now, we will learn how to further investigate the limiting beliefs holding us back. Our realities are a direct reflection of our strongest beliefs. When we get to the root of how these beliefs were formed, it allows us to better understand how we can work through them. In working through our beliefs, we can then release ourselves from the limitations and move towards our growth.

What belief is holding me back?

How old does this belief feel?

Where did this belief come from?

How has this belief shaped your life?

MY IDEAL LIFE

A method used to accomplish your goals can be by working backwards from what you would describe as your ideal life. What would your ideal day consist of? What would your mornings, afternoons, and evenings look like ideally? Where would you be and who would you be with? What experiences would you have? What would your professional life be like? Remember, this exercise is to give you a vision to work towards—you can come back and change it as needed at any time.

_____

_____

_____

_____

_____

_____

_____

_____

_____

_____

_____

_____

_____

_____

_____

_____

_____

_____

_____

_____

_____

_____

_____

FINDING YOUR ZEN

Physical aspects I need to work on...

_____
_____
_____
_____
_____

Emotional aspects I need to work on...

_____
_____
_____
_____
_____

AFFIRMATION:

I am connected to Mother Earth, grounded and secure. I am taking responsibility for my life.

Methods that help me connect...

_____
_____
_____
_____
_____

I feel most grounded when...

Tools I use are...

► _____
► _____
► _____
► _____
► _____

Things that represent abundance to me

● _____
● _____
● _____
● _____
● _____

I FEEL THE MOST SECURE WHEN...

_____
_____
_____
_____
_____
_____

Notes

_____
_____
_____
_____
_____
_____

CHANGES NOTED OVER TIME:

_____
_____

SACRAL CHAKRA

Physical aspects I need to work on...

_____
_____
_____
_____
_____
_____

Emotional aspects I need to work on...

_____
_____
_____
_____
_____
_____

AFFIRMATION:

I trust my feelings and give them room to flourish.

Methods that help me connect...

_____
_____
_____
_____
_____

I honor my body by...

Tools I use are...

► _____
► _____
► _____
► _____
► _____

Things that represent abundance to me

● _____
● _____
● _____
● _____
● _____

I FEEL THE MOST HAPPINESS WHEN...

_____
_____
_____
_____
_____
_____

Notes

_____
_____
_____
_____
_____
_____

CHANGES NOTED OVER TIME:

_____
_____

SOLAR PLEXUS CHAKRA

Physical aspects I need to work on...

_____

_____

_____

_____

_____

Emotional aspects I need to work on...

_____

_____

_____

_____

_____

Methods that help me connect...

I feel most confident when...

_____

_____

_____

_____

_____

Tools I use are...

► _____

► _____

► _____

► _____

► _____

Things that represent abundance to me

● _____

● _____

● _____

● _____

● _____

I FEEL THE MOST INNER-STRENGTH WHEN...

_____

_____

_____

_____

_____

Notes

_____

_____

_____

_____

_____

CHANGES NOTED OVER TIME:

_____

_____

Physical aspects I need to work on...

_____
_____
_____
_____
_____
_____

AFFIRMATION:

I choose to be united
with all beings,
visible and invisible.

Emotional aspects I need to work on...

_____
_____
_____
_____
_____

Methods that help me connect...

_____
_____
_____
_____
_____
_____

I feel most at peace when...

Tools I use are...

▶ _____
▶ _____
▶ _____
▶ _____
▶ _____

Things that represent abundance to me

● _____
● _____
● _____
● _____
● _____

I FEEL THE MOST LOVE & GRATITUDE WHEN...

_____
_____
_____
_____
_____

Notes

_____
_____
_____
_____
_____

CHANGES NOTED OVER TIME:

_____
_____

THROAT CHAKRA

Physical aspects I need to work on...

_____
_____
_____
_____
_____

AFFIRMATION:

I live my truth. I communicate my truth. I am my truth.

Emotional aspects I need to work on...

_____
_____
_____
_____
_____

Methods that help me connect...

I feel most comfortable speaking when...

_____
_____
_____
_____
_____
_____

Tools I use are...

► _____
► _____
► _____
► _____
► _____

Things that represent abundance to me

● _____
● _____
● _____
● _____
● _____

I FEEL FREE TO BE EXPRESSIVE WHEN...

_____
_____
_____
_____
_____
_____

Notes

_____
_____
_____
_____
_____
_____

CHANGES NOTED OVER TIME:

_____
_____

THIRD EYE CHAKRA

Physical aspects I need to work on...

_____
_____
_____
_____
_____
_____

AFFIRMATION:

I open myself to fully knowing my inner guidance and wisdom.

Emotional aspects I need to work on...

_____
_____
_____
_____
_____

Methods that help me connect...

I connect to my intuition when...

_____
_____
_____
_____
_____

Tools I use are...

▶ _____
▶ _____
▶ _____
▶ _____
▶ _____

Things that represent abundance to me

● _____
● _____
● _____
● _____
● _____

I FEEL MOST RECEPTIVE WHEN...

_____
_____
_____
_____
_____
_____

Notes

_____
_____
_____
_____
_____
_____

CHANGES NOTED OVER TIME:

_____
_____

CROWN CHAKRA

Physical aspects I need to work on...

_____
_____
_____
_____
_____

Emotional aspects I need to work on...

_____
_____
_____
_____
_____

Methods that help me connect...

_____
_____
_____
_____
_____

I feel connected when...

Tools I use are...

► _____
► _____
► _____
► _____
► _____

Things that represent abundance to me

● _____
● _____
● _____
● _____
● _____

I APPRECIATE...

_____
_____
_____
_____
_____
_____

Notes

_____
_____
_____
_____
_____
_____

CHANGES NOTED OVER TIME:

_____
_____

NOTES

NATAL CHART

NAME	
DOB	
BIRTH TIME	
BIRTH PLACE	
RULING PLANET	
RULING ELEMENT	
DOMINANT PLANET	
DOMINANT ELEMENT	
NOTES	

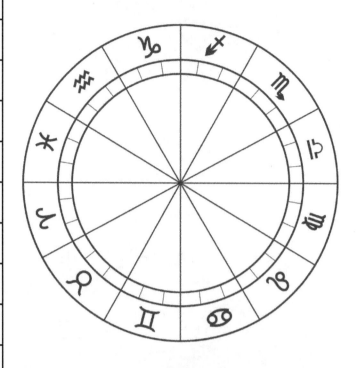

	SIGNS	HOUSES	☌	☍	△	□	✳	NOTES
☉								
☽								
☿								
♀								
♂								
♃								
♄								
♅								
♆								
♇								
AC								
MC								

NOTES

2023 YEAR AHEAD

THE YEAR AHEAD: This section is meant to allow you to use a form of divination (tarot, oracle, rune, etc) to interpret what the year has in store for you. Begin with a pull for the overall energy of the year, continue by writing each month's interpretation in the corresponding text box. This is optional and can be skipped if you do not utilize a divination tool appropriate for this format.

ENERGY THIS YEAR:

JANUARY:

FEBRUARY:

MARCH:

APRIL:

MAY:

JUNE:

JULY:

AUGUST:

SEPTEMBER:

OCTOBER:

NOVEMBER:

DECEMBER:

2023 ASTROLOGICAL DATES

RETROGRADES

MERCURY

12/29/22 - 1/15/23
4/21/23 - 5/14/23
8/23/23 - 9/15/23
12/13/23 - 1/1/24

VENUS

7/22/23 - 9/3/23

MARS

10/30/22 - 1/18/23

JUPITER

9/4/23 - 12/30/23

SATURN

6/17/23 - 11/4/23

NEPTUNE

6/30/23 - 12/6/23

URANUS

8/24/22 - 1/22/23
8/28/23 - 1/27/24

SUPER NEW MOON

1/21/23   2/20/23

SOLAR ECLIPSE

4/20/23   10/14/23

LUNAR ECLIPSE

5/5/23 - 5/6/23   10/28/23 - 10/29/23

SUPER FULL MOON

8/1/23
8/31/23

PLUTO RETROGRADE

5/1/23 - 10/10/23

JANUARY

SUNDAY	MONDAY	TUESDAY	WEDNESDAY
1	2 New Years Day	3	4
8	9	10	11
15	16 MLK Day	17	18
22	23	24	25
29	30	31	

2023

THURSDAY	FRIDAY	SATURDAY	NOTES
5	6 ○	7	
12	13	14 ◐	
19	20	21 ●	
26	27	28 ◑	

WOLF MOON

RITUAL FOCUS:
The wolf moon is a time for connecting with your higher spiritual self, embrace this by looking inward, rest and save your energy for the year to come.

ZODIACS:
Capricorn & Aquarius

CRYSTALS :
Jade & Moonstone

COLORS:
Black, White, Silver, Violet

ELEMENTS:
Earth & Air

DEITIES:
Inanna, Freyja, Skadi, Morrigan, Hecate

FLOWERS:
Carnation, Crocus, Snowdrops

ANIMALS:
Wolves, Foxes, Coyotes, Blue Jay, Pheasants

HERBS:
Marjoram, Thyme, Angelica, Holy Thistle, Patchouli, Pine, Lavender, Mimosa, Peppermint

MAGICAL ASSOCIATIONS:
Protection, Personal Development, Meditation, and focus.

DIVINATION TRACKER

DATE	PULL	MESSAGE

JANUARY TRANSITS

January 2023 Tropical Midnight Ephemeris

Time Zone: **EST (05:00 East)**

Day	☉	☽	+12 Hr	True☊	☿	♀	♂	♃	♄	♅	♆	♇
01 Su	10 ♑ 29 47	06 ♉ 17 36	12 ♉ 35 31	11 ♉ 45 D	23 ♑ 36 R	27 ♑ 39 D	09 ♊ 02 R	01 ♈ 13 D	22 ♒ 26 D	15 ♉ 09 R	22 ♓ 52 D	27 ♑ 40 D
02 Mo	11 30 55	18 49 50	25 00 59	11 45 R	22 57	28 54	08 53	01 20	22 32	15 08	22 53	27 42
03 Tu	12 32 03	01 ♊ 09 25	07 ♊ 15 29	11 43	22 07	00 ♒ 09	08 45	01 28	22 38	15 07	22 54	27 44
04 We	13 33 12	13 19 33	19 21 55	11 38	21 07	01 24	08 37	01 36	22 45	15 06	22 55	27 46
05 Th	14 34 20	25 22 50	01 ♋ 22 33	11 31	19 58	02 39	08 31	01 43	22 51	15 05	22 57	27 48
06 Fr	15 35 28	07 ♋ 21 15	13 19 07	11 21	18 43	03 54	08 25	01 51	22 57	15 04	22 58	27 49
07 Sa	16 36 36	19 16 19	25 13 00	11 09	17 24	05 09	08 20	02 00	23 03	15 03	22 59	27 51
08 Su	17 37 43	01 ♌ 09 20	07 ♌ 05 28	10 55	16 03	06 24	08 16	02 08	23 10	15 02	23 00	27 53
09 Mo	18 38 51	13 01 35	18 57 55	10 42	14 43	07 39	08 13	02 16	23 16	15 01	23 01	27 55
10 Tu	19 39 58	24 54 40	00 ♍ 52 09	10 30	13 27	08 54	08 11	02 25	23 22	15 01	23 02	27 57
11 We	20 41 06	06 ♍ 50 41	12 50 37	10 19	12 17	10 09	08 09	02 33	23 29	15 00	23 04	27 59
12 Th	21 42 13	18 52 23	24 56 25	10 12	11 13	11 24	08 08	02 42	23 35	14 59	23 05	28 01
13 Fr	22 43 20	01 ♎ 03 13	07 ♎ 13 21	10 07	10 19	12 39	08 08 D	02 51	23 42	14 59	23 06	28 03
14 Sa	23 44 27	13 27 20	19 45 48	10 05	09 34	13 54	08 08	03 00	23 48	14 58	23 08	28 05
15 Su	24 45 34	26 09 18	02 ♏ 38 26	10 05 D	08 58	15 09	08 10	03 10	23 55	14 58	23 09	28 07
16 Mo	25 46 41	09 ♏ 13 43	15 55 39	10 05	08 32	16 24	08 12	03 19	24 02	14 58	23 10	28 09
17 Tu	26 47 48	22 44 36	29 40 52	10 04 R	08 16	17 39	08 15	03 28	24 08	14 57	23 12	28 11
18 We	27 48 54	06 ♐ 44 32	13 ♐ 55 34	10 02	08 09	18 54	08 18	03 38	24 15	14 57	23 13	28 13
19 Th	28 50 01	21 13 39	28 38 16	09 57	08 10 D	20 09	08 23	03 48	24 22	14 57	23 15	28 15
20 Fr	29 51 07	06 ♑ 08 39	13 ♑ 43 47	09 49	08 19	21 24	08 28	03 58	24 29	14 57	23 16	28 17
21 Sa	00 ♒ 52 13	21 22 27	29 03 15	09 39	08 36	22 39	08 34	04 08	24 36	14 57	23 18	28 19
22 Su	01 53 18	06 ♒ 44 41	14 ♒ 25 12	09 27	08 59	23 54	08 40	04 18	24 42	14 56	23 19	28 21
23 Mo	02 54 22	22 03 20	29 37 40	09 16	09 29	25 09	08 47	04 28	24 49	14 56 D	23 21	28 23
24 Tu	03 55 25	07 ♓ 07 01	14 ♓ 30 23	09 06	10 04	26 23	08 55	04 39	24 56	14 56	23 23	28 25
25 We	04 56 27	21 47 00	28 56 24	08 58	10 44	27 38	09 03	04 49	25 03	14 57	23 24	28 27
26 Th	05 57 29	05 ♈ 58 18	12 ♈ 52 40	08 53	11 28	28 53	09 12	05 00	25 10	14 57	23 26	28 29
27 Fr	06 58 29	19 39 38	26 19 31	08 50	12 17	00 ♓ 08	09 22	05 10	25 17	14 57	23 27	28 31
28 Sa	07 59 28	02 ♉ 52 45	09 ♉ 19 49	08 50	13 10	01 22	09 32	05 21	25 24	14 57	23 29	28 33
29 Su	09 00 26	15 41 17	21 57 46	08 50	14 06	02 37	09 43	05 32	25 31	14 57	23 31	28 34
30 Mo	10 01 23	28 09 52	04 ♊ 18 11	08 49	15 05	03 52	09 55	05 43	25 38	14 58	23 33	28 36
31 Tu	11 02 18	10 ♊ 23 20	16 25 50	08 46	16 06	05 06	10 07	05 54	25 45	14 58	23 34	28 38

Planetary Data

Ingresses

	Day	Time
♀ ♒	2	9:09 PM
☉ ♒	20	3:29 AM
♀ ♓	26	9:32 PM

Stations

	Day	Time
♂ D	12	3:56 PM
☿ D	18	8:12 AM
♅ D	22	5:58 PM

Lunar Ingresses & Void Moons

Ingresses

	Day	Time
♈	29	5:36 AM
♉	31	12:09 PM
♊	2	9:44 PM
♋	5	9:15 AM
♌	7	9:40 PM
♍	10	10:16 AM
♎	12	9:57 PM
♏	15	7:09 AM
♐	17	12:33 PM
♑	19	2:12 PM
♒	21	1:29 PM
♓	23	12:35 PM
♈	25	1:47 PM
♉	27	6:43 PM
♊	30	3:34 AM

Void Times

Day	Time	Last Aspect
31	7:44 AM	□ ♇
2	5:17 PM	△ ♇
4	7:08 PM	□ ♆
7	5:23 PM	☍ ♇
9	8:53 PM	☍ ♄
12	6:06 PM	△ ♇
15	3:39 AM	□ ♇
17	9:27 AM	⚹ ♇
19	5:08 AM	⚹ ♄
21	10:53 AM	☌ ♇
23	5:19 AM	☌ ♀
25	11:11 AM	⚹ ♇
27	4:01 PM	□ ♇
30	12:52 AM	△ ♇

Phases & Eclipses

Lunar Phases

Day	Time		
6	6:08 PM	○	16♋22
14	9:11 PM	☾	24♎38
21	3:54 PM	●	01♒33
28	10:19 AM	☽	08♉26

Solar Eclipses

Day Time

~ None ~

Lunar Eclipses

Day Time

~ None ~

NOTES

The Moon is in: _____

The Day Ruler is: _____

I AM GRATEFUL FOR

_____

_____

MOOD TRACKER

SELF - CARE

DAILY AFFIRMATION

_____

_____

DREAM JOURNAL

_____

_____

_____

_____

_____

_____

_____

_____

RITUAL TIME   MINDFUL MINUTES

_____5_____
_____10_____
_____15_____
_____20_____
_____25_____
_____30_____

SCRIPTING

3-6-9 MANIFESTATION

_____ _____ _____

_____ _____ _____

_____ _____ _____

1 THING I DID TO MOVE FORWARD

_____

_____

The Moon is in: _____

The Day Ruler is: _____

I AM GRATEFUL FOR

_____

_____

MOOD TRACKER

SELF - CARE

DAILY AFFIRMATION

_____

_____

DREAM JOURNAL

_____

_____

_____

_____

_____

_____

_____

_____

_____

_____ 5 _____
_____ 10 _____
_____ 15 _____
_____ 20 _____
_____ 25 _____
_____ 30 _____

SCRIPTING

3-6-9 MANIFESTATION

_____ _____ _____

_____ _____ _____

_____ _____ _____

1 THING I DID TO MOVE FORWARD

_____

_____

The Moon is in: _____

The Day Ruler is: _____

I AM GRATEFUL FOR

_____

_____

MOOD TRACKER

SELF - CARE

DAILY AFFIRMATION

_____

_____

DREAM JOURNAL

_____

_____

_____

_____

_____

_____

_____

_____

RITUAL TIME   MINDFUL MINUTES

___5___
___10___
___15___
___20___
___25___
___30___

SCRIPTING

3-6-9 MANIFESTATION

_____ _____ _____

_____ _____ _____

1 THING I DID TO MOVE FORWARD

_____

The Moon is in: _____

The Day Ruler is: _____

I AM GRATEFUL FOR

_____

_____

MOOD TRACKER

SELF - CARE

DAILY AFFIRMATION

_____

_____

DREAM JOURNAL

_____

_____

_____

_____

_____

_____

_____

_____

_____

_____

_____ 5 _____
_____ 10 _____
_____ 15 _____
_____ 20 _____
_____ 25 _____
_____ 30 _____

SCRIPTING

3-6-9 MANIFESTATION

_____ _____ _____

_____ _____ _____

_____ _____ _____

1 THING I DID TO MOVE FORWARD

_____

_____

The Moon is in:_____
The Day Ruler is:_____

I AM GRATEFUL FOR

_____
_____

MOOD TRACKER

SELF - CARE

DAILY AFFIRMATION

_____
_____

DREAM JOURNAL

_____
_____
_____
_____
_____
_____
_____
_____

RITUAL TIME   MINDFUL MINUTES

____5____
____10____
____15____
____20____
____25____
____30____

SCRIPTING

3-6-9 MANIFESTATION

_____ _____ _____

_____ _____ _____

1 THING I DID TO MOVE FORWARD

_____
_____

The Moon is in: _____

The Day Ruler is: _____

I AM GRATEFUL FOR

_____

_____

MOOD TRACKER

SELF - CARE

DAILY AFFIRMATION

_____

_____

DREAM JOURNAL

_____

_____

_____

_____

_____

_____

_____

_____

_____

_____

_____ 5 _____
_____ 10 _____
_____ 15 _____
_____ 20 _____
_____ 25 _____
_____ 30 _____

SCRIPTING

3-6-9 MANIFESTATION

_____   _____   _____

_____   _____   _____

_____   _____   _____

1 THING I DID TO MOVE FORWARD

_____

_____

THIS LUNATION

Full Moon ☐   ☐ New Moon

The Moon is in the sign of _____ and transits my _____ house,

meaning _____

_____ for me.

Build your Moon ritual: _____

_____

_____

_____

_____

_____

_____

CANDLES	CRYSTALS
HERBS	OTHER

Card 1	Card 2	Card 3
_____ Deck	_____ Deck	_____ Deck
_____ Card	_____ Card	_____ Card

Interpretation & Meaning: _____

_____

_____

_____

_____

_____

Intentions for this lunation: _____

_____

_____

_____

_____

_____

_____

The Moon is in: _____

The Day Ruler is: _____

I AM GRATEFUL FOR

_____

_____

MOOD TRACKER

SELF - CARE

DAILY AFFIRMATION

_____

_____

DREAM JOURNAL

_____

_____

_____

_____

_____

_____

_____

_____

_____

_____

_____ 5 _____
_____ 10 _____
_____ 15 _____
_____ 20 _____
_____ 25 _____
_____ 30 _____

SCRIPTING

3-6-9 MANIFESTATION

_____ _____ _____

_____ _____ _____

_____ _____ _____

1 THING I DID TO MOVE FORWARD

_____

_____

The Moon is in: _____

The Day Ruler is: _____

I AM GRATEFUL FOR

_____

_____

MOOD TRACKER

SELF - CARE

DAILY AFFIRMATION

_____

_____

DREAM JOURNAL

_____

_____

_____

_____

_____

_____

_____

_____

_____

RITUAL TIME   MINDFUL MINUTES

5
10
15
20
25
30

SCRIPTING

3-6-9 MANIFESTATION

_____ _____ _____

_____ _____ _____

_____ _____ _____

1 THING I DID TO MOVE FORWARD

_____

_____

The Moon is in: _____

The Day Ruler is: _____

I AM GRATEFUL FOR

_____

_____

MOOD TRACKER

SELF - CARE

DAILY AFFIRMATION

_____

_____

DREAM JOURNAL

_____

_____

_____

_____

_____

_____

_____

_____

_____

____ 5 ____
____ 10 ____
____ 15 ____
____ 20 ____
____ 25 ____
____ 30 ____

SCRIPTING

3-6-9 MANIFESTATION

_____ _____ _____

_____ _____ _____

_____ _____ _____

1 THING I DID TO MOVE FORWARD

_____

_____

The Moon is in: _____

The Day Ruler is: _____

I AM GRATEFUL FOR

_____

_____

MOOD TRACKER

SELF - CARE

DAILY AFFIRMATION

_____

_____

DREAM JOURNAL

_____

_____

_____

_____

_____

_____

_____

_____

_____

_____

RITUAL TIME　　MINDFUL MINUTES

____5____
____10____
____15____
____20____
____25____
____30____

SCRIPTING

_____

_____

_____

_____

_____

_____

_____

_____

_____

_____

_____

_____

_____

_____

_____

_____

_____

_____

_____

3-6-9 MANIFESTATION

_____ _____ _____

_____ _____ _____

_____ _____ _____

1 THING I DID TO MOVE FORWARD

_____

_____

The Moon is in: _____

The Day Ruler is: _____

I AM GRATEFUL FOR

_____

_____

MOOD TRACKER

😠 😦 😐 🙂 😃

SELF - CARE

DAILY AFFIRMATION

_____

_____

DREAM JOURNAL

_____

_____

_____

_____

_____

_____

_____

_____

_____

_____

_____5_____
____10_____
____15_____
____20_____
____25_____
____30_____

SCRIPTING

_____
_____
_____
_____
_____
_____
_____
_____
_____
_____
_____
_____
_____
_____
_____
_____
_____
_____
_____

3-6-9 MANIFESTATION

_____ _____ _____

_____ _____ _____

_____ _____ _____

1 THING I DID TO MOVE FORWARD

_____

_____

The Moon is in: _____

The Day Ruler is: _____

I AM GRATEFUL FOR

_____

_____

MOOD TRACKER

SELF - CARE

DAILY AFFIRMATION

_____

_____

DREAM JOURNAL

_____
_____
_____
_____
_____
_____
_____
_____
_____

RITUAL TIME   MINDFUL MINUTES

_____5_____
_____10_____
_____15_____
_____20_____
_____25_____
_____30_____

SCRIPTING

3-6-9 MANIFESTATION

_____ _____ _____
_____ _____ _____
_____ _____ _____

1 THING I DID TO MOVE FORWARD

_____

The Moon is in: _____

The Day Ruler is: _____

I AM GRATEFUL FOR

_____

_____

MOOD TRACKER

SELF - CARE

DAILY AFFIRMATION

_____

_____

DREAM JOURNAL

_____

_____

_____

_____

_____

_____

_____

_____

_____

_____ 5 _____
_____ 10 _____
_____ 15 _____
_____ 20 _____
_____ 25 _____
_____ 30 _____

SCRIPTING

3-6-9 MANIFESTATION

_____ _____ _____

_____ _____ _____

_____ _____ _____

1 THING I DID TO MOVE FORWARD

_____

_____

DAILY 01/14

The Moon is in: _____

The Day Ruler is: _____

I AM GRATEFUL FOR

_____

_____

MOOD TRACKER

SELF - CARE

DAILY AFFIRMATION

_____

_____

DREAM JOURNAL

_____

_____

_____

_____

_____

_____

_____

_____

RITUAL TIME MINDFUL MINUTES

_____ 5 _____
_____ 10 _____
_____ 15 _____
_____ 20 _____
_____ 25 _____
_____ 30 _____

SCRIPTING

3-6-9 MANIFESTATION

_____ _____ _____

_____ _____ _____

1 THING I DID TO MOVE FORWARD

_____

_____

The Moon is in: _____

The Day Ruler is: _____

I AM GRATEFUL FOR

_____

_____

MOOD TRACKER

SELF - CARE

DAILY AFFIRMATION

_____

_____

DREAM JOURNAL

_____

_____

_____

_____

_____

_____

_____

_____

_____

_____

_____5_____
_____10_____
_____15_____
_____20_____
_____25_____
_____30_____

SCRIPTING

3-6-9 MANIFESTATION

_____ _____ _____

_____ _____ _____

_____ _____ _____

1 THING I DID TO MOVE FORWARD

_____

_____

The Moon is in: _____

The Day Ruler is: _____

I AM GRATEFUL FOR

_____

_____

MOOD TRACKER

SELF - CARE

DAILY AFFIRMATION

_____

_____

DREAM JOURNAL

_____

_____

_____

_____

_____

_____

_____

_____

_____

RITUAL TIME   MINDFUL MINUTES

____5____
____10____
____15____
____20____
____25____
____30____

SCRIPTING

3-6-9 MANIFESTATION

_____ _____ _____

_____ _____ _____

_____ _____ _____

1 THING I DID TO MOVE FORWARD

_____

The Moon is in: _____

The Day Ruler is: _____

I AM GRATEFUL FOR

_____

_____

MOOD TRACKER

SELF - CARE

DAILY AFFIRMATION

_____

_____

DREAM JOURNAL

_____

_____

_____

_____

_____

_____

_____

_____

_____

_____ 5 _____
_____ 10 _____
_____ 15 _____
_____ 20 _____
_____ 25 _____
_____ 30 _____

SCRIPTING

3-6-9 MANIFESTATION

_____ _____ _____

_____ _____ _____

_____ _____ _____

1 THING I DID TO MOVE FORWARD

_____

_____

The Moon is in: _____

The Day Ruler is: _____

I AM GRATEFUL FOR

_____

_____

MOOD TRACKER

SELF - CARE

DAILY AFFIRMATION

_____

_____

DREAM JOURNAL

_____

_____

_____

_____

_____

_____

_____

_____

_____

SCRIPTING

RITUAL TIME

MINDFUL MINUTES

_____ 5 _____
_____ 10 _____
_____ 15 _____
_____ 20 _____
_____ 25 _____
_____ 30 _____

3-6-9 MANIFESTATION

_____ _____ _____
_____ _____ _____
_____ _____ _____

1 THING I DID TO MOVE FORWARD

_____

_____

The Moon is in: _____

The Day Ruler is: _____

I AM GRATEFUL FOR

_____

_____

MOOD TRACKER

SELF - CARE

DAILY AFFIRMATION

_____

_____

DREAM JOURNAL

_____

_____

_____

_____

_____

_____

_____

_____

_____

_____5_____
_____10_____
_____15_____
_____20_____
_____25_____
_____30_____

SCRIPTING

3-6-9 MANIFESTATION

_____ _____ _____

_____ _____ _____

_____ _____ _____

1 THING I DID TO MOVE FORWARD

_____

_____

The Moon is in: _____

The Day Ruler is: _____

I AM GRATEFUL FOR

_____

_____

MOOD TRACKER

SELF - CARE

DAILY AFFIRMATION

_____

_____

DREAM JOURNAL

_____

_____

_____

_____

_____

_____

_____

_____

RITUAL TIME   MINDFUL MINUTES

_____ 5 _____
_____ 10 _____
_____ 15 _____
_____ 20 _____
_____ 25 _____
_____ 30 _____

SCRIPTING

3-6-9 MANIFESTATION

_____ _____ _____

_____ _____ _____

_____ _____ _____

1 THING I DID TO MOVE FORWARD

_____

_____

The Moon is in: _____
The Day Ruler is: _____

I AM GRATEFUL FOR

_____

_____

MOOD TRACKER

SELF - CARE

DAILY AFFIRMATION

_____

_____

DREAM JOURNAL

_____

_____

_____

_____

_____

_____

_____

_____

5
10
15
20
25
30

SCRIPTING

3-6-9 MANIFESTATION

_____ _____ _____

_____ _____ _____

_____ _____ _____

1 THING I DID TO MOVE FORWARD

_____

_____

THIS LUNATION

Full Moon ☐   ☐ New Moon

The Moon is in the sign of _____ and transits my _____ house,

meaning _____

_____ for me.

Build your Moon ritual: _____

_____

_____

_____

_____

_____

_____

CANDLES	CRYSTALS
HERBS	OTHER

Card 1	Card 2	Card 3
___ Deck	___ Deck	___ Deck
___ Card	___ Card	___ Card

Interpretation & Meaning: _____

_____

_____

_____

_____

Intentions for this lunation: _____

_____

_____

_____

_____

_____

_____

The Moon is in: _____

The Day Ruler is: _____

I AM GRATEFUL FOR

_____

_____

MOOD TRACKER

SELF - CARE

DAILY AFFIRMATION

_____

_____

DREAM JOURNAL

_____

_____

_____

_____

_____

_____

_____

_____

_____

_____

____5____
____10____
____15____
____20____
____25____
____30____

SCRIPTING

3-6-9 MANIFESTATION

_____ _____ _____

_____ _____ _____

_____ _____ _____

1 THING I DID TO MOVE FORWARD

_____

_____

The Moon is in: _____

The Day Ruler is: _____

I AM GRATEFUL FOR

_____

_____

MOOD TRACKER

SELF - CARE

DAILY AFFIRMATION

_____

_____

DREAM JOURNAL

_____

_____

_____

_____

_____

_____

_____

_____

_____

RITUAL TIME   MINDFUL MINUTES

_____5_____
_____10_____
_____15_____
_____20_____
_____25_____
_____30_____

SCRIPTING

3-6-9 MANIFESTATION

_____ _____ _____

_____ _____ _____

1 THING I DID TO MOVE FORWARD

_____

_____

The Moon is in: _____

The Day Ruler is: _____

I AM GRATEFUL FOR

_____

_____

MOOD TRACKER

SELF - CARE

DAILY AFFIRMATION

_____

_____

DREAM JOURNAL

_____

_____

_____

_____

_____

_____

_____

_____

_____

_____5_____
_____10_____
_____15_____
_____20_____
_____25_____
_____30_____

SCRIPTING

3-6-9 MANIFESTATION

_____ _____ _____

_____ _____ _____

_____ _____ _____

1 THING I DID TO MOVE FORWARD

_____

_____

The Moon is in: _____

The Day Ruler is: _____

I AM GRATEFUL FOR

_____

_____

MOOD TRACKER

😠 😦 😐 🙂 😃

SELF - CARE

DAILY AFFIRMATION

_____

_____

DREAM JOURNAL

_____

_____

_____

_____

_____

_____

_____

_____

_____

RITUAL TIME   MINDFUL MINUTES

___5___
___10___
___15___
___20___
___25___
___30___

SCRIPTING

_____
_____
_____
_____
_____
_____
_____
_____
_____
_____
_____
_____
_____
_____
_____
_____
_____
_____
_____
_____
_____

3-6-9 MANIFESTATION

_____ _____ _____

_____ _____ _____

_____ _____ _____

1 THING I DID TO MOVE FORWARD

_____

_____

The Moon is in: _____

The Day Ruler is: _____

I AM GRATEFUL FOR

_____

_____

MOOD TRACKER

SELF - CARE

DAILY AFFIRMATION

_____

_____

DREAM JOURNAL

_____

_____

_____

_____

_____

_____

_____

_____

_____

_____5_____
_____10_____
_____15_____
_____20_____
_____25_____
_____30_____

SCRIPTING

3-6-9 MANIFESTATION

_____ _____ _____

_____ _____ _____

_____ _____ _____

1 THING I DID TO MOVE FORWARD

_____

_____

The Moon is in: _____

The Day Ruler is: _____

I AM GRATEFUL FOR

_____

_____

MOOD TRACKER

SELF - CARE

DAILY AFFIRMATION

_____

_____

DREAM JOURNAL

_____

_____

_____

_____

_____

_____

_____

_____

RITUAL TIME   MINDFUL MINUTES

_____5_____
_____10_____
_____15_____
_____20_____
_____25_____
_____30_____

SCRIPTING

3-6-9 MANIFESTATION

_____ _____ _____

_____ _____ _____

_____ _____ _____

1 THING I DID TO MOVE FORWARD

_____

_____

The Moon is in: _____

The Day Ruler is: _____

I AM GRATEFUL FOR

_____

_____

MOOD TRACKER

SELF - CARE

DAILY AFFIRMATION

_____

_____

DREAM JOURNAL

_____

_____

_____

_____

_____

_____

_____

_____

_____

_____5_____
_____10_____
_____15_____
_____20_____
_____25_____
_____30_____

SCRIPTING

3-6-9 MANIFESTATION

_____ _____ _____

_____ _____ _____

_____ _____ _____

1 THING I DID TO MOVE FORWARD

_____

_____

The Moon is in: _____

The Day Ruler is: _____

I AM GRATEFUL FOR

_____

_____

MOOD TRACKER

SELF - CARE

DAILY AFFIRMATION

_____

_____

DREAM JOURNAL

_____

_____

_____

_____

_____

_____

_____

_____

_____

_____

RITUAL TIME   MINDFUL MINUTES

_____ 5 _____
_____ 10 _____
_____ 15 _____
_____ 20 _____
_____ 25 _____
_____ 30 _____

SCRIPTING

_____

_____

_____

_____

_____

_____

_____

_____

_____

_____

_____

_____

_____

_____

3-6-9 MANIFESTATION

_____ _____ _____

_____ _____ _____

_____ _____ _____

1 THING I DID TO MOVE FORWARD

_____

_____

The Moon is in: _____

The Day Ruler is: _____

I AM GRATEFUL FOR

_____

_____

MOOD TRACKER

SELF - CARE

DAILY AFFIRMATION

_____

_____

DREAM JOURNAL

_____

_____

_____

_____

_____

_____

_____

_____

_____

_____

_____5_____
_____10_____
_____15_____
_____20_____
_____25_____
_____30_____

SCRIPTING

_____

_____

_____

_____

_____

_____

_____

_____

_____

_____

_____

_____

_____

_____

_____

_____

_____

_____

_____

_____

3-6-9 MANIFESTATION

_____ _____ _____

_____ _____ _____

_____ _____ _____

1 THING I DID TO MOVE FORWARD

_____

_____

The Moon is in: _____

The Day Ruler is: _____

I AM GRATEFUL FOR

_____

_____

MOOD TRACKER

SELF - CARE

DAILY AFFIRMATION

_____

_____

DREAM JOURNAL

_____

_____

_____

_____

_____

_____

_____

_____

RITUAL TIME   MINDFUL MINUTES

_____5_____
_____10_____
_____15_____
_____20_____
_____25_____
_____30_____

SCRIPTING

3-6-9 MANIFESTATION

_____ _____ _____

_____ _____ _____

_____ _____ _____

1 THING I DID TO MOVE FORWARD

_____

_____

NOTES

FEBRUARY

SUNDAY	MONDAY	TUESDAY	WEDNESDAY
			1 Imbolc
5 ○	**6**	**7**	**8**
12 Lincoln's Birthday	**13** ◑	**14** Valentine's Day	**15**
19	**20** ● President's Day	**21**	**22**
26	**27** ◑	**28**	

2023

THURSDAY	FRIDAY	SATURDAY	NOTES
2	3	4	
9	10	11	
16	17	18	
23	24	25	

SNOW MOON

RITUAL FOCUS:
This is the perfect time to make plans for the future. Center your magick around dreams, ambition, career, education, health, etc. Magical workings this month should focus on ambition, clarity, new beginnings, enlightenment.

ZODIACS:
Aquarius & Pices

CRYSTALS:
Opal & Howlite

COLORS:
Purple, Blue, Violet

ELEMENTS:
Air, Water

DEITIES:
Brighid, Aprodite, Juno, Mars, Persephone

FLOWERS:
Violet, Primrose

ANIMALS:
Otter, Unicorn

HERBS:
Myrtle, Sage

MAGICAL ASSOCIATIONS:
Healing, Motivation, Planning, Love
Crystals: Rose Quartz, Jasper, Amethyst

DIVINATION TRACKER

DATE	PULL	MESSAGE

February 2023 Tropical Midnight Ephemeris

Time Zone: **EST (05:00 East)**

Day	☉	☽	+12 Hr	True☊	☿	♀	♂	♃	♄	♅	♆	♇
01 We	12 ♒ 03 13	22 ♊ 26 13	28 ♊ 24 57	08 ♉ 41 R	17 ♑ 11 D	06 ♓ 21 D	10 ♊ 19 D	06 ♈ 06 D	25 ♒ 53 D	14 ♉ 59 D	23 ♓ 36 D	28 ♑ 40 D
02 Th	13 04 06	04 ♋ 22 28	10 ♋ 19 08	08 33	18 18	07 35	10 32	06 17	26 00	14 59	23 38	28 42
03 Fr	14 04 58	16 15 17	22 11 12	08 22	19 26	08 50	10 46	06 28	26 07	15 00	23 40	28 44
04 Sa	15 05 49	28 07 08	04 ♌ 03 16	08 08	20 37	10 04	11 00	06 40	26 14	15 00	23 42	28 46
05 Su	16 06 38	09 ♌ 59 48	15 56 53	07 53	21 50	11 19	11 15	06 52	26 21	15 01	23 44	28 48
06 Mo	17 07 27	21 54 40	27 53 17	07 38	23 04	12 33	11 30	07 03	26 28	15 02	23 46	28 50
07 Tu	18 08 14	03 ♍ 52 52	09 ♍ 53 37	07 25	24 20	13 48	11 46	07 15	26 36	15 03	23 47	28 52
08 We	19 09 00	15 55 41	21 59 17	07 13	25 38	15 02	12 02	07 27	26 43	15 03	23 49	28 54
09 Th	20 09 45	28 04 41	04 ♎ 12 09	07 04	26 57	16 16	12 19	07 39	26 50	15 04	23 51	28 55
10 Fr	21 10 28	10 ♎ 22 02	16 34 41	06 59	28 17	17 30	12 36	07 51	26 57	15 05	23 53	28 57
11 Sa	22 11 11	22 50 32	29 09 59	06 56	29 38	18 45	12 53	08 03	27 04	15 06	23 55	28 59
12 Su	23 11 53	05 ♏ 33 33	12 ♏ 01 40	06 55	01 ♒ 01	19 59	13 11	08 16	27 12	15 07	23 57	29 01
13 Mo	24 12 33	18 34 50	25 13 30	06 55 D	02 25	21 13	13 29	08 28	27 19	15 08	23 59	29 03
14 Tu	25 13 13	01 ♐ 58 04	08 ♐ 48 52	06 55 R	03 50	22 27	13 48	08 40	27 26	15 09	24 01	29 05
15 We	26 13 51	15 46 08	22 49 58	06 54	05 15	23 41	14 07	08 53	27 33	15 11	24 03	29 06
16 Th	27 14 29	00 ♑ 00 18	07 ♑ 16 52	06 50	06 42	24 55	14 26	09 05	27 41	15 12	24 06	29 08
17 Fr	28 15 05	14 39 13	22 06 39	06 44	08 11	26 09	14 46	09 18	27 48	15 13	24 08	29 10
18 Sa	29 15 40	29 38 16	07 ♒ 12 59	06 35	09 40	27 23	15 07	09 31	27 55	15 14	24 10	29 12
19 Su	00 ♓ 16 13	14 ♒ 49 31	22 26 32	06 25	11 10	28 37	15 27	09 44	28 03	15 16	24 12	29 13
20 Mo	01 16 46	00 ♓ 02 37	07 ♓ 36 24	06 14	12 41	29 51	15 48	09 56	28 10	15 17	24 14	29 15
21 Tu	02 17 16	15 06 34	22 31 59	06 05	14 13	01 ♈ 05	16 09	10 09	28 17	15 19	24 16	29 17
22 We	03 17 45	29 51 42	07 ♈ 04 58	05 58	15 46	02 19	16 31	10 22	28 24	15 20	24 18	29 19
23 Th	04 18 12	14 ♈ 11 15	21 10 16	05 54	17 19	03 32	16 53	10 35	28 31	15 22	24 20	29 20
24 Fr	05 18 37	28 01 56	04 ♉ 46 19	05 52	18 54	04 46	17 15	10 48	28 39	15 23	24 23	29 22
25 Sa	06 19 00	11 ♉ 23 42	17 54 26	05 51 D	20 30	06 00	17 38	11 02	28 46	15 25	24 25	29 24
26 Su	07 19 21	24 19 00	00 ♊ 37 57	05 52	22 07	07 13	18 01	11 15	28 53	15 27	24 27	29 25
27 Mo	08 19 41	06 ♊ 51 52	13 01 23	05 53	23 45	08 27	18 24	11 28	29 00	15 29	24 29	29 27
28 Tu	09 19 58	19 07 09	25 09 46	05 52 R	25 24	09 40	18 48	11 42	29 08	15 30	24 31	29 28
01 We	10 20 14	01 ♋ 09 51	07 ♋ 07 59	05 50	27 03	10 54	19 12	11 55	29 15	15 32	24 34	29 30
02 Th	11 20 28	13 04 44	19 00 37	05 45	28 44	12 07	19 36	12 08	29 22	15 34	24 36	29 32
03 Fr	12 20 39	24 56 05	00 ♌ 51 35	05 38	00 ♓ 26	13 20	20 00	12 22	29 29	15 36	24 38	29 33

Planetary Data

Ingresses

		Day	Time
☿	♒	11	6:22 AM
☉	♓	18	5:34 PM
♀	♈	20	2:55 AM
☿	♓	2	5:51 PM

Stations

Day Time

~ None ~

Lunar Ingresses & Void Moons

Ingresses	Day	Time	Void Times	Last Aspect	
♊	30	3:34 AM	1 6:58 AM	△	♄
♋	1	3:12 PM	4 1:19 AM	☍	♇
♌	4	3:49 AM	6 9:16 AM	☍	♄
♍	6	4:14 PM	9 1:40 AM	△	♇
♎	9	3:46 AM	11 11:42 AM	□	♇
♏	11	1:35 PM	13 6:52 PM	⚹	♇
♐	13	8:30 PM	15 8:05 PM	⚹	♄
♑	16	12:00 AM	17 11:18 PM	☌	♇
♒	18	12:34 AM	19 9:00 PM	☌	♄
♓	19	11:55 PM	21 11:05 PM	⚹	♇
♈	22	12:14 AM	24 2:22 AM	□	♇
♉	24	3:29 AM	26 9:43 AM	△	♇
♊	26	10:47 AM	28 8:07 PM	△	♄
♋	28	9:41 PM	3 9:23 AM	☍	♇
♌	3	10:16 AM			

Phases & Eclipses

Lunar Phases

Day	Time		
5	1:29 PM	○	16♌41
13	11:01 AM	☽	24♏40
20	2:05 AM	●	01♓22
27	3:06 AM	☽	08♊27

Solar Eclipses

Day Time

~ None ~

Lunar Eclipses

Day Time

~ None ~

NOTES

The Moon is in: _____

The Day Ruler is: _____

I AM GRATEFUL FOR

_____

_____

MOOD TRACKER

SELF - CARE

DAILY AFFIRMATION

_____

_____

DREAM JOURNAL

_____

_____

_____

_____

_____

_____

_____

_____

RITUAL TIME MINDFUL MINUTES

_____5_____
_____10_____
_____15_____
_____20_____
_____25_____
_____30_____

SCRIPTING

3-6-9 MANIFESTATION

_____ _____ _____

_____ _____ _____

1 THING I DID TO MOVE FORWARD

_____

_____

The Moon is in: _____
The Day Ruler is: _____

I AM GRATEFUL FOR

_____

_____

MOOD TRACKER

SELF - CARE

DAILY AFFIRMATION

_____

_____

DREAM JOURNAL

_____

_____

_____

_____

_____

_____

_____

_____

_____

_____5_____
_____10_____
_____15_____
_____20_____
_____25_____
_____30_____

SCRIPTING

3-6-9 MANIFESTATION

_____ _____ _____

_____ _____ _____

_____ _____ _____

1 THING I DID TO MOVE FORWARD

_____

_____

The Moon is in: _____

The Day Ruler is: _____

I AM GRATEFUL FOR

_____

_____

MOOD TRACKER

SELF - CARE

DAILY AFFIRMATION

_____

_____

DREAM JOURNAL

_____

_____

_____

_____

_____

_____

_____

_____

RITUAL TIME   MINDFUL MINUTES

_____5_____
_____10_____
_____15_____
_____20_____
_____25_____
_____30_____

SCRIPTING

3-6-9 MANIFESTATION

_____ _____ _____

_____ _____ _____

_____ _____ _____

1 THING I DID TO MOVE FORWARD

_____

_____

The Moon is in: _____

The Day Ruler is: _____

I AM GRATEFUL FOR

_____

_____

MOOD TRACKER

SELF - CARE

DAILY AFFIRMATION

_____

_____

DREAM JOURNAL

_____

_____

_____

_____

_____

_____

_____

_____

_____

_____ 5 _____
_____ 10 _____
_____ 15 _____
_____ 20 _____
_____ 25 _____
_____ 30 _____

SCRIPTING

3-6-9 MANIFESTATION

_____ _____ _____

_____ _____ _____

_____ _____ _____

1 THING I DID TO MOVE FORWARD

_____

_____

The Moon is in: _____

The Day Ruler is: _____

I AM GRATEFUL FOR

_____

_____

MOOD TRACKER

SELF - CARE

DAILY AFFIRMATION

_____

_____

DREAM JOURNAL

_____

_____

_____

_____

_____

_____

_____

_____

_____

RITUAL TIME   MINDFUL MINUTES

_____ 5 _____
_____ 10 _____
_____ 15 _____
_____ 20 _____
_____ 25 _____
_____ 30 _____

SCRIPTING

3-6-9 MANIFESTATION

_____ _____ _____

_____ _____ _____

_____ _____ _____

1 THING I DID TO MOVE FORWARD

_____

_____

THIS LUNATION

Full Moon ☐   ☐ New Moon

The Moon is in the sign of _____ and transits my _____ house,

meaning _____

_____ for me.

Build your Moon ritual: _____

_____
_____
_____
_____
_____
_____
_____
_____

CANDLES	CRYSTALS
HERBS	OTHER

Card 1	Card 2	Card 3
____ Deck	____ Deck	____ Deck
____ Card	____ Card	____ Card

Interpretation & Meaning: _____

_____
_____
_____
_____
_____

Intentions for this lunation: _____

_____
_____
_____
_____
_____
_____
_____

The Moon is in: _____

The Day Ruler is: _____

I AM GRATEFUL FOR

_____

_____

MOOD TRACKER

SELF - CARE

DAILY AFFIRMATION

_____

_____

DREAM JOURNAL

_____

_____

_____

_____

_____

_____

_____

_____

_____

RITUAL TIME   MINDFUL MINUTES

_____ 5
_____ 10
_____ 15
_____ 20
_____ 25
_____ 30

SCRIPTING

3-6-9 MANIFESTATION

_____ _____ _____

_____ _____ _____

_____ _____ _____

1 THING I DID TO MOVE FORWARD

_____

_____

The Moon is in: _____
The Day Ruler is: _____

I AM GRATEFUL FOR

_____
_____

MOOD TRACKER

SELF - CARE

DAILY AFFIRMATION

_____
_____

DREAM JOURNAL

_____
_____
_____
_____
_____
_____
_____
_____

_____ 5 _____
_____ 10 _____
_____ 15 _____
_____ 20 _____
_____ 25 _____
_____ 30 _____

SCRIPTING

3-6-9 MANIFESTATION

_____ _____ _____
_____ _____ _____
_____ _____ _____

1 THING I DID TO MOVE FORWARD

_____
_____

The Moon is in: _____

The Day Ruler is: _____

I AM GRATEFUL FOR

_____

_____

MOOD TRACKER

SELF - CARE

DAILY AFFIRMATION

_____

_____

DREAM JOURNAL

_____

_____

_____

_____

_____

_____

_____

_____

_____

RITUAL TIME   MINDFUL MINUTES

5
10
15
20
25
30

SCRIPTING

3-6-9 MANIFESTATION

_____ _____ _____

_____ _____ _____

_____ _____ _____

1 THING I DID TO MOVE FORWARD

_____

The Moon is in: _____

The Day Ruler is: _____

I AM GRATEFUL FOR

_____

_____

MOOD TRACKER

SELF - CARE

DAILY AFFIRMATION

_____

_____

DREAM JOURNAL

_____

_____

_____

_____

_____

_____

_____

_____

_____

_____

```
_____5_____
____10____
____15____
____20____
____25____
____30____
```

SCRIPTING

3-6-9 MANIFESTATION

_____ _____ _____

_____ _____ _____

_____ _____ _____

1 THING I DID TO MOVE FORWARD

_____

_____

The Moon is in: _____

The Day Ruler is: _____

I AM GRATEFUL FOR

_____

_____

MOOD TRACKER

SELF - CARE

DAILY AFFIRMATION

_____

_____

DREAM JOURNAL

_____

_____

_____

_____

_____

_____

_____

_____

_____

SCRIPTING

RITUAL TIME   MINDFUL MINUTES

___5___
___10___
___15___
___20___
___25___
___30___

3-6-9 MANIFESTATION

_____ _____ _____

_____ _____ _____

1 THING I DID TO MOVE FORWARD

_____

_____

The Moon is in: _____
The Day Ruler is: _____

I AM GRATEFUL FOR

_____
_____

MOOD TRACKER

SELF - CARE

DAILY AFFIRMATION

_____
_____

DREAM JOURNAL

_____
_____
_____
_____
_____
_____
_____
_____
_____

5
10
15
20
25
30

SCRIPTING

3-6-9 MANIFESTATION

_____ _____ _____
_____ _____ _____
_____ _____ _____

1 THING I DID TO MOVE FORWARD

_____
_____

The Moon is in: _____

The Day Ruler is: _____

I AM GRATEFUL FOR

_____

_____

MOOD TRACKER

😠 😟 😐 🙂 😄

SELF - CARE

DAILY AFFIRMATION

_____

_____

DREAM JOURNAL

_____

_____

_____

_____

_____

_____

_____

_____

_____

RITUAL TIME   MINDFUL MINUTES

_____ 5 _____
_____ 10 _____
_____ 15 _____
_____ 20 _____
_____ 25 _____
_____ 30 _____

SCRIPTING

3-6-9 MANIFESTATION

_____ _____ _____

_____ _____ _____

_____ _____ _____

1 THING I DID TO MOVE FORWARD

_____

_____

The Moon is in: _____

The Day Ruler is: _____

I AM GRATEFUL FOR

_____

_____

MOOD TRACKER

SELF - CARE

DAILY AFFIRMATION

_____

_____

DREAM JOURNAL

_____

_____

_____

_____

_____

_____

_____

_____

_____

_____5_____
_____10_____
_____15_____
_____20_____
_____25_____
_____30_____

SCRIPTING

3-6-9 MANIFESTATION

_____ _____ _____

_____ _____ _____

_____ _____ _____

1 THING I DID TO MOVE FORWARD

_____

_____

The Moon is in: _____

The Day Ruler is: _____

I AM GRATEFUL FOR

_____

_____

MOOD TRACKER

SELF - CARE

DAILY AFFIRMATION

_____

_____

DREAM JOURNAL

_____

_____

_____

_____

_____

_____

_____

_____

_____

RITUAL TIME   MINDFUL MINUTES

_____ 5 _____
_____ 10 _____
_____ 15 _____
_____ 20 _____
_____ 25 _____
_____ 30 _____

SCRIPTING

3-6-9 MANIFESTATION

_____ _____ _____

_____ _____ _____

_____ _____ _____

1 THING I DID TO MOVE FORWARD

_____

_____

The Moon is in: _____

The Day Ruler is: _____

I AM GRATEFUL FOR

_____

_____

MOOD TRACKER

SELF - CARE

DAILY AFFIRMATION

_____

_____

DREAM JOURNAL

_____

_____

_____

_____

_____

_____

_____

_____

_____

_____5_____
_____10_____
_____15_____
_____20_____
_____25_____
_____30_____

SCRIPTING

3-6-9 MANIFESTATION

_____ _____ _____

_____ _____ _____

_____ _____ _____

1 THING I DID TO MOVE FORWARD

_____

_____

The Moon is in: _____

The Day Ruler is: _____

I AM GRATEFUL FOR

_____

_____

MOOD TRACKER

SELF - CARE

DAILY AFFIRMATION

_____

_____

DREAM JOURNAL

_____

_____

_____

_____

_____

_____

_____

_____

_____

RITUAL TIME   MINDFUL MINUTES

_____5_____
_____10_____
_____15_____
_____20_____
_____25_____
_____30_____

SCRIPTING

3-6-9 MANIFESTATION

_____ _____ _____

_____ _____ _____

_____ _____ _____

1 THING I DID TO MOVE FORWARD

_____

_____

The Moon is in: _____
The Day Ruler is: _____

I AM GRATEFUL FOR

_____
_____

MOOD TRACKER

SELF - CARE

DAILY AFFIRMATION

_____
_____

DREAM JOURNAL

_____
_____
_____
_____
_____
_____
_____
_____
_____

_____ 5 _____
_____ 10 _____
_____ 15 _____
_____ 20 _____
_____ 25 _____
_____ 30 _____

SCRIPTING

3-6-9 MANIFESTATION

_____ _____ _____
_____ _____ _____
_____ _____ _____

1 THING I DID TO MOVE FORWARD

_____
_____

The Moon is in: _____

The Day Ruler is: _____

I AM GRATEFUL FOR

_____

_____

MOOD TRACKER

😠 😟 😐 🙂 😃

SELF - CARE

DAILY AFFIRMATION

_____

_____

DREAM JOURNAL

_____

_____

_____

_____

_____

_____

_____

_____

_____

SCRIPTING

_____

_____

_____

_____

_____

_____

_____

_____

_____

_____

_____

_____

_____

_____

_____

_____

_____

_____

_____

RITUAL TIME

MINDFUL MINUTES
5
10
15
20
25
30

3-6-9 MANIFESTATION

_____ _____ _____

_____ _____ _____

_____ _____ _____

1 THING I DID TO MOVE FORWARD

_____

_____

The Moon is in: _____

The Day Ruler is: _____

I AM GRATEFUL FOR

_____

_____

MOOD TRACKER

SELF - CARE

DAILY AFFIRMATION

_____

_____

DREAM JOURNAL

_____

_____

_____

_____

_____

_____

_____

_____

_____

_____5_____
_____10_____
_____15_____
_____20_____
_____25_____
_____30_____

SCRIPTING

_____
_____
_____
_____
_____
_____
_____
_____
_____
_____
_____
_____
_____
_____
_____
_____
_____
_____

3-6-9 MANIFESTATION

_____ _____ _____

_____ _____ _____

_____ _____ _____

1 THING I DID TO MOVE FORWARD

_____

_____

DAILY 02/20

The Moon is in:_____
The Day Ruler is:_____

I AM GRATEFUL FOR

_____
_____

MOOD TRACKER

😠 ☹️ 😐 🙂 😃

SELF - CARE

DAILY AFFIRMATION

_____
_____

DREAM JOURNAL

_____
_____
_____
_____
_____
_____
_____
_____

RITUAL TIME   MINDFUL MINUTES

___5___
___10___
___15___
___20___
___25___
___30___

SCRIPTING

3-6-9 MANIFESTATION

_____ _____ _____
_____ _____ _____
_____ _____ _____

1 THING I DID TO MOVE FORWARD

_____
_____

THIS LUNATION

Full Moon ☐   ☐ New Moon

The Moon is in the sign of _____ and transits my _____ house,

meaning _____

_____ for me.

Build your Moon ritual: _____

_____

_____

_____

_____

_____

_____

_____

_____

CANDLES	CRYSTALS
HERBS	OTHER

Card 1	Card 2	Card 3
___ Deck	___ Deck	___ Deck
___ Card	___ Card	___ Card

Interpretation & Meaning: _____

_____

_____

_____

_____

_____

Intentions for this lunation: _____

_____

_____

_____

_____

_____

_____

_____

The Moon is in: _____

The Day Ruler is: _____

I AM GRATEFUL FOR

_____

_____

MOOD TRACKER

😠   ☹️   😐   🙂   😄

SELF - CARE

DAILY AFFIRMATION

_____

_____

DREAM JOURNAL

_____

_____

_____

_____

_____

_____

_____

_____

_____

RITUAL TIME	MINDFUL MINUTES

_____ 5 _____
_____ 10 _____
_____ 15 _____
_____ 20 _____
_____ 25 _____
_____ 30 _____

SCRIPTING

_____
_____
_____
_____
_____
_____
_____
_____
_____
_____
_____
_____
_____
_____
_____
_____
_____
_____

3-6-9 MANIFESTATION

_____ _____ _____

_____ _____ _____

_____ _____ _____

1 THING I DID TO MOVE FORWARD

_____

_____

The Moon is in: _____

The Day Ruler is: _____

I AM GRATEFUL FOR

_____

_____

MOOD TRACKER

SELF - CARE

DAILY AFFIRMATION

_____

_____

DREAM JOURNAL

_____

_____

_____

_____

_____

_____

_____

_____

_____

_____

_____5_____
_____10_____
_____15_____
_____20_____
_____25_____
_____30_____
_____

SCRIPTING

3-6-9 MANIFESTATION

_____ _____ _____

_____ _____ _____

_____ _____ _____

1 THING I DID TO MOVE FORWARD

_____

_____

The Moon is in: _____

The Day Ruler is: _____

I AM GRATEFUL FOR

_____

_____

MOOD TRACKER

😠 😞 😐 🙂 😃

SELF - CARE

DAILY AFFIRMATION

_____

_____

DREAM JOURNAL

_____

_____

_____

_____

_____

_____

_____

_____

RITUAL TIME   MINDFUL MINUTES

```
____5____
____10____
____15____
____20____
____25____
____30____
```

SCRIPTING

_____

_____

_____

_____

_____

_____

_____

_____

_____

_____

_____

_____

_____

_____

_____

_____

_____

_____

_____

_____

3-6-9 MANIFESTATION

_____ _____ _____

_____ _____ _____

_____ _____ _____

1 THING I DID TO MOVE FORWARD

_____

_____

The Moon is in: _____

The Day Ruler is: _____

I AM GRATEFUL FOR

_____

_____

MOOD TRACKER

SELF - CARE

DAILY AFFIRMATION

_____

_____

DREAM JOURNAL

_____

_____

_____

_____

_____

_____

_____

_____

_____

_____

_____ 5 _____
_____ 10 _____
_____ 15 _____
_____ 20 _____
_____ 25 _____
_____ 30 _____

SCRIPTING

3-6-9 MANIFESTATION

_____ _____ _____

_____ _____ _____

_____ _____ _____

1 THING I DID TO MOVE FORWARD

_____

_____

The Moon is in: _____

The Day Ruler is: _____

I AM GRATEFUL FOR

_____

_____

MOOD TRACKER

SELF - CARE

DAILY AFFIRMATION

_____

_____

DREAM JOURNAL

_____

_____

_____

_____

_____

_____

_____

_____

_____

RITUAL TIME   MINDFUL MINUTES

_____5_____
_____10_____
_____15_____
_____20_____
_____25_____
_____30_____

SCRIPTING

3-6-9 MANIFESTATION

_____ _____ _____

_____ _____ _____

_____ _____ _____

1 THING I DID TO MOVE FORWARD

_____

_____

The Moon is in: _____

The Day Ruler is: _____

I AM GRATEFUL FOR

_____

_____

MOOD TRACKER

SELF - CARE

DAILY AFFIRMATION

_____

_____

DREAM JOURNAL

_____

_____

_____

_____

_____

_____

_____

_____

_____

_____

_____ 5 _____
_____ 10 _____
_____ 15 _____
_____ 20 _____
_____ 25 _____
_____ 30 _____

SCRIPTING

3-6-9 MANIFESTATION

_____ _____ _____

_____ _____ _____

_____ _____ _____

1 THING I DID TO MOVE FORWARD

_____

_____

The Moon is in: _____
The Day Ruler is: _____

I AM GRATEFUL FOR

_____
_____

MOOD TRACKER

😠 😕 😐 🙂 😄

SELF - CARE

DAILY AFFIRMATION

_____
_____

DREAM JOURNAL

_____
_____
_____
_____
_____
_____
_____
_____

RITUAL TIME   MINDFUL MINUTES

_____ 5 _____
_____ 10 _____
_____ 15 _____
_____ 20 _____
_____ 25 _____
_____ 30 _____

SCRIPTING

3-6-9 MANIFESTATION

_____ _____ _____
_____ _____ _____
_____ _____ _____

1 THING I DID TO MOVE FORWARD

_____
_____

The Moon is in: _____

The Day Ruler is: _____

I AM GRATEFUL FOR

_____

_____

MOOD TRACKER

SELF - CARE

DAILY AFFIRMATION

_____

_____

DREAM JOURNAL

_____

_____

_____

_____

_____

_____

_____

_____

_____

_____ 5 _____
_____ 10 _____
_____ 15 _____
_____ 20 _____
_____ 25 _____
_____ 30 _____

SCRIPTING

3-6-9 MANIFESTATION

_____ _____ _____

_____ _____ _____

_____ _____ _____

1 THING I DID TO MOVE FORWARD

_____

_____

MARCH

SUNDAY	MONDAY	TUESDAY	WEDNESDAY
			1
5	6	7 ○	8
12 Daylight Savings	13	14 ◑	15
19	20 Ostara	21 ●	22
26	27	28 ◑	29

2023

THURSDAY	FRIDAY	SATURDAY	NOTES
2	3	4	
9	10	11	
16	17 St. Patrick's Day	18	
23	24	25	
30	31		

WORM MOON

RITUAL FOCUS:
You can celebrate by tending to your garden. Maybe it's time to plant seeds so you can sow them in time. Not just the physical tending, you can start thinking of what you would like to grow in your life.

ZODIACS:
Pices & Aries

CRYSTALS:
Aquamarine, Jade, Amethyst

COLORS:
Pale Green, Red, Violet

ELEMENTS:
Water & Fire

DEITIES:
Mars, Tyr, Athena, Minerva, Morrigan, Ostara, Libera, Pater, Isis, Hecate

FLOWERS:

ANIMALS:
Cougar, Hedgehog, Boar

HERBS:
Yellow Dock, Wood Betony, Irish Moss, Jasmine, Sage, Star Anise

MAGICAL ASSOCIATIONS:
Growing, Prospering, Exploration, Growth, Balance, New Beginnings, Planting, Renewal

DIVINATION TRACKER

DATE	PULL	MESSAGE

March 2023 — Tropical Midnight Ephemeris — Time Zone: EDT (04:00 East)

Day	☉	☽	+12 Hr	True☊	☿	♀	♂	♃	♄	♅	♆	♇
01 We	10♓17 43	00♋39 55	06♋38 12	05♉50 R	26♒59 D	10♈51 D	19♊11 D	11♈54 D	29♒14 D	15♉32 D	24♓33 D	29♑30 D
02 Th	11 17 57	12 35 03	18 30 59	05 45	28 40	12 04	19 35	12 08	29 22	15 34	24 36	29 32
03 Fr	12 18 09	24 26 28	00♌21 56	05 38	00♓22	13 17	19 59	12 21	29 29	15 36	24 38	29 33
04 Sa	13 18 18	06♌17 47	12 14 19	05 29	02 05	14 30	20 24	12 35	29 36	15 38	24 40	29 35
05 Su	14 18 26	18 11 51	24 10 38	05 20	03 49	15 44	20 48	12 49	29 43	15 40	24 42	29 36
06 Mo	15 18 31	00♍10 51	06♍12 43	05 09	05 34	16 57	21 14	13 02	29 50	15 42	24 45	29 38
07 Tu	16 18 35	12 16 21	18 21 55	05 00	07 20	18 10	21 39	13 16	29 57	15 44	24 47	29 39
08 We	17 18 37	24 29 30	00♎39 15	04 52	09 07	19 23	22 04	13 30	00♓04	15 46	24 49	29 41
09 Th	18 18 37	06♎51 16	13 05 41	04 46	10 55	20 36	22 30	13 43	00 11	15 48	24 51	29 42
10 Fr	19 18 35	19 22 39	25 42 20	04 43	12 45	21 48	22 56	13 57	00 18	15 51	24 54	29 43
11 Sa	20 18 31	02♏04 55	08♏30 37	04 42	14 35	23 01	23 23	14 11	00 25	15 53	24 56	29 45
12 Su	21 18 26	14 59 40	21 32 19	04 42 D	16 27	24 14	23 49	14 25	00 32	15 55	24 58	29 46
13 Mo	22 18 19	28 08 49	04♐49 25	04 43	18 20	25 26	24 16	14 39	00 39	15 57	25 01	29 47
14 Tu	23 18 10	11♐34 22	18 23 51	04 45	20 13	26 39	24 43	14 53	00 46	16 00	25 03	29 49
15 We	24 18 00	25 18 01	02♑16 57	04 45 R	22 08	27 52	25 10	15 07	00 53	16 02	25 05	29 50
16 Th	25 17 48	09♑20 36	16 28 51	04 44	24 04	29 04	25 37	15 21	01 00	16 05	25 07	29 51
17 Fr	26 17 35	23 41 26	00♒57 55	04 42	26 01	00♉16	26 04	15 35	01 07	16 07	25 10	29 53
18 Sa	27 17 20	08♒17 46	15 40 15	04 38	27 59	01 29	26 32	15 49	01 13	16 10	25 12	29 54
19 Su	28 17 03	23 04 35	00♓29 48	04 32	29 58	02 41	27 00	16 04	01 20	16 12	25 14	29 55
20 Mo	29 16 44	07♓54 54	15 18 52	04 27	01♈58	03 53	27 28	16 18	01 27	16 15	25 16	29 56
21 Tu	00♈16 23	22 40 40	29 59 19	04 22	03 58	05 05	27 56	16 32	01 34	16 17	25 19	29 57
22 We	01 16 01	07♈13 57	14♈23 48	04 18	05 58	06 17	28 24	16 46	01 40	16 20	25 21	29 59
23 Th	02 15 36	21 28 14	28 26 48	04 16	07 59	07 29	28 53	17 00	01 47	16 23	25 23	29 59
24 Fr	03 15 09	05♉19 12	12♉05 18	04 15 D	10 00	08 41	29 22	17 15	01 53	16 26	25 26	00♒01
25 Sa	04 14 40	18 45 05	25 18 41	04 16	12 01	09 53	29 51	17 29	02 00	16 28	25 28	00 02
26 Su	05 14 09	01♊46 23	08♊08 31	04 17	14 01	11 04	00♋20	17 43	02 07	16 31	25 30	00 03
27 Mo	06 13 35	14 25 31	20 37 53	04 19	16 01	12 16	00 49	17 58	02 13	16 34	25 32	00 04
28 Tu	07 13 00	26 46 09	02♋50 54	04 20	18 00	13 27	01 18	18 12	02 19	16 37	25 35	00 05
29 We	08 12 22	08♋52 43	14 52 13	04 21 R	19 57	14 39	01 48	18 26	02 26	16 40	25 37	00 06
30 Th	09 11 41	20 49 59	26 46 36	04 20	21 52	15 50	02 17	18 41	02 32	16 42	25 39	00 07
31 Fr	10 10 59	02♌42 38	08♌38 38	04 18	23 46	17 01	02 47	18 55	02 38	16 45	25 41	00 08

Planetary Data

Ingresses

		Day	Time
☿	♓	2	6:51 PM
♄	♓	7	9:34 AM
♀	♉	16	6:34 PM
☿	♈	19	12:23 AM
☉	♈	20	5:24 PM
♇	♒	23	8:14 AM
♂	♋	25	7:45 AM

Stations

Day Time

~ None ~

Lunar Ingresses & Void Moons

Ingresses	Day	Time	Void Times		Last Aspect	
♊	26	11:47 AM	28	9:07 PM	△	♄
♋	28	10:41 PM	3	10:23 AM	☍	♇
♌	3	11:16 AM	5	11:19 PM	☍	♄
♍	5	11:38 PM	8	10:08 AM	△	♇
♎	8	10:44 AM	10	7:37 PM	□	♇
♏	10	8:06 PM	13	2:59 AM	⚹	♇
♐	13	3:21 AM	15	4:50 AM	△	♀
♑	15	8:06 AM	17	10:14 AM	☌	♇
♒	17	10:25 AM	19	6:33 AM	△	♂
♓	19	11:12 AM	21	11:58 AM	⚹	♇
♈	21	12:01 PM	23	1:13 PM	⚹	♂
♉	23	2:41 PM	25	12:19 PM	⚹	♆
♊	25	8:42 PM	27	9:40 PM	□	♆
♋	28	6:22 AM	30	9:46 AM	△	♆
♌	30	6:31 PM				

Phases & Eclipses

Lunar Phases

Day	Time		
7	8:41 AM	○	16♍40
14	10:09 PM	☽	24♐13
21	1:23 PM	●	00♈50
28	10:33 PM	☽	08♋09

Solar Eclipses

Day Time

~ None ~

Lunar Eclipses

Day Time

~ None ~

NOTES

The Moon is in: _____

The Day Ruler is: _____

I AM GRATEFUL FOR

_____

_____

MOOD TRACKER

SELF - CARE

DAILY AFFIRMATION

_____

_____

DREAM JOURNAL

_____

_____

_____

_____

_____

_____

_____

_____

_____

RITUAL TIME   MINDFUL MINUTES

_____ 5 _____

_____ 10 _____

_____ 15 _____

_____ 20 _____

_____ 25 _____

_____ 30 _____

SCRIPTING

3-6-9 MANIFESTATION

_____ _____ _____

_____ _____ _____

1 THING I DID TO MOVE FORWARD

_____

_____

The Moon is in: _____
The Day Ruler is: _____

I AM GRATEFUL FOR

_____
_____

MOOD TRACKER

😠   😞   😐   🙂   😄

SELF - CARE

DAILY AFFIRMATION

_____
_____

DREAM JOURNAL

_____
_____
_____
_____
_____
_____
_____
_____
_____

```
____5____
____10____
____15____
____20____
____25____
____30____
```

SCRIPTING

_____
_____
_____
_____
_____
_____
_____
_____
_____
_____
_____
_____
_____
_____
_____
_____
_____
_____
_____

3-6-9 MANIFESTATION

_____ _____ _____
_____ _____ _____
_____ _____ _____

1 THING I DID TO MOVE FORWARD

_____
_____

The Moon is in: _____

The Day Ruler is: _____

I AM GRATEFUL FOR

_____

_____

MOOD TRACKER

SELF - CARE

DAILY AFFIRMATION

_____

_____

DREAM JOURNAL

_____

_____

_____

_____

_____

_____

_____

_____

_____

RITUAL TIME   MINDFUL MINUTES

5
10
15
20
25
30

SCRIPTING

3-6-9 MANIFESTATION

____ ____ ____

____ ____ ____

____ ____ ____

1 THING I DID TO MOVE FORWARD

_____

_____

The Moon is in: _____

The Day Ruler is: _____

I AM GRATEFUL FOR

_____

_____

MOOD TRACKER

SELF - CARE

DAILY AFFIRMATION

_____

_____

DREAM JOURNAL

_____

_____

_____

_____

_____

_____

_____

_____

_____

_____5_____
_____10_____
_____15_____
_____20_____
_____25_____
_____30_____

SCRIPTING

3-6-9 MANIFESTATION

_____ _____ _____

_____ _____ _____

_____ _____ _____

1 THING I DID TO MOVE FORWARD

_____

_____

The Moon is in: _____

The Day Ruler is: _____

I AM GRATEFUL FOR

_____
_____

MOOD TRACKER

😠 😞 😐 😊 😃

SELF - CARE

DAILY AFFIRMATION

_____
_____

DREAM JOURNAL

_____
_____
_____
_____
_____
_____
_____
_____

RITUAL TIME   MINDFUL MINUTES

___5___
___10___
___15___
___20___
___25___
___30___

SCRIPTING

3-6-9 MANIFESTATION

_____ _____ _____
_____ _____ _____

1 THING I DID TO MOVE FORWARD

_____
_____

The Moon is in: _____
The Day Ruler is: _____

I AM GRATEFUL FOR

_____
_____

MOOD TRACKER

😠 😞 😐 🙂 😃

SELF - CARE

DAILY AFFIRMATION

_____
_____

DREAM JOURNAL

_____
_____
_____
_____
_____
_____
_____
_____
_____

_____5_____
_____10_____
_____15_____
_____20_____
_____25_____
_____30_____

SCRIPTING

3-6-9 MANIFESTATION

_____ _____ _____
_____ _____ _____
_____ _____ _____

1 THING I DID TO MOVE FORWARD

_____
_____

The Moon is in: _____

The Day Ruler is: _____

SCRIPTING

I AM GRATEFUL FOR

_____

_____

MOOD TRACKER

SELF - CARE

DAILY AFFIRMATION

_____

_____

DREAM JOURNAL

_____

_____

_____

_____

_____

_____

_____

_____

RITUAL TIME   MINDFUL MINUTES

_____ 5 _____
_____ 10 _____
_____ 15 _____
_____ 20 _____
_____ 25 _____
_____ 30 _____

3-6-9 MANIFESTATION

_____ _____ _____

_____ _____ _____

_____ _____ _____

1 THING I DID TO MOVE FORWARD

_____

_____

THIS LUNATION

Full Moon ☐   ☐ New Moon

The Moon is in the sign of _____ and transits my _____ house,

meaning _____

_____ for me.

Build your Moon ritual: _____

_____

_____

_____

_____

_____

_____

_____

CANDLES	CRYSTALS
HERBS	OTHER

Card 1	Card 2	Card 3
___ Deck	___ Deck	___ Deck
___ Card	___ Card	___ Card

Interpretation & Meaning: _____

_____

_____

_____

_____

_____

Intentions for this lunation: _____

_____

_____

_____

_____

_____

_____

The Moon is in: _____

The Day Ruler is: _____

I AM GRATEFUL FOR

_____

_____

MOOD TRACKER

SELF - CARE

DAILY AFFIRMATION

_____

_____

DREAM JOURNAL

_____

_____

_____

_____

_____

_____

_____

_____

RITUAL TIME   MINDFUL MINUTES

_____ 5 _____
_____ 10 _____
_____ 15 _____
_____ 20 _____
_____ 25 _____
_____ 30 _____

SCRIPTING

3-6-9 MANIFESTATION

_____ _____ _____

_____ _____ _____

_____ _____ _____

1 THING I DID TO MOVE FORWARD

_____

_____

The Moon is in: _____

The Day Ruler is: _____

I AM GRATEFUL FOR

_____

_____

MOOD TRACKER

😠　😞　😐　🙂　😄

SELF - CARE

DAILY AFFIRMATION

_____

_____

DREAM JOURNAL

_____

_____

_____

_____

_____

_____

_____

_____

_____

_____5_____
_____10_____
_____15_____
_____20_____
_____25_____
_____30_____

SCRIPTING

3-6-9 MANIFESTATION

_____ _____ _____

_____ _____ _____

_____ _____ _____

1 THING I DID TO MOVE FORWARD

_____

_____

The Moon is in: _____

The Day Ruler is: _____

I AM GRATEFUL FOR

_____

_____

MOOD TRACKER

SELF - CARE

DAILY AFFIRMATION

_____

_____

DREAM JOURNAL

_____

_____

_____

_____

_____

_____

_____

_____

RITUAL TIME   MINDFUL MINUTES

___ 5 ___
___ 10 ___
___ 15 ___
___ 20 ___
___ 25 ___
___ 30 ___

SCRIPTING

3-6-9 MANIFESTATION

_____ _____ _____

_____ _____ _____

1 THING I DID TO MOVE FORWARD

_____

_____

The Moon is in: _____

The Day Ruler is: _____

I AM GRATEFUL FOR

_____

_____

MOOD TRACKER

SELF - CARE

DAILY AFFIRMATION

_____

_____

DREAM JOURNAL

_____

_____

_____

_____

_____

_____

_____

_____

_____

_____5_____
_____10_____
_____15_____
_____20_____
_____25_____
_____30_____

SCRIPTING

3-6-9 MANIFESTATION

_____ _____ _____

_____ _____ _____

_____ _____ _____

1 THING I DID TO MOVE FORWARD

_____

_____

The Moon is in: _____

The Day Ruler is: _____

I AM GRATEFUL FOR

_____

_____

MOOD TRACKER

SELF - CARE

DAILY AFFIRMATION

_____

_____

DREAM JOURNAL

_____

_____

_____

_____

_____

_____

_____

RITUAL TIME   MINDFUL MINUTES

```
___5___
___10___
___15___
___20___
___25___
___30___
```

SCRIPTING

3-6-9 MANIFESTATION

_____ _____ _____

_____ _____ _____

1 THING I DID TO MOVE FORWARD

_____

_____

The Moon is in: _____
The Day Ruler is: _____

I AM GRATEFUL FOR

_____

_____

MOOD TRACKER

SELF - CARE

DAILY AFFIRMATION

_____

_____

DREAM JOURNAL

_____
_____
_____
_____
_____
_____
_____
_____
_____

_____5_____
_____10_____
_____15_____
_____20_____
_____25_____
_____30_____

SCRIPTING

3-6-9 MANIFESTATION

_____ _____ _____
_____ _____ _____
_____ _____ _____

1 THING I DID TO MOVE FORWARD

_____
_____

The Moon is in: _____

The Day Ruler is: _____

I AM GRATEFUL FOR

_____

_____

MOOD TRACKER

😠　😟　😐　🙂　😃

SELF - CARE

DAILY AFFIRMATION

_____

_____

DREAM JOURNAL

_____

_____

_____

_____

_____

_____

_____

SCRIPTING

_____

RITUAL TIME　　MINDFUL MINUTES

_____5_____
_____10_____
_____15_____
_____20_____
_____25_____
_____30_____

3-6-9 MANIFESTATION

_____　_____　_____

_____　_____　_____

_____　_____　_____

1 THING I DID TO MOVE FORWARD

_____

_____

The Moon is in: _____

The Day Ruler is: _____

I AM GRATEFUL FOR

_____

_____

MOOD TRACKER

SELF - CARE

DAILY AFFIRMATION

_____

_____

DREAM JOURNAL

_____

_____

_____

_____

_____

_____

_____

_____

_____

_____

| _____ 5 _____ |
| _____ 10 _____ |
| _____ 15 _____ |
| _____ 20 _____ |
| _____ 25 _____ |
| _____ 30 _____ |

SCRIPTING

3-6-9 MANIFESTATION

_____ _____ _____

_____ _____ _____

_____ _____ _____

1 THING I DID TO MOVE FORWARD

_____

_____

The Moon is in:_____

The Day Ruler is:_____

I AM GRATEFUL FOR

_____

_____

MOOD TRACKER

SELF - CARE

DAILY AFFIRMATION

_____

_____

DREAM JOURNAL

_____
_____
_____
_____
_____
_____
_____
_____

RITUAL TIME   MINDFUL MINUTES

___5___
___10___
___15___
___20___
___25___
___30___

SCRIPTING

3-6-9 MANIFESTATION

_____ _____ _____
_____ _____ _____

_____ _____ _____

1 THING I DID TO MOVE FORWARD

_____
_____

The Moon is in: _____

The Day Ruler is: _____

I AM GRATEFUL FOR

_____

_____

MOOD TRACKER

😠 😞 😐 🙂 😄

SELF - CARE

DAILY AFFIRMATION

_____

_____

DREAM JOURNAL

_____

_____

_____

_____

_____

_____

_____

_____

_____

_____ 5 _____
_____ 10 _____
_____ 15 _____
_____ 20 _____
_____ 25 _____
_____ 30 _____

SCRIPTING

3-6-9 MANIFESTATION

_____ _____ _____

_____ _____ _____

_____ _____ _____

1 THING I DID TO MOVE FORWARD

_____

_____

The Moon is in: _____

The Day Ruler is: _____

I AM GRATEFUL FOR

_____

_____

MOOD TRACKER

SELF - CARE

DAILY AFFIRMATION

_____

_____

DREAM JOURNAL

_____

_____

_____

_____

_____

_____

_____

_____

RITUAL TIME   MINDFUL MINUTES

_____5_____
_____10_____
_____15_____
_____20_____
_____25_____
_____30_____

SCRIPTING

3-6-9 MANIFESTATION

_____ _____ _____

_____ _____ _____

_____ _____ _____

1 THING I DID TO MOVE FORWARD

_____

_____

The Moon is in: _____

The Day Ruler is: _____

I AM GRATEFUL FOR

_____

_____

MOOD TRACKER

SELF - CARE

DAILY AFFIRMATION

_____

_____

DREAM JOURNAL

_____

_____

_____

_____

_____

_____

_____

_____

_____

_____

_____

_____

5
10
15
20
25
30

SCRIPTING

_____

_____

_____

_____

_____

_____

_____

_____

_____

_____

_____

_____

_____

_____

_____

_____

_____

_____

_____

3-6-9 MANIFESTATION

_____ _____ _____

_____ _____ _____

_____ _____ _____

1 THING I DID TO MOVE FORWARD

_____

_____

The Moon is in: _____

The Day Ruler is: _____

I AM GRATEFUL FOR

_____

_____

MOOD TRACKER

SELF - CARE

DAILY AFFIRMATION

_____

_____

DREAM JOURNAL

_____

_____

_____

_____

_____

_____

_____

_____

RITUAL TIME   MINDFUL MINUTES

_____ 5 _____
_____ 10 _____
_____ 15 _____
_____ 20 _____
_____ 25 _____
_____ 30 _____

SCRIPTING

3-6-9 MANIFESTATION

_____ _____ _____

_____ _____ _____

_____ _____ _____

_____ _____ _____

1 THING I DID TO MOVE FORWARD

_____

_____

The Moon is in: _____

The Day Ruler is: _____

I AM GRATEFUL FOR

_____

_____

MOOD TRACKER

SELF - CARE

DAILY AFFIRMATION

_____

_____

DREAM JOURNAL

_____

_____

_____

_____

_____

_____

_____

_____

_____

_____5_____
_____10_____
_____15_____
_____20_____
_____25_____
_____30_____

SCRIPTING

3-6-9 MANIFESTATION

_____ _____ _____

_____ _____ _____

_____ _____ _____

1 THING I DID TO MOVE FORWARD

_____

_____

THIS LUNATION

Full Moon ☐   ☐ New Moon

The Moon is in the sign of _____ and transits my _____ house,

meaning _____

_____ for me.

Build your Moon ritual: _____

_____

_____

_____

_____

_____

_____

CANDLES	CRYSTALS
HERBS	OTHER

Card 1	Card 2	Card 3
Deck	Deck	Deck
Card	Card	Card

Interpretation & Meaning: _____

_____

_____

_____

_____

_____

Intentions for this lunation: _____

_____

_____

_____

_____

_____

The Moon is in: _____

The Day Ruler is: _____

I AM GRATEFUL FOR

_____

_____

MOOD TRACKER

SELF - CARE

DAILY AFFIRMATION

_____

_____

DREAM JOURNAL

_____

_____

_____

_____

_____

_____

_____

_____

_____

_____ 5 _____
_____ 10 _____
_____ 15 _____
_____ 20 _____
_____ 25 _____
_____ 30 _____

SCRIPTING

3-6-9 MANIFESTATION

_____ _____ _____

_____ _____ _____

_____ _____ _____

1 THING I DID TO MOVE FORWARD

_____

_____

The Moon is in: _____

The Day Ruler is: _____

I AM GRATEFUL FOR

_____

_____

MOOD TRACKER

SELF - CARE

DAILY AFFIRMATION

_____

_____

DREAM JOURNAL

_____

_____

_____

_____

_____

_____

_____

_____

RITUAL TIME   MINDFUL MINUTES

_____ 5 _____
_____ 10 _____
_____ 15 _____
_____ 20 _____
_____ 25 _____
_____ 30 _____

SCRIPTING

3-6-9 MANIFESTATION

_____ _____ _____

_____ _____ _____

_____ _____ _____

1 THING I DID TO MOVE FORWARD

_____

The Moon is in: _____

The Day Ruler is: _____

I AM GRATEFUL FOR

_____

_____

MOOD TRACKER

SELF - CARE

DAILY AFFIRMATION

_____

_____

DREAM JOURNAL

_____

_____

_____

_____

_____

_____

_____

_____

_____5_____
_____10_____
_____15_____
_____20_____
_____25_____
_____30_____

SCRIPTING

3-6-9 MANIFESTATION

_____ _____ _____

_____ _____ _____

_____ _____ _____

1 THING I DID TO MOVE FORWARD

_____

_____

The Moon is in: _____

The Day Ruler is: _____

I AM GRATEFUL FOR

_____

_____

MOOD TRACKER

😠 😦 😐 🙂 😃

SELF - CARE

DAILY AFFIRMATION

_____

_____

DREAM JOURNAL

_____

_____

_____

_____

_____

_____

_____

_____

_____

SCRIPTING

_____

_____

_____

_____

_____

_____

_____

_____

_____

_____

_____

_____

_____

_____

_____

_____

_____

_____

3-6-9 MANIFESTATION

_____ _____ _____

_____ _____ _____

_____ _____ _____

RITUAL TIME   MINDFUL MINUTES

_____ 5 _____
_____ 10 _____
_____ 15 _____
_____ 20 _____
_____ 25 _____
_____ 30 _____

1 THING I DID TO MOVE FORWARD

_____

_____

The Moon is in: _____

The Day Ruler is: _____

I AM GRATEFUL FOR

_____

_____

MOOD TRACKER

SELF - CARE

DAILY AFFIRMATION

_____

_____

DREAM JOURNAL

_____
_____
_____
_____
_____
_____
_____
_____
_____

5
10
15
20
25
30

SCRIPTING

3-6-9 MANIFESTATION

_____ _____ _____
_____ _____ _____
_____ _____ _____

1 THING I DID TO MOVE FORWARD

_____
_____

The Moon is in: _____

The Day Ruler is: _____

I AM GRATEFUL FOR

_____

_____

MOOD TRACKER

SELF - CARE

DAILY AFFIRMATION

_____

_____

DREAM JOURNAL

_____

_____

_____

_____

_____

_____

_____

_____

RITUAL TIME　　MINDFUL MINUTES

_____5_____
_____10_____
_____15_____
_____20_____
_____25_____
_____30_____

SCRIPTING

3-6-9 MANIFESTATION

_____ _____ _____

_____ _____ _____

_____ _____ _____

1 THING I DID TO MOVE FORWARD

_____

_____

The Moon is in: _____

The Day Ruler is: _____

I AM GRATEFUL FOR

_____

_____

MOOD TRACKER

SELF - CARE

DAILY AFFIRMATION

_____

_____

DREAM JOURNAL

_____

_____

_____

_____

_____

_____

_____

_____

_____

SCRIPTING

_____

_____

_____

_____

_____

_____

_____

_____

_____

_____

_____

_____

_____

_____

_____

_____

3-6-9 MANIFESTATION

_____ _____ _____

_____ _____ _____

_____ _____ _____

1 THING I DID TO MOVE FORWARD

_____

_____

5
10
15
20
25
30

The Moon is in: _____

The Day Ruler is: _____

I AM GRATEFUL FOR

_____

_____

MOOD TRACKER

SELF - CARE

DAILY AFFIRMATION

_____

_____

DREAM JOURNAL

_____

_____

_____

_____

_____

_____

_____

_____

RITUAL TIME

MINDFUL MINUTES

5
10
15
20
25
30

SCRIPTING

3-6-9 MANIFESTATION

___ ___ ___

___ ___ ___

___ ___ ___

1 THING I DID TO MOVE FORWARD

_____

_____

The Moon is in: _____

The Day Ruler is: _____

I AM GRATEFUL FOR

_____

_____

MOOD TRACKER

SELF - CARE

DAILY AFFIRMATION

_____

_____

DREAM JOURNAL

_____

_____

_____

_____

_____

_____

_____

_____

_____

_____ 5 _____
_____ 10 _____
_____ 15 _____
_____ 20 _____
_____ 25 _____
_____ 30 _____

SCRIPTING

3-6-9 MANIFESTATION

_____ _____ _____

_____ _____ _____

_____ _____ _____

1 THING I DID TO MOVE FORWARD

_____

_____

DAILY

The Moon is in: _____

The Day Ruler is: _____

I AM GRATEFUL FOR

_____

_____

MOOD TRACKER

SELF - CARE

DAILY AFFIRMATION

_____

_____

DREAM JOURNAL

_____

_____

_____

_____

_____

_____

_____

_____

RITUAL TIME   MINDFUL MINUTES

_____5_____
_____10_____
_____15_____
_____20_____
_____25_____
_____30_____

SCRIPTING

3-6-9 MANIFESTATION

_____ _____ _____
_____ _____ _____
_____ _____ _____

1 THING I DID TO MOVE FORWARD

_____

_____

NOTES

APRIL

SUNDAY	MONDAY	TUESDAY	WEDNESDAY
2	3	4	5
9 Easter	10	11	12
16	17	18	19
23	24	25	26
30 Beltane			

2023

THURSDAY	FRIDAY	SATURDAY	NOTES
		1	
6 ○	7 Good Friday	8	
13 ◐	14	15	
20 ● Total Solar Eclipse	21	22 Earth Day	
27 ◑	28	29	

PINK MOON

RITUAL FOCUS:
The pink moon is a time of great transformation, is good for banishing bad habits, and gaining confidence.

ZODIACS:
Aries & Taurus

CRYSTALS:
Diamond, Quartz, Kyanite

COLORS:
Pale Yellow, Pink, Gold

ELEMENTS:
Fire & Earth

DEITIES:
Aprodite, Venus, Hathor, Ishtar, Kali, Ceres, Bast

FLOWERS:
Daisy, Sweet Pea

ANIMALS:
Rabbits

HERBS:
Basil, Comfrey, Chives, Dragon's Blood, Allspice, Fennel, Frankincense.

MAGICAL ASSOCIATIONS:
Fertility, Creativity, Openings, Opportunities, Prosperity

DIVINATION TRACKER

DATE	PULL	MESSAGE

APRIL TRANSITS

April 2023

Tropical Midnight Ephemeris Time Zone: **EDT (04:00 East)**

Day	☉	☽	+12 Hr	True☊	☿	♀	♂	♃	♄	♅	♆	♇
01 Sa	11 ♈ 10 14	14 ♌ 35 06	20 ♌ 32 31	04 ♉ 16 R	25 ♈ 36 D	18 ♉ 12 D	03 ♋ 17 D	19 ♈ 10 D	02 ♓ 45 D	16 ♉ 48 D	25 ♓ 43 D	00 ♒ 08 D
02 Su	12 09 27	26 31 19	02 ♍ 31 54	04 12	27 24	19 23	03 47	19 24	02 51	16 51	25 46	00 09
03 Mo	13 08 37	08 ♍ 34 36	14 39 43	04 09	29 08	20 34	04 17	19 39	02 57	16 54	25 48	00 10
04 Tu	14 07 45	20 47 32	26 58 13	04 06	00 ♉ 48	21 45	04 48	19 53	03 03	16 57	25 50	00 11
05 We	15 06 51	03 ♎ 11 59	09 ♎ 28 54	04 03	02 24	22 56	05 18	20 07	03 09	17 00	25 52	00 12
06 Th	16 05 55	15 49 06	22 12 37	04 01	03 56	24 06	05 48	20 22	03 15	17 03	25 54	00 12
07 Fr	17 04 57	28 39 28	05 ♏ 09 38	04 00	05 23	25 17	06 19	20 36	03 21	17 07	25 57	00 13
08 Sa	18 03 57	11 ♏ 43 08	18 19 54	04 00 D	06 45	26 27	06 50	20 51	03 27	17 10	25 59	00 14
09 Su	19 02 56	24 59 55	01 ♐ 43 05	04 01	08 02	27 38	07 21	21 05	03 33	17 13	26 01	00 15
10 Mo	20 01 52	08 ♐ 29 23	15 18 43	04 02	09 13	28 48	07 52	21 20	03 38	17 16	26 03	00 15
11 Tu	21 00 47	22 11 01	29 06 12	04 03	10 18	29 58	08 23	21 34	03 44	17 19	26 05	00 16
12 We	21 59 40	06 ♑ 04 08	13 ♑ 04 40	04 04	11 18	01 ♊ 08	08 54	21 49	03 50	17 22	26 07	00 16
13 Th	22 58 31	20 07 40	27 12 55	04 04	12 11	02 17	09 25	22 03	03 55	17 26	26 09	00 17
14 Fr	23 57 21	04 ♒ 20 08	11 ♒ 29 01	04 04 R	12 59	03 27	09 57	22 18	04 01	17 29	26 11	00 17
15 Sa	24 56 08	18 39 14	25 50 19	04 04	13 40	04 37	10 28	22 32	04 06	17 32	26 13	00 18
16 Su	25 54 54	03 ♓ 01 51	10 ♓ 13 16	04 03	14 15	05 46	11 00	22 47	04 12	17 35	26 15	00 18
17 Mo	26 53 39	17 24 03	24 33 36	04 02	14 44	06 56	11 32	23 01	04 17	17 39	26 18	00 19
18 Tu	27 52 21	01 ♈ 41 20	08 ♈ 46 41	04 01	15 07	08 05	12 04	23 16	04 22	17 42	26 20	00 19
19 We	28 51 02	15 49 06	22 48 03	04 01	15 23	09 14	12 35	23 30	04 28	17 45	26 22	00 20
20 Th	29 49 41	29 43 05	06 ♉ 33 50	04 01	15 33	10 23	13 07	23 44	04 33	17 49	26 24	00 20
21 Fr	00 ♉ 48 18	13 ♉ 20 00	20 01 21	04 01 D	15 37	11 32	13 40	23 59	04 38	17 52	26 25	00 20
22 Sa	01 46 53	26 37 47	03 ♊ 09 16	04 01	15 35 R	12 40	14 12	24 13	04 43	17 55	26 27	00 21
23 Su	02 45 26	09 ♊ 35 51	15 57 43	04 01	15 28	13 49	14 44	24 28	04 48	17 59	26 29	00 21
24 Mo	03 43 57	22 15 03	28 28 12	04 01	15 15	14 57	15 16	24 42	04 53	18 02	26 31	00 21
25 Tu	04 42 26	04 ♋ 37 31	10 ♋ 43 26	04 01 R	14 57	16 06	15 49	24 56	04 58	18 06	26 33	00 21
26 We	05 40 53	16 46 25	22 46 58	04 01	14 35	17 14	16 21	25 11	05 02	18 09	26 35	00 21
27 Th	06 39 17	28 45 39	04 ♌ 43 00	04 01	14 08	18 22	16 54	25 25	05 07	18 12	26 37	00 22
28 Fr	07 37 40	10 ♌ 39 37	16 36 04	04 01 D	13 38	19 29	17 27	25 39	05 12	18 16	26 39	00 22
29 Sa	08 36 00	22 32 57	28 30 48	04 01	13 04	20 37	18 00	25 54	05 16	18 19	26 41	00 22
30 Su	09 34 19	04 ♍ 30 12	10 ♍ 31 40	04 01	12 28	21 44	18 32	26 08	05 21	18 23	26 42	00 22
01 Mo	10 32 35	16 35 43	22 42 48	04 02	11 51	22 52	19 05	26 22	05 25	18 26	26 44	00 22

Planetary Data

Ingresses

		Day	Time
☿	♉	3	12:22 PM
♀	♊	11	12:47 AM
☉	♉	20	4:13 AM

Stations

	Day	Time
☿R	21	4:35 AM
♇R	1	1:08 PM

Lunar Ingresses & Void Moons

Ingresses

	Day	Time
♌	30	6:31 PM
♍	2	6:58 AM
♎	4	5:51 PM
♏	7	2:30 AM
♐	9	8:56 AM
♑	11	1:32 PM
♒	13	4:42 PM
♓	15	6:57 PM
♈	17	9:10 PM
♉	20	12:30 AM
♊	22	6:11 AM
♋	24	2:59 PM
♌	27	2:30 AM
♍	29	3:00 PM

Void Times

Day	Time	Last Aspect	
2	2:03 AM	△	☿
4	9:50 AM	☍	♆
6	8:43 AM	☍	♃
9	5:10 AM	☍	♀
11	6:48 AM	□	♆
13	10:14 AM	⚹	♆
15	11:16 AM	⚹	☉
17	2:56 PM	☌	♆
20	12:13 AM	☌	☉
21	11:42 PM	⚹	♆
24	8:15 AM	□	♆
26	7:41 PM	△	♆
29	6:53 AM	△	♃

Phases & Eclipses

Lunar Phases

Day	Time		
6	12:34 AM	○	16♎07
13	5:11 AM	☽	23♑11
20	12:13 AM	●	29♈50
27	5:20 PM	☽	07♌21

Solar Eclipses

Day	Time	
20	12:17 AM	AT1'16

Lunar Eclipses

Day Time

~ None ~

NOTES

The Moon is in: _____

The Day Ruler is: _____

I AM GRATEFUL FOR

_____

_____

MOOD TRACKER

SELF - CARE

DAILY AFFIRMATION

_____

_____

DREAM JOURNAL

_____

_____

_____

_____

_____

_____

_____

_____

RITUAL TIME   MINDFUL MINUTES

_____5_____
_____10_____
_____15_____
_____20_____
_____25_____
_____30_____

SCRIPTING

3-6-9 MANIFESTATION

_____ _____ _____

_____ _____ _____

_____ _____ _____

1 THING I DID TO MOVE FORWARD

_____

_____

The Moon is in: _____

The Day Ruler is: _____

I AM GRATEFUL FOR

_____

_____

MOOD TRACKER

SELF - CARE

DAILY AFFIRMATION

_____

_____

DREAM JOURNAL

_____

_____

_____

_____

_____

_____

_____

_____

_____

_____ 5 _____
_____ 10 _____
_____ 15 _____
_____ 20 _____
_____ 25 _____
_____ 30 _____

SCRIPTING

3-6-9 MANIFESTATION

_____ _____ _____

_____ _____ _____

_____ _____ _____

1 THING I DID TO MOVE FORWARD

_____

_____

The Moon is in: _____

The Day Ruler is: _____

I AM GRATEFUL FOR

_____

_____

MOOD TRACKER

😠 😟 😐 🙂 😄

SELF - CARE

DAILY AFFIRMATION

_____

_____

DREAM JOURNAL

_____

_____

_____

_____

_____

_____

_____

_____

_____

RITUAL TIME   MINDFUL MINUTES

5
10
15
20
25
30

SCRIPTING

3-6-9 MANIFESTATION

____ ____ ____

____ ____ ____

1 THING I DID TO MOVE FORWARD

_____

_____

The Moon is in: _____

The Day Ruler is: _____

I AM GRATEFUL FOR

_____

_____

MOOD TRACKER

SELF - CARE

DAILY AFFIRMATION

_____

_____

DREAM JOURNAL

_____

_____

_____

_____

_____

_____

_____

_____

_____

_____5_____
_____10_____
_____15_____
_____20_____
_____25_____
_____30_____

SCRIPTING

3-6-9 MANIFESTATION

_____ _____ _____

_____ _____ _____

_____ _____ _____

1 THING I DID TO MOVE FORWARD

_____

_____

The Moon is in: _____

The Day Ruler is: _____

I AM GRATEFUL FOR

_____

_____

MOOD TRACKER

SELF - CARE

DAILY AFFIRMATION

_____

_____

DREAM JOURNAL

_____

_____

_____

_____

_____

_____

_____

_____

RITUAL TIME   MINDFUL MINUTES

_____ 5 _____
_____ 10 _____
_____ 15 _____
_____ 20 _____
_____ 25 _____
_____ 30 _____

SCRIPTING

3-6-9 MANIFESTATION

_____ _____ _____

_____ _____ _____

_____ _____ _____

1 THING I DID TO MOVE FORWARD

_____

_____

The Moon is in: _____

The Day Ruler is: _____

I AM GRATEFUL FOR

_____

_____

MOOD TRACKER

SELF - CARE

DAILY AFFIRMATION

_____

_____

DREAM JOURNAL

_____

_____

_____

_____

_____

_____

_____

_____

_____

_____

_____5_____
_____10_____
_____15_____
_____20_____
_____25_____
_____30_____

SCRIPTING

3-6-9 MANIFESTATION

_____ _____ _____

_____ _____ _____

_____ _____ _____

1 THING I DID TO MOVE FORWARD

_____

_____

THIS LUNATION

Full Moon ☐   ☐ New Moon

The Moon is in the sign of _____ and transits my _____ house,

meaning _____

_____ for me.

Build your Moon ritual: _____

_____

_____

_____

_____

_____

_____

_____

CANDLES	CRYSTALS
HERBS	OTHER

Card 1	Card 2	Card 3
____ Deck	____ Deck	____ Deck
____ Card	____ Card	____ Card

Interpretation & Meaning: _____

_____

_____

_____

_____

_____

Intentions for this lunation: _____

_____

_____

_____

_____

_____

_____

The Moon is in: _____
The Day Ruler is: _____

I AM GRATEFUL FOR

_____
_____

MOOD TRACKER

SELF - CARE

DAILY AFFIRMATION

_____
_____

DREAM JOURNAL

_____
_____
_____
_____
_____
_____
_____
_____
_____

5
10
15
20
25
30

SCRIPTING

3-6-9 MANIFESTATION

_____ _____ _____
_____ _____ _____
_____ _____ _____

1 THING I DID TO MOVE FORWARD

_____
_____

The Moon is in: _____

The Day Ruler is: _____

I AM GRATEFUL FOR

_____

_____

MOOD TRACKER

SELF - CARE

DAILY AFFIRMATION

_____

_____

DREAM JOURNAL

_____

_____

_____

_____

_____

_____

_____

_____

_____

RITUAL TIME   MINDFUL MINUTES

_____ 5 _____
_____ 10 _____
_____ 15 _____
_____ 20 _____
_____ 25 _____
_____ 30 _____

SCRIPTING

_____

_____

_____

_____

_____

_____

_____

_____

_____

_____

_____

_____

_____

_____

_____

_____

_____

_____

_____

3-6-9 MANIFESTATION

_____ _____ _____

_____ _____ _____

_____ _____ _____

1 THING I DID TO MOVE FORWARD

_____

_____

The Moon is in: _____

The Day Ruler is: _____

I AM GRATEFUL FOR

_____

_____

MOOD TRACKER

😠 🙁 😐 🙂 😃

SELF - CARE

DAILY AFFIRMATION

_____

_____

DREAM JOURNAL

_____

_____

_____

_____

_____

_____

_____

_____

_____

_____

_____ 5 _____
_____ 10 _____
_____ 15 _____
_____ 20 _____
_____ 25 _____
_____ 30 _____

SCRIPTING

3-6-9 MANIFESTATION

_____ _____ _____

_____ _____ _____

_____ _____ _____

1 THING I DID TO MOVE FORWARD

_____

_____

The Moon is in: _____

The Day Ruler is: _____

I AM GRATEFUL FOR

_____

_____

MOOD TRACKER

SELF - CARE

DAILY AFFIRMATION

_____

_____

DREAM JOURNAL

_____

_____

_____

_____

_____

_____

_____

_____

RITUAL TIME   MINDFUL MINUTES

_____5_____
_____10_____
_____15_____
_____20_____
_____25_____
_____30_____

SCRIPTING

3-6-9 MANIFESTATION

_____ _____ _____

_____ _____ _____

_____ _____ _____

1 THING I DID TO MOVE FORWARD

_____

_____

The Moon is in: _____

The Day Ruler is: _____

I AM GRATEFUL FOR

_____

_____

MOOD TRACKER

SELF - CARE

DAILY AFFIRMATION

_____

_____

DREAM JOURNAL

_____

_____

_____

_____

_____

_____

_____

_____

_____

_____

_____5_____
_____10_____
_____15_____
_____20_____
_____25_____
_____30_____

SCRIPTING

3-6-9 MANIFESTATION

_____ _____ _____

_____ _____ _____

_____ _____ _____

1 THING I DID TO MOVE FORWARD

_____

_____

The Moon is in: _____
The Day Ruler is: _____

I AM GRATEFUL FOR

_____
_____

MOOD TRACKER

SELF - CARE

DAILY AFFIRMATION

_____
_____

DREAM JOURNAL

_____
_____
_____
_____
_____
_____
_____
_____

RITUAL TIME   MINDFUL MINUTES

_____5_____
_____10_____
_____15_____
_____20_____
_____25_____
_____30_____

SCRIPTING

3-6-9 MANIFESTATION

_____ _____ _____
_____ _____ _____

_____ _____ _____

1 THING I DID TO MOVE FORWARD

_____
_____

The Moon is in: _____

The Day Ruler is: _____

I AM GRATEFUL FOR

_____

_____

MOOD TRACKER

SELF - CARE

DAILY AFFIRMATION

_____

_____

DREAM JOURNAL

_____

_____

_____

_____

_____

_____

_____

_____

_____

_____

_____ 5 _____
_____ 10 _____
_____ 15 _____
_____ 20 _____
_____ 25 _____
_____ 30 _____

SCRIPTING

3-6-9 MANIFESTATION

_____ _____ _____

_____ _____ _____

_____ _____ _____

1 THING I DID TO MOVE FORWARD

_____

_____

The Moon is in: _____

The Day Ruler is: _____

I AM GRATEFUL FOR

_____

_____

MOOD TRACKER

SELF - CARE

DAILY AFFIRMATION

_____

_____

DREAM JOURNAL

_____

_____

_____

_____

_____

_____

_____

_____

RITUAL TIME

MINDFUL MINUTES

_____5_____
_____10_____
_____15_____
_____20_____
_____25_____
_____30_____

SCRIPTING

3-6-9 MANIFESTATION

_____ _____ _____

_____ _____ _____

_____ _____ _____

1 THING I DID TO MOVE FORWARD

_____

_____

The Moon is in: _____

The Day Ruler is: _____

I AM GRATEFUL FOR

_____

_____

MOOD TRACKER

SELF - CARE

DAILY AFFIRMATION

_____

_____

DREAM JOURNAL

_____

_____

_____

_____

_____

_____

_____

_____

_____

_____5_____
_____10_____
_____15_____
_____20_____
_____25_____
_____30_____

SCRIPTING

3-6-9 MANIFESTATION

_____ _____ _____

_____ _____ _____

_____ _____ _____

1 THING I DID TO MOVE FORWARD

_____

_____

The Moon is in:_____

The Day Ruler is:_____

I AM GRATEFUL FOR

_____

_____

MOOD TRACKER

SELF - CARE

DAILY AFFIRMATION

_____

_____

DREAM JOURNAL

_____

_____

_____

_____

_____

_____

_____

_____

_____

RITUAL TIME   MINDFUL MINUTES

_____5_____
_____10_____
_____15_____
_____20_____
_____25_____
_____30_____

SCRIPTING

3-6-9 MANIFESTATION

_____ _____ _____

_____ _____ _____

_____ _____ _____

1 THING I DID TO MOVE FORWARD

_____

_____

The Moon is in: _____

The Day Ruler is: _____

I AM GRATEFUL FOR

_____

_____

MOOD TRACKER

SELF - CARE

DAILY AFFIRMATION

_____

_____

DREAM JOURNAL

_____

_____

_____

_____

_____

_____

_____

_____

_____

_____5_____
_____10_____
_____15_____
_____20_____
_____25_____
_____30_____

SCRIPTING

3-6-9 MANIFESTATION

_____ _____ _____

_____ _____ _____

_____ _____ _____

1 THING I DID TO MOVE FORWARD

_____

_____

The Moon is in:_____

The Day Ruler is:_____

I AM GRATEFUL FOR

_____

_____

MOOD TRACKER

😠 😦 😐 🙂 😃

SELF - CARE

DAILY AFFIRMATION

_____

_____

DREAM JOURNAL

_____

_____

_____

_____

_____

_____

_____

_____

RITUAL TIME   MINDFUL MINUTES

_____5_____
_____10_____
_____15_____
_____20_____
_____25_____
_____30_____

SCRIPTING

3-6-9 MANIFESTATION

_____ _____ _____

_____ _____ _____

_____ _____ _____

1 THING I DID TO MOVE FORWARD

_____

_____

The Moon is in: _____

The Day Ruler is: _____

I AM GRATEFUL FOR

_____

_____

MOOD TRACKER

SELF - CARE

DAILY AFFIRMATION

_____

_____

DREAM JOURNAL

_____

_____

_____

_____

_____

_____

_____

_____

_____

_____ 5 _____
_____ 10 _____
_____ 15 _____
_____ 20 _____
_____ 25 _____
_____ 30 _____

SCRIPTING

3-6-9 MANIFESTATION

_____ _____ _____

_____ _____ _____

_____ _____ _____

1 THING I DID TO MOVE FORWARD

_____

_____

The Moon is in: _____
The Day Ruler is: _____

I AM GRATEFUL FOR

_____
_____

MOOD TRACKER

SELF - CARE

DAILY AFFIRMATION

_____
_____

DREAM JOURNAL

_____
_____
_____
_____
_____
_____
_____
_____

RITUAL TIME   MINDFUL MINUTES

_____5_____
_____10_____
_____15_____
_____20_____
_____25_____
_____30_____

SCRIPTING

3-6-9 MANIFESTATION

_____ _____ _____
_____ _____ _____
_____ _____ _____

1 THING I DID TO MOVE FORWARD

_____
_____

THIS LUNATION

Full Moon ☐   ☐ New Moon

The Moon is in the sign of _____ and transits my _____ house,

meaning _____

_____ for me.

Build your Moon ritual: _____

_____

_____

_____

_____

_____

_____

_____

CANDLES	CRYSTALS
HERBS	OTHER

Card 1	Card 2	Card 3
Deck	Deck	Deck
Card	Card	Card

Interpretation & Meaning: _____

_____

_____

_____

_____

_____

Intentions for this lunation: _____

_____

_____

_____

_____

_____

_____

The Moon is in: _____

The Day Ruler is: _____

I AM GRATEFUL FOR

_____

_____

MOOD TRACKER

SELF - CARE

DAILY AFFIRMATION

_____

_____

DREAM JOURNAL

_____

_____

_____

_____

_____

_____

_____

_____

RITUAL TIME   MINDFUL MINUTES

_____5_____
_____10_____
_____15_____
_____20_____
_____25_____
_____30_____

SCRIPTING

3-6-9 MANIFESTATION

_____ _____ _____

_____ _____ _____

_____ _____ _____

1 THING I DID TO MOVE FORWARD

_____

The Moon is in: _____

The Day Ruler is: _____

I AM GRATEFUL FOR

_____

_____

MOOD TRACKER

SELF - CARE

DAILY AFFIRMATION

_____

_____

DREAM JOURNAL

_____

_____

_____

_____

_____

_____

_____

_____

_____

_____

_____ 5 _____
_____ 10 _____
_____ 15 _____
_____ 20 _____
_____ 25 _____
_____ 30 _____

SCRIPTING

3-6-9 MANIFESTATION

_____ _____ _____

_____ _____ _____

_____ _____ _____

1 THING I DID TO MOVE FORWARD

_____

_____

The Moon is in: _____

The Day Ruler is: _____

I AM GRATEFUL FOR

_____

_____

MOOD TRACKER

😠 😞 😐 🙂 😄

SELF - CARE

DAILY AFFIRMATION

_____

_____

DREAM JOURNAL

_____

_____

_____

_____

_____

_____

_____

_____

_____

RITUAL TIME   MINDFUL MINUTES

_____ 5 _____
_____ 10 _____
_____ 15 _____
_____ 20 _____
_____ 25 _____
_____ 30 _____

SCRIPTING

3-6-9 MANIFESTATION

_____ _____ _____
_____ _____ _____
_____ _____ _____

1 THING I DID TO MOVE FORWARD

_____

_____

The Moon is in: _____

The Day Ruler is: _____

I AM GRATEFUL FOR

_____

_____

MOOD TRACKER

SELF - CARE

DAILY AFFIRMATION

_____

_____

DREAM JOURNAL

_____

_____

_____

_____

_____

_____

_____

_____

_____

_____

_____ 5 _____
_____ 10 _____
_____ 15 _____
_____ 20 _____
_____ 25 _____
_____ 30 _____

SCRIPTING

3-6-9 MANIFESTATION

_____ _____ _____

_____ _____ _____

_____ _____ _____

1 THING I DID TO MOVE FORWARD

_____

_____

The Moon is in: _____

The Day Ruler is: _____

I AM GRATEFUL FOR

_____
_____

MOOD TRACKER

😠   🙁   😐   🙂   😃

SELF - CARE

DAILY AFFIRMATION

_____
_____

DREAM JOURNAL

_____
_____
_____
_____
_____
_____
_____
_____

RITUAL TIME   MINDFUL MINUTES

____5____
____10____
____15____
____20____
____25____
____30____

SCRIPTING

3-6-9 MANIFESTATION

_____ _____ _____
_____ _____ _____
_____ _____ _____

1 THING I DID TO MOVE FORWARD

_____
_____

The Moon is in: _____

The Day Ruler is: _____

I AM GRATEFUL FOR

_____

_____

MOOD TRACKER

SELF - CARE

DAILY AFFIRMATION

_____

_____

DREAM JOURNAL

_____

_____

_____

_____

_____

_____

_____

_____

_____

_____

_____ 5 _____
_____ 10 _____
_____ 15 _____
_____ 20 _____
_____ 25 _____
_____ 30 _____

SCRIPTING

3-6-9 MANIFESTATION

_____ _____ _____

_____ _____ _____

_____ _____ _____

1 THING I DID TO MOVE FORWARD

_____

_____

The Moon is in: _____
The Day Ruler is: _____

I AM GRATEFUL FOR

_____
_____

MOOD TRACKER

SELF - CARE

DAILY AFFIRMATION

_____
_____

DREAM JOURNAL

_____
_____
_____
_____
_____
_____
_____
_____
_____

SCRIPTING

_____
_____
_____
_____
_____
_____
_____
_____
_____
_____
_____
_____
_____
_____
_____
_____
_____
_____
_____
_____
_____

3-6-9 MANIFESTATION

_____ _____ _____
_____ _____ _____
_____ _____ _____

1 THING I DID TO MOVE FORWARD

_____
_____

RITUAL TIME   MINDFUL MINUTES

_____5_____
_____10_____
_____15_____
_____20_____
_____25_____
_____30_____

The Moon is in: _____

The Day Ruler is: _____

I AM GRATEFUL FOR

_____

_____

MOOD TRACKER

SELF - CARE

DAILY AFFIRMATION

_____

_____

DREAM JOURNAL

_____

_____

_____

_____

_____

_____

_____

_____

_____

_____

_____ 5 _____
_____ 10 _____
_____ 15 _____
_____ 20 _____
_____ 25 _____
_____ 30 _____

SCRIPTING

3-6-9 MANIFESTATION

_____ _____ _____

_____ _____ _____

_____ _____ _____

1 THING I DID TO MOVE FORWARD

_____

_____

The Moon is in: _____

The Day Ruler is: _____

I AM GRATEFUL FOR

_____

_____

MOOD TRACKER

SELF - CARE

DAILY AFFIRMATION

_____

_____

DREAM JOURNAL

_____

_____

_____

_____

_____

_____

_____

_____

RITUAL TIME   MINDFUL MINUTES

___5___
___10___
___15___
___20___
___25___
___30___

SCRIPTING

_____
_____
_____
_____
_____
_____
_____
_____
_____
_____
_____
_____
_____
_____
_____
_____
_____
_____

3-6-9 MANIFESTATION

_____ _____ _____
_____ _____ _____
_____ _____ _____

1 THING I DID TO MOVE FORWARD

_____

_____

The Moon is in: _____

The Day Ruler is: _____

I AM GRATEFUL FOR

_____

_____

MOOD TRACKER

SELF - CARE

DAILY AFFIRMATION

_____

_____

DREAM JOURNAL

_____

_____

_____

_____

_____

_____

_____

_____

_____ 5 _____
_____ 10 _____
_____ 15 _____
_____ 20 _____
_____ 25 _____
_____ 30 _____

SCRIPTING

3-6-9 MANIFESTATION

_____ _____ _____

_____ _____ _____

_____ _____ _____

1 THING I DID TO MOVE FORWARD

_____

_____

MAY

SUNDAY	MONDAY	TUESDAY	WEDNESDAY
	1	2	3
7	8	9	10
14 Mother's Day	15	16	17
21	22	23	24
28	29 Memorial Day	30	31

THURSDAY	FRIDAY	SATURDAY	NOTES
4	5 Cinco de Mayo ◯ Penumbral Lunar Eclispse	6	
11	12 ◑	13	
18	19 ●	20	
25	26	27 ◐	

URSDAY   FRIDAY SATURDAY   NOTES

FLOWER MOON

RITUAL FOCUS:
During the Flower Moon focus on your development, spiritual growth, maturity, and intuition.

ZODIACS:
Taurus & Gemini

CRYSTALS:
Emerald, Sapphire, Septarian

COLORS:
Pink, Green, Brown

ELEMENTS:
Earth & Air

DEITIES:
Maia, Bast, Venus, Diana, Artemis

FLOWERS:
Lily of the Valley, Hawthorn, Magnolia

ANIMALS:
Wolves, Foxes, Coyotes, Blue Jay, Pheasants

HERBS:
Mint, Rose, Mugwort, Thyme, Yarrow, Apple Blossom

MAGICAL ASSOCIATIONS:
Duality, Expanding Horizons, Sex Magic,

DIVINATION TRACKER

DATE	PULL	MESSAGE

MAY TRANSITS

May 2023

Tropical Midnight Ephemeris Time Zone: **EDT (04:00 East)**

Day	☉	☽	+12 Hr	True☊	☿	♀	♂	♃	♄	♅	♆	♇
01 Mo	10 ♉ 32 35	16 ♍ 35 43	22 ♍ 42 48	04 ♉ 02 D	11 ♉ 51 ℞	22 ♊ 52 D	19 ♋ 05 D	26 ♈ 22 D	05 ♓ 25 D	18 ♉ 26 D	26 ♓ 44 D	00 ♒ 22 D
02 Tu	11 30 49	28 53 19	05 ♎ 07 39	04 03	11 12	23 59	19 38	26 37	05 29	18 30	26 46	00 22 ℞
03 We	12 29 02	11 ♎ 26 05	17 48 53	04 03	10 34	25 06	20 11	26 51	05 34	18 33	26 48	00 22
04 Th	13 27 12	24 16 10	00 ♏ 48 04	04 04	09 55	26 12	20 45	27 05	05 38	18 36	26 49	00 22
05 Fr	14 25 21	07 ♏ 24 33	14 05 34	04 04 ℞	09 18	27 19	21 18	27 19	05 42	18 40	26 51	00 22
06 Sa	15 23 28	20 50 58	27 40 30	04 04	08 42	28 25	21 51	27 33	05 46	18 43	26 53	00 22
07 Su	16 21 33	04 ♐ 33 52	11 ♐ 30 43	04 03	08 09	29 31	22 24	27 47	05 50	18 47	26 54	00 21
08 Mo	17 19 37	18 30 38	25 33 10	04 01	07 38	00 ♋ 37	22 58	28 01	05 53	18 50	26 56	00 21
09 Tu	18 17 39	02 ♑ 37 50	09 ♑ 44 10	03 59	07 10	01 43	23 31	28 15	05 57	18 54	26 58	00 21
10 We	19 15 40	16 51 40	23 59 52	03 58	06 47	02 49	24 05	28 29	06 01	18 57	26 59	00 21
11 Th	20 13 40	01 ♒ 08 19	08 ♒ 16 38	03 56	06 27	03 54	24 38	28 43	06 04	19 01	27 01	00 21
12 Fr	21 11 38	15 24 25	22 31 20	03 55	06 11	04 59	25 12	28 57	06 08	19 04	27 02	00 20
13 Sa	22 09 35	29 37 05	06 ♓ 41 25	03 56 D	06 00	06 04	25 46	29 11	06 11	19 08	27 04	00 20
14 Su	23 07 31	13 ♓ 44 04	20 44 50	03 56	05 53	07 08	26 20	29 25	06 15	19 11	27 05	00 20
15 Mo	24 05 25	27 43 32	04 ♈ 39 57	03 58	05 51 D	08 13	26 53	29 39	06 18	19 15	27 07	00 19
16 Tu	25 03 18	11 ♈ 33 56	18 25 17	03 59	05 53	09 17	27 27	29 52	06 21	19 18	27 08	00 19
17 We	26 01 10	25 13 51	01 ♉ 59 27	04 00	06 00	10 21	28 01	00 ♉ 06	06 24	19 22	27 09	00 19
18 Th	26 59 01	08 ♉ 41 55	15 21 07	04 00 ℞	06 12	11 25	28 35	00 20	06 27	19 25	27 11	00 18
19 Fr	27 56 50	21 56 55	28 29 12	03 59	06 28	12 28	29 09	00 33	06 30	19 29	27 12	00 18
20 Sa	28 54 38	04 ♊ 57 53	11 ♊ 22 55	03 57	06 49	13 31	29 44	00 47	06 33	19 32	27 13	00 17
21 Su	29 52 25	17 44 19	24 02 06	03 53	07 14	14 34	00 ♌ 18	01 01	06 35	19 35	27 15	00 17
22 Mo	00 ♊ 50 10	00 ♋ 16 23	06 ♋ 27 20	03 49	07 43	15 37	00 52	01 14	06 38	19 39	27 16	00 16
23 Tu	01 47 54	12 35 08	18 40 04	03 45	08 16	16 39	01 26	01 27	06 41	19 42	27 17	00 16
24 We	02 45 36	24 42 27	00 ♌ 42 39	03 40	08 53	17 41	02 01	01 41	06 43	19 46	27 18	00 15
25 Th	03 43 17	06 ♌ 41 06	12 38 16	03 36	09 34	18 42	02 35	01 54	06 45	19 49	27 20	00 14
26 Fr	04 40 56	18 34 39	24 30 48	03 34	10 19	19 44	03 10	02 07	06 48	19 52	27 21	00 14
27 Sa	05 38 34	00 ♍ 27 17	06 ♍ 24 41	03 33	11 07	20 45	03 44	02 21	06 50	19 56	27 22	00 13
28 Su	06 36 10	12 23 37	18 24 41	03 33 D	11 59	21 45	04 19	02 34	06 52	19 59	27 23	00 12
29 Mo	07 33 45	24 28 29	00 ♎ 35 36	03 34	12 55	22 46	04 53	02 47	06 54	20 03	27 24	00 12
30 Tu	08 31 18	06 ♎ 46 37	13 02 04	03 35	13 53	23 46	05 28	03 00	06 56	20 06	27 25	00 11
31 We	09 28 50	19 22 24	25 48 01	03 37	14 55	24 45	06 03	03 13	06 57	20 09	27 26	00 10

Planetary Data

Ingresses

	Day	Time
♀ ♋	7	10:24 AM
♃ ♉	16	1:19 PM
♂ ♌	20	11:31 AM
☉ ♊	21	3:09 AM

Stations

	Day	Time
♇ ℞	1	1:08 PM
☿ D	14	11:17 PM

Lunar Ingresses & Void Moons

Ingresses

	Day	Time
♍	29	3:00 PM
♎	2	2:09 AM
♏	4	10:33 AM
♐	6	4:03 PM
♑	8	7:33 PM
♒	10	10:05 PM
♓	13	12:38 AM
♈	15	3:56 AM
♉	17	8:28 AM
♊	19	2:48 PM
♋	21	11:29 PM
♌	24	10:35 AM
♍	26	11:04 PM
♎	29	10:51 AM
♏	31	7:45 PM

Void Times

Day	Time	Last Aspect	
1	7:53 PM	☍	♆
4	5:17 AM	☍	♃
6	10:37 AM	△	♆
8	4:28 PM	△	♃
10	7:52 PM	□	♃
12	11:16 PM	⚹	♃
14	10:57 PM	☌	♆
17	5:10 AM	□	♂
19	1:50 PM	⚹	♂
21	6:11 PM	□	♆
24	5:12 AM	△	♆
26	2:39 AM	□	♅
29	5:46 AM	☍	♆
31	10:54 AM	□	♀

Phases & Eclipses

Lunar Phases

Day	Time		
5	1:34 PM	○	14♏58
12	10:29 AM	☽	21♒37
19	11:54 AM	●	28♉25
27	11:23 AM	☽	06♍06

Solar Eclipses

Day Time

~ None ~

Lunar Eclipses

Day	Time		
5	1:23 PM	A	.2f

NOTES

The Moon is in: _____
The Day Ruler is: _____

I AM GRATEFUL FOR

_____
_____

MOOD TRACKER

☹ ☹ 😐 🙂 😄

SELF - CARE

DAILY AFFIRMATION

_____
_____

DREAM JOURNAL

_____
_____
_____
_____
_____
_____
_____
_____

SCRIPTING

_____
_____
_____
_____
_____
_____
_____
_____
_____
_____
_____
_____
_____
_____
_____
_____
_____
_____

3-6-9 MANIFESTATION

_____ _____ _____
_____ _____ _____
_____ _____ _____

1 THING I DID TO MOVE FORWARD

_____
_____

RITUAL TIME   MINDFUL MINUTES

____5____
____10____
____15____
____20____
____25____
____30____

The Moon is in: _____

The Day Ruler is: _____

I AM GRATEFUL FOR

_____

_____

MOOD TRACKER

SELF - CARE

DAILY AFFIRMATION

_____

_____

DREAM JOURNAL

_____

_____

_____

_____

_____

_____

_____

_____

_____

_____5_____
_____10_____
_____15_____
_____20_____
_____25_____
_____30_____

SCRIPTING

3-6-9 MANIFESTATION

_____ _____ _____

_____ _____ _____

_____ _____ _____

1 THING I DID TO MOVE FORWARD

_____

_____

The Moon is in: _____

The Day Ruler is: _____

I AM GRATEFUL FOR

_____

_____

MOOD TRACKER

SELF - CARE

DAILY AFFIRMATION

_____

_____

DREAM JOURNAL

_____

_____

_____

_____

_____

_____

_____

_____

RITUAL TIME   MINDFUL MINUTES

_____5_____
_____10_____
_____15_____
_____20_____
_____25_____
_____30_____

SCRIPTING

3-6-9 MANIFESTATION

_____ _____ _____

_____ _____ _____

_____ _____ _____

1 THING I DID TO MOVE FORWARD

_____

The Moon is in: _____

The Day Ruler is: _____

I AM GRATEFUL FOR

_____

_____

MOOD TRACKER

😠   😦   😐   🙂   😃

SELF - CARE

DAILY AFFIRMATION

_____

_____

DREAM JOURNAL

_____

_____

_____

_____

_____

_____

_____

_____

_____

_____

_____5_____
_____10_____
_____15_____
_____20_____
_____25_____
_____30_____

SCRIPTING

_____

_____

_____

_____

_____

_____

_____

_____

_____

_____

_____

_____

_____

_____

_____

_____

3-6-9 MANIFESTATION

_____ _____ _____

_____ _____ _____

_____ _____ _____

1 THING I DID TO MOVE FORWARD

_____

_____

The Moon is in: _____

The Day Ruler is: _____

I AM GRATEFUL FOR

_____

_____

MOOD TRACKER

SELF - CARE

DAILY AFFIRMATION

_____

_____

DREAM JOURNAL

_____

_____

_____

_____

_____

_____

_____

_____

RITUAL TIME   MINDFUL MINUTES

_____ 5 _____
_____ 10 _____
_____ 15 _____
_____ 20 _____
_____ 25 _____
_____ 30 _____

SCRIPTING

3-6-9 MANIFESTATION

_____ _____ _____

_____ _____ _____

_____ _____ _____

1 THING I DID TO MOVE FORWARD

_____

_____

THIS LUNATION

Full Moon ☐   ☐ New Moon

The Moon is in the sign of _____ and transits my _____ house,

meaning _____

_____ for me.

Build your Moon ritual: _____

_____

_____

_____

_____

_____

_____

_____

CANDLES	CRYSTALS
HERBS	OTHER

Card 1	Card 2	Card 3
_____ Deck	_____ Deck	_____ Deck
_____ Card	_____ Card	_____ Card

Interpretation & Meaning: _____

_____

_____

_____

_____

_____

Intentions for this lunation: _____

_____

_____

_____

_____

_____

_____

_____

The Moon is in:_____

The Day Ruler is:_____

I AM GRATEFUL FOR

_____
_____

MOOD TRACKER

SELF - CARE

DAILY AFFIRMATION

_____
_____

DREAM JOURNAL

_____
_____
_____
_____
_____
_____
_____
_____

RITUAL TIME   MINDFUL MINUTES

5
10
15
20
25
30

SCRIPTING

3-6-9 MANIFESTATION

____ ____ ____
____ ____ ____
____ ____ ____

1 THING I DID TO MOVE FORWARD

_____

The Moon is in: _____

The Day Ruler is: _____

I AM GRATEFUL FOR

_____

_____

MOOD TRACKER

SELF - CARE

DAILY AFFIRMATION

_____

_____

DREAM JOURNAL

_____

_____

_____

_____

_____

_____

_____

_____

_____

_____

_____5_____
_____10_____
_____15_____
_____20_____
_____25_____
_____30_____

SCRIPTING

3-6-9 MANIFESTATION

_____ _____ _____

_____ _____ _____

_____ _____ _____

1 THING I DID TO MOVE FORWARD

_____

_____

The Moon is in:_____

The Day Ruler is:_____

I AM GRATEFUL FOR

_____

_____

MOOD TRACKER

SELF - CARE

DAILY AFFIRMATION

_____

_____

DREAM JOURNAL

_____

_____

_____

_____

_____

_____

_____

_____

RITUAL TIME   MINDFUL MINUTES

_____5_____
_____10_____
_____15_____
_____20_____
_____25_____
_____30_____

SCRIPTING

3-6-9 MANIFESTATION

_____ _____ _____

_____ _____ _____

_____ _____ _____

1 THING I DID TO MOVE FORWARD

_____

_____

The Moon is in: _____
The Day Ruler is: _____

I AM GRATEFUL FOR

_____
_____

MOOD TRACKER

SELF - CARE

DAILY AFFIRMATION

_____
_____

DREAM JOURNAL

_____
_____
_____
_____
_____
_____
_____
_____
_____

_____ 5 _____
_____ 10 _____
_____ 15 _____
_____ 20 _____
_____ 25 _____
_____ 30 _____

SCRIPTING

3-6-9 MANIFESTATION

_____ _____ _____
_____ _____ _____

1 THING I DID TO MOVE FORWARD

_____
_____

The Moon is in: _____
The Day Ruler is: _____

I AM GRATEFUL FOR

_____
_____

MOOD TRACKER

SELF - CARE

DAILY AFFIRMATION

_____
_____

DREAM JOURNAL

_____
_____
_____
_____
_____
_____
_____

RITUAL TIME   MINDFUL MINUTES

5
10
15
20
25
30

SCRIPTING

3-6-9 MANIFESTATION

_____ _____ _____
_____ _____ _____
_____ _____ _____

1 THING I DID TO MOVE FORWARD

_____
_____

The Moon is in: _____

The Day Ruler is: _____

I AM GRATEFUL FOR

_____

_____

MOOD TRACKER

😠   🙁   😐   🙂   😃

SELF - CARE

DAILY AFFIRMATION

_____

_____

DREAM JOURNAL

_____

_____

_____

_____

_____

_____

_____

_____

_____

_____5_____
_____10_____
_____15_____
_____20_____
_____25_____
_____30_____

SCRIPTING

_____
_____
_____
_____
_____
_____
_____
_____
_____
_____
_____
_____
_____
_____
_____
_____
_____
_____
_____
_____
_____
_____

3-6-9 MANIFESTATION

_____ _____ _____
_____ _____ _____
_____ _____ _____

1 THING I DID TO MOVE FORWARD

_____

_____

The Moon is in: _____

The Day Ruler is: _____

I AM GRATEFUL FOR

_____

_____

MOOD TRACKER

SELF - CARE

DAILY AFFIRMATION

_____

_____

DREAM JOURNAL

_____

_____

_____

_____

_____

_____

_____

_____

_____

SCRIPTING

RITUAL TIME   MINDFUL MINUTES

_____5_____
_____10_____
_____15_____
_____20_____
_____25_____
_____30_____

3-6-9 MANIFESTATION

_____ _____ _____

_____ _____ _____

1 THING I DID TO MOVE FORWARD

_____

_____

The Moon is in: _____

The Day Ruler is: _____

I AM GRATEFUL FOR

_____

_____

MOOD TRACKER

SELF - CARE

DAILY AFFIRMATION

_____

_____

DREAM JOURNAL

_____

_____

_____

_____

_____

_____

_____

_____

_____ 5 _____
_____ 10 _____
_____ 15 _____
_____ 20 _____
_____ 25 _____
_____ 30 _____

SCRIPTING

3-6-9 MANIFESTATION

_____ _____ _____

_____ _____ _____

_____ _____ _____

1 THING I DID TO MOVE FORWARD

_____

_____

The Moon is in: _____

The Day Ruler is: _____

I AM GRATEFUL FOR

_____
_____

MOOD TRACKER

😠 🙁 😐 🙂 😃

SELF - CARE

DAILY AFFIRMATION

_____
_____

DREAM JOURNAL

_____
_____
_____
_____
_____
_____
_____
_____
_____

RITUAL TIME   MINDFUL MINUTES

___5___
___10___
___15___
___20___
___25___
___30___

SCRIPTING

_____
_____
_____
_____
_____
_____
_____
_____
_____
_____
_____
_____
_____
_____
_____
_____
_____
_____
_____
_____

3-6-9 MANIFESTATION

_____ _____ _____
_____ _____ _____
_____ _____ _____

1 THING I DID TO MOVE FORWARD

_____
_____

The Moon is in: _____

The Day Ruler is: _____

I AM GRATEFUL FOR

_____

_____

MOOD TRACKER

SELF - CARE

DAILY AFFIRMATION

_____

_____

DREAM JOURNAL

_____

_____

_____

_____

_____

_____

_____

_____

_____

_____

_____ 5 _____
_____ 10 _____
_____ 15 _____
_____ 20 _____
_____ 25 _____
_____ 30 _____

SCRIPTING

_____

_____

_____

_____

_____

_____

_____

_____

_____

_____

_____

_____

_____

_____

_____

_____

_____

_____

_____

_____

_____

3-6-9 MANIFESTATION

_____ _____ _____

_____ _____ _____

_____ _____ _____

1 THING I DID TO MOVE FORWARD

_____

_____

The Moon is in: _____

The Day Ruler is: _____

I AM GRATEFUL FOR

_____

_____

MOOD TRACKER

😠   ☹️   😐   🙂   😀

SELF - CARE

◉   🏋️   ᶻᶻᶻ   🍶   💊

DAILY AFFIRMATION

_____

_____

DREAM JOURNAL

_____

_____

_____

_____

_____

_____

_____

_____

RITUAL TIME   MINDFUL MINUTES

_____ 5 _____
_____ 10 _____
_____ 15 _____
_____ 20 _____
_____ 25 _____
_____ 30 _____

SCRIPTING

_____
_____
_____
_____
_____
_____
_____
_____
_____
_____
_____
_____
_____
_____
_____
_____
_____
_____
_____

3-6-9 MANIFESTATION

_____ _____ _____
_____ _____ _____
_____ _____ _____

1 THING I DID TO MOVE FORWARD

_____

The Moon is in: _____

The Day Ruler is: _____

I AM GRATEFUL FOR

_____

_____

MOOD TRACKER

SELF - CARE

DAILY AFFIRMATION

_____

_____

DREAM JOURNAL

_____

_____

_____

_____

_____

_____

_____

_____

_____

_____

| 5 |
| 10 |
| 15 |
| 20 |
| 25 |
| 30 |

SCRIPTING

3-6-9 MANIFESTATION

_____   _____   _____

_____   _____   _____

1 THING I DID TO MOVE FORWARD

_____

_____

The Moon is in: _____

The Day Ruler is: _____

I AM GRATEFUL FOR

_____

_____

MOOD TRACKER

☹ ☹ 😐 🙂 😃

SELF - CARE

DAILY AFFIRMATION

_____

_____

DREAM JOURNAL

_____

_____

_____

_____

_____

_____

_____

_____

RITUAL TIME   MINDFUL MINUTES

___5___
___10___
___15___
___20___
___25___
___30___

SCRIPTING

3-6-9 MANIFESTATION

_____ _____ _____

_____ _____ _____

_____ _____ _____

1 THING I DID TO MOVE FORWARD

_____

The Moon is in: _____

The Day Ruler is: _____

I AM GRATEFUL FOR

_____

_____

MOOD TRACKER

SELF - CARE

DAILY AFFIRMATION

_____

_____

DREAM JOURNAL

_____

_____

_____

_____

_____

_____

_____

_____

_____

_____ 5 _____
_____ 10 _____
_____ 15 _____
_____ 20 _____
_____ 25 _____
_____ 30 _____

SCRIPTING

3-6-9 MANIFESTATION

_____   _____   _____

_____   _____   _____

_____   _____   _____

1 THING I DID TO MOVE FORWARD

_____

_____

THIS LUNATION

Full Moon ☐   ☐ New Moon

The Moon is in the sign of _____ and transits my _____ house,

meaning _____

_____ for me.

Build your Moon ritual: _____

_____

_____

_____

_____

_____

_____

CANDLES	CRYSTALS
HERBS	OTHER

Card 1	Card 2	Card 3
_____	_____	_____
Deck	Deck	Deck
_____	_____	_____
Card	Card	Card

Interpretation & Meaning: _____

_____

_____

_____

_____

_____

Intentions for this lunation: _____

_____

_____

_____

_____

_____

_____

The Moon is in: _____

The Day Ruler is: _____

I AM GRATEFUL FOR

_____

_____

MOOD TRACKER

SELF - CARE

DAILY AFFIRMATION

_____

_____

DREAM JOURNAL

_____

_____

_____

_____

_____

_____

_____

_____

_____

_____ 5 _____
_____ 10 _____
_____ 15 _____
_____ 20 _____
_____ 25 _____
_____ 30 _____

SCRIPTING

3-6-9 MANIFESTATION

_____   _____   _____

_____   _____   _____

_____   _____   _____

1 THING I DID TO MOVE FORWARD

_____

_____

The Moon is in: _____

The Day Ruler is: _____

I AM GRATEFUL FOR

_____

_____

MOOD TRACKER

SELF - CARE

DAILY AFFIRMATION

_____

_____

DREAM JOURNAL

_____

_____

_____

_____

_____

_____

_____

_____

_____

RITUAL TIME   MINDFUL MINUTES

___5___
___10___
___15___
___20___
___25___
___30___

SCRIPTING

3-6-9 MANIFESTATION

_____ _____ _____

_____ _____ _____

_____ _____ _____

1 THING I DID TO MOVE FORWARD

_____

_____

The Moon is in: _____

The Day Ruler is: _____

I AM GRATEFUL FOR

_____

_____

MOOD TRACKER

SELF - CARE

DAILY AFFIRMATION

_____

_____

DREAM JOURNAL

_____

_____

_____

_____

_____

_____

_____

_____

_____

_____5_____
_____10_____
_____15_____
_____20_____
_____25_____
_____30_____

SCRIPTING

3-6-9 MANIFESTATION

_____ _____ _____

_____ _____ _____

_____ _____ _____

1 THING I DID TO MOVE FORWARD

_____

_____

The Moon is in: _____

The Day Ruler is: _____

I AM GRATEFUL FOR

_____

_____

MOOD TRACKER

SELF - CARE

DAILY AFFIRMATION

_____

_____

DREAM JOURNAL

_____

_____

_____

_____

_____

_____

_____

_____

RITUAL TIME   MINDFUL MINUTES

___5___
___10___
___15___
___20___
___25___
___30___

SCRIPTING

3-6-9 MANIFESTATION

_____ _____ _____

_____ _____ _____

_____ _____ _____

1 THING I DID TO MOVE FORWARD

_____

_____

The Moon is in: _____
The Day Ruler is: _____

I AM GRATEFUL FOR

_____

_____

MOOD TRACKER

SELF - CARE

DAILY AFFIRMATION

_____

_____

DREAM JOURNAL

_____

_____

_____

_____

_____

_____

_____

_____

_____

_____5_____
_____10_____
_____15_____
_____20_____
_____25_____
_____30_____

SCRIPTING

3-6-9 MANIFESTATION

_____ _____ _____

_____ _____ _____

_____ _____ _____

1 THING I DID TO MOVE FORWARD

_____

_____

The Moon is in: _____

The Day Ruler is: _____

I AM GRATEFUL FOR

_____

_____

MOOD TRACKER

SELF - CARE

DAILY AFFIRMATION

_____

_____

DREAM JOURNAL

_____

_____

_____

_____

_____

_____

_____

_____

RITUAL TIME   MINDFUL MINUTES

_____ 5 _____
_____ 10 _____
_____ 15 _____
_____ 20 _____
_____ 25 _____
_____ 30 _____

SCRIPTING

3-6-9 MANIFESTATION

_____ _____ _____

_____ _____ _____

_____ _____ _____

1 THING I DID TO MOVE FORWARD

_____

_____

The Moon is in: _____

The Day Ruler is: _____

I AM GRATEFUL FOR

_____

_____

MOOD TRACKER

SELF - CARE

DAILY AFFIRMATION

_____

_____

DREAM JOURNAL

_____

_____

_____

_____

_____

_____

_____

_____

_____

_____ 5 _____
_____ 10 _____
_____ 15 _____
_____ 20 _____
_____ 25 _____
_____ 30 _____

SCRIPTING

3-6-9 MANIFESTATION

_____ _____ _____

_____ _____ _____

_____ _____ _____

1 THING I DID TO MOVE FORWARD

_____

_____

DAILY
05/27

The Moon is in: _____
The Day Ruler is: _____

I AM GRATEFUL FOR
_____
_____

MOOD TRACKER

SELF - CARE

DAILY AFFIRMATION
_____
_____

DREAM JOURNAL
_____
_____
_____
_____
_____
_____
_____
_____

RITUAL TIME   MINDFUL MINUTES
___5___
___10___
___15___
___20___
___25___
___30___

SCRIPTING

3-6-9 MANIFESTATION
___ ___ ___
___ ___ ___
___ ___ ___

1 THING I DID TO MOVE FORWARD
_____
_____

The Moon is in: _____
The Day Ruler is: _____

I AM GRATEFUL FOR

_____
_____

MOOD TRACKER

SELF - CARE

DAILY AFFIRMATION

_____
_____

DREAM JOURNAL

_____
_____
_____
_____
_____
_____
_____
_____

_____5_____
_____10_____
_____15_____
_____20_____
_____25_____
_____30_____

SCRIPTING

3-6-9 MANIFESTATION

_____ _____ _____
_____ _____ _____
_____ _____ _____

1 THING I DID TO MOVE FORWARD

_____
_____

The Moon is in: _____

The Day Ruler is: _____

I AM GRATEFUL FOR

_____

_____

MOOD TRACKER

SELF - CARE

DAILY AFFIRMATION

_____

_____

DREAM JOURNAL

_____

_____

_____

_____

_____

_____

_____

_____

RITUAL TIME   MINDFUL MINUTES

_____ 5 _____
_____ 10 _____
_____ 15 _____
_____ 20 _____
_____ 25 _____
_____ 30 _____

SCRIPTING

3-6-9 MANIFESTATION

_____ _____ _____

_____ _____ _____

_____ _____ _____

1 THING I DID TO MOVE FORWARD

_____

_____

The Moon is in: _____

The Day Ruler is: _____

I AM GRATEFUL FOR

_____

_____

MOOD TRACKER

SELF - CARE

DAILY AFFIRMATION

_____

_____

DREAM JOURNAL

_____

_____

_____

_____

_____

_____

_____

_____

_____

_____ 5 _____
_____ 10 _____
_____ 15 _____
_____ 20 _____
_____ 25 _____
_____ 30 _____

SCRIPTING

3-6-9 MANIFESTATION

_____ _____ _____

_____ _____ _____

_____ _____ _____

1 THING I DID TO MOVE FORWARD

_____

_____

The Moon is in:_____
The Day Ruler is:_____

I AM GRATEFUL FOR

_____

_____

MOOD TRACKER

😠 😟 😐 🙂 😄

SELF - CARE

DAILY AFFIRMATION

_____

_____

DREAM JOURNAL

_____

_____

_____

_____

_____

_____

_____

_____

SCRIPTING

RITUAL TIME   MINDFUL MINUTES

___5___
___10___
___15___
___20___
___25___
___30___

3-6-9 MANIFESTATION

_____ _____ _____

_____ _____ _____

1 THING I DID TO MOVE FORWARD

_____

_____

NOTES

JUNE

SUNDAY	MONDAY	TUESDAY	WEDNESDAY
4	5	6	7
11	12	13	14
18 ● Father's Day	19	20	21 Litha
25	26 ◑	27	28

2023

THURSDAY	FRIDAY	SATURDAY	NOTES
1	2	3 ○	
8	9	10 ◐	
15	16	17	
22	23	24	
29	30		

STRAWBERRY MOON

RITUAL FOCUS:
The strawberry moon is a time for connecting with your commitment, love and evolution. It is a good time for workings to encourage good health and increased energy.

ZODIACS:
Gemini & Cancer

CRYSTALS:
Pearl, Citrine, & Alexandrite

COLORS:
Yellow, Green, Orange

ELEMENTS:
Air & Water

DEITIES:
Juno, Hera, Isis, Neith, Cerridwen, Green Man

FLOWERS:
Lilly & Tansy

ANIMALS:
Crab, Fish

HERBS:
Meadowsweet, Vervain, Almond Dill, Clover, Lemongrass

MAGICAL ASSOCIATIONS:
Communication, Transformation, Clarification, Fairy Magic, Empowerment

DIVINATION TRACKER

DATE	PULL	MESSAGE

JUNE TRANSITS

June 2023 — Tropical Midnight Ephemeris — Time Zone: **EDT (04:00 East)**

Day	☉	☽	+12 Hr	True☊	☿	♀	♂	♃	♄	♅	♆	♇
01 Th	10♊ 26 21	02♏ 19 17	08♏ 56 23	03♉ 37 D	16♉ 00 D	25♋ 44 D	06♌ 38 D	03♉ 26 D	06♓ 59 D	20♉ 13 D	27♓ 27 D	00♒ 09 R
02 Fr	11 23 50	15 39 27	22 28 29	03 37 R	17 09	26 43	07 12	03 39	07 01	20 16	27 28	00 08
03 Sa	12 21 19	29 23 17	06♐ 23 36	03 35	18 20	27 41	07 47	03 52	07 02	20 19	27 29	00 08
04 Su	13 18 46	13♐ 28 58	20 38 50	03 31	19 34	28 39	08 22	04 04	07 04	20 22	27 30	00 07
05 Mo	14 16 12	27 52 28	05♑ 09 05	03 25	20 51	29 37	08 57	04 17	07 05	20 26	27 31	00 06
06 Tu	15 13 38	12♑ 27 49	19 47 46	03 19	22 11	00♌ 34	09 32	04 30	07 06	20 29	27 31	00 05
07 We	16 11 02	27 08 02	04♒ 27 45	03 13	23 34	01 30	10 07	04 42	07 07	20 32	27 32	00 04
08 Th	17 08 26	11♒ 46 06	19 02 23	03 08	25 00	02 26	10 42	04 55	07 08	20 35	27 33	00 03
09 Fr	18 05 50	26 16 02	03♓ 26 32	03 04	26 29	03 22	11 17	05 07	07 09	20 39	27 34	00 02
10 Sa	19 03 12	10♓ 33 33	17 36 51	03 02	28 00	04 17	11 53	05 19	07 10	20 42	27 34	00 01
11 Su	20 00 35	24 36 18	01♈ 31 51	03 02 D	29 34	05 11	12 28	05 32	07 11	20 45	27 35	00 00
12 Mo	20 57 56	08♈ 23 32	15 11 26	03 03	01♊ 11	06 05	13 03	05 44	07 11	20 48	27 36	29♑ 59
13 Tu	21 55 18	21 55 40	28 36 23	03 04	02 51	06 59	13 39	05 56	07 12	20 51	27 36	29 58
14 We	22 52 38	05♉ 13 42	11♉ 47 46	03 04 R	04 33	07 51	14 14	06 08	07 12	20 54	27 37	29 57
15 Th	23 49 59	18 18 44	24 46 42	03 03	06 18	08 43	14 49	06 20	07 12	20 57	27 37	29 56
16 Fr	24 47 19	01♊ 11 45	07♊ 33 59	03 00	08 06	09 35	15 25	06 32	07 13	21 00	27 38	29 55
17 Sa	25 44 38	13 53 26	20 10 11	02 54	09 56	10 26	16 00	06 43	07 13	21 03	27 38	29 54
18 Su	26 41 57	26 24 17	02♋ 35 46	02 46	11 49	11 16	16 36	06 55	07 13 R	21 06	27 39	29 53
19 Mo	27 39 15	08♋ 44 45	14 51 18	02 37	13 44	12 05	17 11	07 07	07 13	21 09	27 39	29 52
20 Tu	28 36 33	20 55 33	26 57 41	02 26	15 42	12 54	17 47	07 18	07 12	21 12	27 39	29 50
21 We	29 33 50	02♌ 57 52	08♌ 56 23	02 16	17 42	13 42	18 23	07 30	07 12	21 15	27 40	29 49
22 Th	00♋ 31 07	14 53 32	20 49 39	02 07	19 44	14 29	18 58	07 41	07 12	21 18	27 40	29 48
23 Fr	01 28 23	26 45 08	02♍ 40 27	02 00	21 48	15 16	19 34	07 52	07 11	21 21	27 40	29 47
24 Sa	02 25 38	08♍ 36 04	14 32 32	01 55	23 54	16 01	20 10	08 03	07 11	21 24	27 41	29 46
25 Su	03 22 53	20 30 26	26 30 22	01 52	26 01	16 46	20 46	08 14	07 10	21 26	27 41	29 44
26 Mo	04 20 06	02♎ 32 58	08♎ 38 51	01 51	28 10	17 30	21 22	08 25	07 09	21 29	27 41	29 43
27 Tu	05 17 20	14 48 41	21 03 05	01 51 D	00♋ 20	18 12	21 58	08 36	07 08	21 32	27 41	29 42
28 We	06 14 33	27 22 40	03♏ 48 00	01 52	02 30	18 54	22 34	08 47	07 07	21 35	27 41	29 41
29 Th	07 11 45	10♏ 19 33	16 57 45	01 51 R	04 41	19 35	23 10	08 58	07 06	21 37	27 41	29 39
30 Fr	08 08 57	23 42 51	00♐ 35 01	01 49	06 52	20 14	23 46	09 08	07 05	21 40	27 41	29 38
01 Sa	09 06 09	07♐ 34 14	14 40 16	01 45	09 03	20 53	24 22	09 19	07 04	21 43	27 41 R	29 37

Planetary Data

Ingresses

		Day	Time
♀	♌	5	9:46 AM
♇	♑	11	5:45 AM
☿	♊	11	6:26 AM
☉	♋	21	10:57 AM
☿	♋	26	8:23 PM

Stations

	Day	Time
♄ R	17	1:27 PM
♆ R	30	5:06 PM

Lunar Ingresses & Void Moons

Ingresses

	Day	Time
♎	29	10:51 AM
♏	31	7:45 PM
♐	3	1:03 AM
♑	5	3:30 AM
♒	7	4:42 AM
♓	9	6:14 AM
♈	11	9:20 AM
♉	13	2:32 PM
♊	15	9:46 PM
♋	18	6:58 AM
♌	20	6:03 PM
♍	23	6:35 AM
♎	25	6:57 PM
♏	28	4:56 AM
♐	30	10:59 AM

Void Times

Day	Time	Last Aspect	
31	10:54 AM	□	♀
2	8:51 PM	△	♀
4	11:24 PM	□	♆
7	12:39 AM	⚹	♆
9	12:24 AM	□	☿
11	9:20 AM	⚹	♇
13	2:27 PM	□	♇
15	9:37 PM	△	♇
18	2:24 AM	□	♆
20	5:44 PM	☍	♇
22	1:01 PM	□	♅
25	6:25 PM	△	♇
28	4:19 AM	□	♇
30	10:21 AM	⚹	♇

Phases & Eclipses

Lunar Phases

Day	Time		
3	11:41 PM	○	13♐18
10	3:31 PM	☽	19♓40
18	12:37 AM	●	26♊43
26	3:50 AM	☽	04♎29

Solar Eclipses

Day Time

~ None ~

Lunar Eclipses

Day Time

~ None ~

NOTES

The Moon is in: _____

The Day Ruler is: _____

I AM GRATEFUL FOR

_____

_____

MOOD TRACKER

SELF - CARE

DAILY AFFIRMATION

_____

_____

DREAM JOURNAL

_____

_____

_____

_____

_____

_____

_____

_____

RITUAL TIME   MINDFUL MINUTES

_____ 5 _____
_____ 10 _____
_____ 15 _____
_____ 20 _____
_____ 25 _____
_____ 30 _____

SCRIPTING

3-6-9 MANIFESTATION

_____ _____ _____

_____ _____ _____

_____ _____ _____

1 THING I DID TO MOVE FORWARD

_____

_____

The Moon is in: _____

The Day Ruler is: _____

I AM GRATEFUL FOR

_____

_____

MOOD TRACKER

SELF - CARE

DAILY AFFIRMATION

_____

_____

DREAM JOURNAL

_____

_____

_____

_____

_____

_____

_____

_____

_____

_____5_____
_____10_____
_____15_____
_____20_____
_____25_____
_____30_____

SCRIPTING

_____

_____

_____

_____

_____

_____

_____

_____

_____

_____

_____

_____

_____

_____

_____

3-6-9 MANIFESTATION

_____ _____ _____

_____ _____ _____

_____ _____ _____

1 THING I DID TO MOVE FORWARD

_____

_____

The Moon is in: _____

The Day Ruler is: _____

I AM GRATEFUL FOR

_____

_____

MOOD TRACKER

SELF - CARE

DAILY AFFIRMATION

_____

_____

DREAM JOURNAL

_____

_____

_____

_____

_____

_____

_____

_____

RITUAL TIME   MINDFUL MINUTES

_____5_____
_____10_____
_____15_____
_____20_____
_____25_____
_____30_____

SCRIPTING

3-6-9 MANIFESTATION

_____ _____ _____
_____ _____ _____
_____ _____ _____

1 THING I DID TO MOVE FORWARD

_____

_____

THIS LUNATION

Full Moon ☐   ☐ New Moon

The Moon is in the sign of _____ and transits my _____ house,

meaning _____

_____ for me.

Build your Moon ritual: _____

_____

_____

_____

_____

_____

_____

CANDLES	CRYSTALS
HERBS	OTHER

Card 1	Card 2	Card 3
_____	_____	_____
Deck	Deck	Deck
_____	_____	_____
Card	Card	Card

Interpretation & Meaning: _____

_____

_____

_____

_____

_____

Intentions for this lunation: _____

_____

_____

_____

_____

_____

_____

The Moon is in: _____

The Day Ruler is: _____

I AM GRATEFUL FOR

_____

_____

MOOD TRACKER

😠 😟 😐 🙂 😃

SELF - CARE

DAILY AFFIRMATION

_____

_____

DREAM JOURNAL

_____

_____

_____

_____

_____

_____

_____

RITUAL TIME   MINDFUL MINUTES

_____5_____
_____10_____
_____15_____
_____20_____
_____25_____
_____30_____

SCRIPTING

_____

_____

_____

_____

_____

_____

_____

_____

_____

_____

_____

_____

_____

_____

_____

_____

_____

3-6-9 MANIFESTATION

_____ _____ _____
_____ _____ _____
_____ _____ _____

1 THING I DID TO MOVE FORWARD

_____

_____

The Moon is in: _____

The Day Ruler is: _____

I AM GRATEFUL FOR

_____

_____

MOOD TRACKER

SELF - CARE

DAILY AFFIRMATION

_____

_____

DREAM JOURNAL

_____

_____

_____

_____

_____

_____

_____

_____

_____

_____5_____
_____10_____
_____15_____
_____20_____
_____25_____
_____30_____

SCRIPTING

_____

_____

_____

_____

_____

_____

_____

_____

_____

_____

_____

_____

_____

_____

_____

_____

3-6-9 MANIFESTATION

_____ _____ _____

_____ _____ _____

_____ _____ _____

1 THING I DID TO MOVE FORWARD

_____

_____

The Moon is in: _____

The Day Ruler is: _____

I AM GRATEFUL FOR

_____

_____

MOOD TRACKER

SELF - CARE

DAILY AFFIRMATION

_____

_____

DREAM JOURNAL

_____

_____

_____

_____

_____

_____

_____

_____

_____

RITUAL TIME   MINDFUL MINUTES

____5____
____10____
____15____
____20____
____25____
____30____

SCRIPTING

3-6-9 MANIFESTATION

_____ _____ _____

_____ _____ _____

_____ _____ _____

1 THING I DID TO MOVE FORWARD

_____

_____

The Moon is in: _____

The Day Ruler is: _____

I AM GRATEFUL FOR

_____

_____

MOOD TRACKER

SELF - CARE

DAILY AFFIRMATION

_____

_____

DREAM JOURNAL

_____

_____

_____

_____

_____

_____

_____

_____

_____

_____

_____5_____
_____10_____
_____15_____
_____20_____
_____25_____
_____30_____

SCRIPTING

3-6-9 MANIFESTATION

_____ _____ _____

_____ _____ _____

_____ _____ _____

1 THING I DID TO MOVE FORWARD

_____

_____

The Moon is in: _____

The Day Ruler is: _____

I AM GRATEFUL FOR

_____

_____

MOOD TRACKER

😠 😦 😐 🙂 😃

SELF - CARE

DAILY AFFIRMATION

_____

_____

DREAM JOURNAL

_____

_____

_____

_____

_____

_____

_____

_____

RITUAL TIME   MINDFUL MINUTES

___5___
___10___
___15___
___20___
___25___
___30___

SCRIPTING

_____
_____
_____
_____
_____
_____
_____
_____
_____
_____
_____
_____
_____
_____
_____
_____
_____
_____
_____
_____
_____

3-6-9 MANIFESTATION

_____ _____ _____
_____ _____ _____
_____ _____ _____

1 THING I DID TO MOVE FORWARD

_____

_____

The Moon is in: _____

The Day Ruler is: _____

I AM GRATEFUL FOR

_____

_____

MOOD TRACKER

SELF - CARE

DAILY AFFIRMATION

_____

_____

DREAM JOURNAL

_____

_____

_____

_____

_____

_____

_____

_____

_____

_____5_____
_____10_____
_____15_____
_____20_____
_____25_____
_____30_____

SCRIPTING

3-6-9 MANIFESTATION

_____ _____ _____

_____ _____ _____

_____ _____ _____

1 THING I DID TO MOVE FORWARD

_____

_____

The Moon is in: _____
The Day Ruler is: _____

I AM GRATEFUL FOR

_____

_____

MOOD TRACKER

SELF - CARE

DAILY AFFIRMATION

_____

_____

DREAM JOURNAL

_____

_____

_____

_____

_____

_____

_____

_____

RITUAL TIME   MINDFUL MINUTES

```
___5___
___10___
___15___
___20___
___25___
___30___
```

SCRIPTING

3-6-9 MANIFESTATION

_____ _____ _____

_____ _____ _____

_____ _____ _____

1 THING I DID TO MOVE FORWARD

_____

_____

The Moon is in: _____

The Day Ruler is: _____

I AM GRATEFUL FOR

_____

_____

MOOD TRACKER

SELF - CARE

DAILY AFFIRMATION

_____

_____

DREAM JOURNAL

_____

_____

_____

_____

_____

_____

_____

_____

_____

_____ 5 _____
_____ 10 _____
_____ 15 _____
_____ 20 _____
_____ 25 _____
_____ 30 _____

SCRIPTING

3-6-9 MANIFESTATION

_____ _____ _____

_____ _____ _____

_____ _____ _____

1 THING I DID TO MOVE FORWARD

_____

_____

The Moon is in: _____

The Day Ruler is: _____

I AM GRATEFUL FOR

_____

_____

MOOD TRACKER

😠 ☹️ 😐 🙂 😃

SELF - CARE

DAILY AFFIRMATION

_____

_____

DREAM JOURNAL

_____

_____

_____

_____

_____

_____

_____

RITUAL TIME   MINDFUL MINUTES

_____ 5 _____
_____ 10 _____
_____ 15 _____
_____ 20 _____
_____ 25 _____
_____ 30 _____

SCRIPTING

3-6-9 MANIFESTATION

_____ _____ _____

_____ _____ _____

1 THING I DID TO MOVE FORWARD

_____

_____

The Moon is in: _____

The Day Ruler is: _____

I AM GRATEFUL FOR

_____

_____

MOOD TRACKER

SELF - CARE

DAILY AFFIRMATION

_____

_____

DREAM JOURNAL

_____

_____

_____

_____

_____

_____

_____

_____

_____

_____

_____ 5 _____
_____ 10 _____
_____ 15 _____
_____ 20 _____
_____ 25 _____
_____ 30 _____

SCRIPTING

3-6-9 MANIFESTATION

_____ _____ _____

_____ _____ _____

_____ _____ _____

1 THING I DID TO MOVE FORWARD

_____

_____

The Moon is in: _____

The Day Ruler is: _____

I AM GRATEFUL FOR

_____

_____

MOOD TRACKER

SELF - CARE

DAILY AFFIRMATION

_____

_____

DREAM JOURNAL

_____

_____

_____

_____

_____

_____

_____

_____

_____

RITUAL TIME   MINDFUL MINUTES

_____ 5 _____
_____ 10 _____
_____ 15 _____
_____ 20 _____
_____ 25 _____
_____ 30 _____

SCRIPTING

3-6-9 MANIFESTATION

_____ _____ _____

_____ _____ _____

_____ _____ _____

1 THING I DID TO MOVE FORWARD

_____

_____

The Moon is in: _____

The Day Ruler is: _____

I AM GRATEFUL FOR

_____

_____

MOOD TRACKER

SELF - CARE

DAILY AFFIRMATION

_____

_____

DREAM JOURNAL

_____

_____

_____

_____

_____

_____

_____

_____

_____

_____

```
_____ 5 _____
_____ 10 _____
_____ 15 _____
_____ 20 _____
_____ 25 _____
_____ 30 _____
```

SCRIPTING

3-6-9 MANIFESTATION

_____ _____ _____

_____ _____ _____

_____ _____ _____

1 THING I DID TO MOVE FORWARD

_____

_____

The Moon is in: _____

The Day Ruler is: _____

I AM GRATEFUL FOR

_____

_____

MOOD TRACKER

😠 😞 😐 🙂 😄

SELF - CARE

DAILY AFFIRMATION

_____

_____

DREAM JOURNAL

_____

_____

_____

_____

_____

_____

_____

_____

RITUAL TIME   MINDFUL MINUTES

__5__
__10__
__15__
__20__
__25__
__30__

SCRIPTING

_____

_____

_____

_____

_____

_____

_____

_____

_____

_____

_____

_____

_____

_____

_____

3-6-9 MANIFESTATION

_____ _____ _____

_____ _____ _____

_____ _____ _____

1 THING I DID TO MOVE FORWARD

_____

_____

The Moon is in: _____

The Day Ruler is: _____

I AM GRATEFUL FOR

_____

_____

MOOD TRACKER

SELF - CARE

DAILY AFFIRMATION

_____

_____

DREAM JOURNAL

_____

_____

_____

_____

_____

_____

_____

_____

_____ 5 _____
_____ 10 _____
_____ 15 _____
_____ 20 _____
_____ 25 _____
_____ 30 _____

SCRIPTING

3-6-9 MANIFESTATION

_____   _____   _____

_____   _____   _____

_____   _____   _____

1 THING I DID TO MOVE FORWARD

_____

_____

The Moon is in: _____

The Day Ruler is: _____

I AM GRATEFUL FOR

_____

_____

MOOD TRACKER

SELF - CARE

DAILY AFFIRMATION

_____

_____

DREAM JOURNAL

_____

_____

_____

_____

_____

_____

_____

_____

_____

RITUAL TIME   MINDFUL MINUTES

_____ 5 _____
_____ 10 _____
_____ 15 _____
_____ 20 _____
_____ 25 _____
_____ 30 _____

SCRIPTING

3-6-9 MANIFESTATION

_____ _____ _____
_____ _____ _____
_____ _____ _____

1 THING I DID TO MOVE FORWARD

_____

_____

THIS LUNATION

Full Moon ☐   ☐ New Moon

The Moon is in the sign of _____ and transits my _____ house,

meaning _____

_____ for me.

Build your Moon ritual: _____

_____

_____

_____

_____

_____

_____

CANDLES	CRYSTALS
HERBS	OTHER

Card 1	Card 2	Card 3
_____ Deck	_____ Deck	_____ Deck
_____ Card	_____ Card	_____ Card

Interpretation & Meaning: _____

_____

_____

_____

_____

_____

Intentions for this lunation: _____

_____

_____

_____

_____

_____

_____

_____

The Moon is in: _____

The Day Ruler is: _____

I AM GRATEFUL FOR

_____

_____

MOOD TRACKER

SELF - CARE

DAILY AFFIRMATION

_____

_____

DREAM JOURNAL

_____

_____

_____

_____

_____

_____

_____

_____

RITUAL TIME   MINDFUL MINUTES

_____ 5 _____
_____ 10 _____
_____ 15 _____
_____ 20 _____
_____ 25 _____
_____ 30 _____

SCRIPTING

3-6-9 MANIFESTATION

_____ _____ _____

_____ _____ _____

_____ _____ _____

1 THING I DID TO MOVE FORWARD

_____

_____

The Moon is in: _____

The Day Ruler is: _____

I AM GRATEFUL FOR

_____

_____

MOOD TRACKER

SELF - CARE

DAILY AFFIRMATION

_____

_____

DREAM JOURNAL

_____

_____

_____

_____

_____

_____

_____

_____

_____ 5 _____
_____ 10 _____
_____ 15 _____
_____ 20 _____
_____ 25 _____
_____ 30 _____

SCRIPTING

3-6-9 MANIFESTATION

_____ _____ _____

_____ _____ _____

_____ _____ _____

1 THING I DID TO MOVE FORWARD

_____

_____

The Moon is in: _____

The Day Ruler is: _____

I AM GRATEFUL FOR

_____

_____

MOOD TRACKER

SELF - CARE

DAILY AFFIRMATION

_____

_____

DREAM JOURNAL

_____

_____

_____

_____

_____

_____

_____

SCRIPTING

RITUAL TIME   MINDFUL MINUTES

5
10
15
20
25
30

3-6-9 MANIFESTATION

_____ _____ _____

_____ _____ _____

_____ _____ _____

1 THING I DID TO MOVE FORWARD

_____

_____

The Moon is in: _____

The Day Ruler is: _____

I AM GRATEFUL FOR

_____

_____

MOOD TRACKER

SELF - CARE

DAILY AFFIRMATION

_____

_____

DREAM JOURNAL

_____

_____

_____

_____

_____

_____

_____

_____

_____

_____5_____
_____10_____
_____15_____
_____20_____
_____25_____
_____30_____

SCRIPTING

3-6-9 MANIFESTATION

_____ _____ _____

_____ _____ _____

_____ _____ _____

1 THING I DID TO MOVE FORWARD

_____

_____

The Moon is in: _____

The Day Ruler is: _____

I AM GRATEFUL FOR

_____

_____

MOOD TRACKER

☹ ☹ 😐 🙂 😀

SELF - CARE

DAILY AFFIRMATION

_____

_____

DREAM JOURNAL

_____

_____

_____

_____

_____

_____

_____

_____

RITUAL TIME   MINDFUL MINUTES

_____ 5 _____
_____ 10 _____
_____ 15 _____
_____ 20 _____
_____ 25 _____
_____ 30 _____

SCRIPTING

_____
_____
_____
_____
_____
_____
_____
_____
_____
_____
_____
_____
_____
_____
_____
_____
_____
_____

3-6-9 MANIFESTATION

_____ _____ _____
_____ _____ _____
_____ _____ _____

1 THING I DID TO MOVE FORWARD

_____

_____

The Moon is in: _____

The Day Ruler is: _____

I AM GRATEFUL FOR

_____

_____

MOOD TRACKER

SELF - CARE

DAILY AFFIRMATION

_____

_____

DREAM JOURNAL

_____

_____

_____

_____

_____

_____

_____

_____

_____

_____ 5 _____
_____ 10 _____
_____ 15 _____
_____ 20 _____
_____ 25 _____
_____ 30 _____

SCRIPTING

3-6-9 MANIFESTATION

_____ _____ _____

_____ _____ _____

_____ _____ _____

1 THING I DID TO MOVE FORWARD

_____

_____

The Moon is in: _____

The Day Ruler is: _____

I AM GRATEFUL FOR

_____

_____

MOOD TRACKER

SELF - CARE

DAILY AFFIRMATION

_____

_____

DREAM JOURNAL

_____

_____

_____

_____

_____

_____

_____

_____

_____

RITUAL TIME   MINDFUL MINUTES

_____5_____
_____10_____
_____15_____
_____20_____
_____25_____
_____30_____

SCRIPTING

3-6-9 MANIFESTATION

_____ _____ _____

_____ _____ _____

_____ _____ _____

1 THING I DID TO MOVE FORWARD

_____

_____

The Moon is in: _____

The Day Ruler is: _____

I AM GRATEFUL FOR

_____

_____

MOOD TRACKER

SELF - CARE

DAILY AFFIRMATION

_____

_____

DREAM JOURNAL

_____

_____

_____

_____

_____

_____

_____

_____

_____

_____ 5 _____
_____ 10 _____
_____ 15 _____
_____ 20 _____
_____ 25 _____
_____ 30 _____

SCRIPTING

_____

_____

_____

_____

_____

_____

_____

_____

_____

_____

_____

_____

_____

_____

_____

_____

3-6-9 MANIFESTATION

_____ _____ _____

_____ _____ _____

_____ _____ _____

1 THING I DID TO MOVE FORWARD

_____

_____

The Moon is in: _____

The Day Ruler is: _____

I AM GRATEFUL FOR

_____

_____

MOOD TRACKER

SELF - CARE

DAILY AFFIRMATION

_____

_____

DREAM JOURNAL

_____

_____

_____

_____

_____

_____

_____

RITUAL TIME   MINDFUL MINUTES

_____ 5 _____
_____ 10 _____
_____ 15 _____
_____ 20 _____
_____ 25 _____
_____ 30 _____

SCRIPTING

3-6-9 MANIFESTATION

_____ _____ _____
_____ _____ _____
_____ _____ _____

1 THING I DID TO MOVE FORWARD

_____

_____

The Moon is in: _____
The Day Ruler is: _____

I AM GRATEFUL FOR

_____

_____

MOOD TRACKER

SELF - CARE

DAILY AFFIRMATION

_____

_____

DREAM JOURNAL

_____

_____

_____

_____

_____

_____

_____

_____

_____

_____ 5 _____
_____ 10 _____
_____ 15 _____
_____ 20 _____
_____ 25 _____
_____ 30 _____

SCRIPTING

3-6-9 MANIFESTATION

_____ _____ _____

_____ _____ _____

_____ _____ _____

1 THING I DID TO MOVE FORWARD

_____

_____

The Moon is in: _____

The Day Ruler is: _____

I AM GRATEFUL FOR

_____

_____

MOOD TRACKER

SELF - CARE

DAILY AFFIRMATION

_____

_____

DREAM JOURNAL

_____

_____

_____

_____

_____

_____

_____

RITUAL TIME

MINDFUL MINUTES

____ 5 ____
____ 10 ____
____ 15 ____
____ 20 ____
____ 25 ____
____ 30 ____

SCRIPTING

3-6-9 MANIFESTATION

_____ _____ _____

_____ _____ _____

_____ _____ _____

1 THING I DID TO MOVE FORWARD

_____

_____

The Moon is in: _____

The Day Ruler is: _____

I AM GRATEFUL FOR

_____

_____

MOOD TRACKER

SELF - CARE

DAILY AFFIRMATION

_____

_____

DREAM JOURNAL

_____

_____

_____

_____

_____

_____

_____

_____

_____ 5 _____
_____ 10 _____
_____ 15 _____
_____ 20 _____
_____ 25 _____
_____ 30 _____

SCRIPTING

3-6-9 MANIFESTATION

_____ _____ _____

_____ _____ _____

_____ _____ _____

1 THING I DID TO MOVE FORWARD

_____

_____

JULY

SUNDAY	MONDAY	TUESDAY	WEDNESDAY
2	3 ○	4 Independence Day	5
9 ◐	10	11	12
16	17 ●	18	19
23	24	25 ◑	26
30	31 Lammas		

2023

THURSDAY	FRIDAY	SATURDAY	NOTES
		1	
6	7	8	
13	14	15	
20	21	22	
27	28	29	

BUCK MOON

RITUAL FOCUS:
The buck moon is a time for connecting with your inner leader, set long-term goals, do divination, and dreamscaping.

ZODIACS:
Cancer & Leo

CRYSTALS:
Ruby, Carnelian, Peacock Ore

COLORS:
Blue, Gray & Silver

ELEMENTS:
Water & Fire

DEITIES:
Hel, Athena, Venus, Juno, Khephri

FLOWERS:
Larkspur, Waterlilly & Delphinum

ANIMALS:
Deer, Frogs & Bees

HERBS:
Honeysuckle, Lemon Balm, Hyssop, Agrimony, Gardenia & Myrrh

MAGICAL ASSOCIATIONS:
Self-regulation & Divination

DIVINATION TRACKER

DATE	PULL	MESSAGE

JULY TRANSITS

July 2023 — Tropical Midnight Ephemeris — Time Zone: EDT (04:00 East)

Day	☉	☽	+12 Hr	True☊	☿	♀	♂	♃	♄	♅	♆	♇
01 Sa	09♋06 09	07♐34 14	14♐40 16	01♉45 R	09♋03 D	20♌53 D	24♌22 D	09♉19 D	07♓04 R	21♉43 D	27♓41 R	29♑37 R
02 Su	10 03 20	21 52 43	29 11 00	01 39	11 13	21 30	24 58	09 29	07 02	21 45	27 41	29 35
03 Mo	11 00 31	06♑34 16	14♑01 33	01 30	13 23	22 06	25 34	09 39	07 01	21 48	27 41	29 34
04 Tu	11 57 42	21 31 44	29 03 35	01 20	15 33	22 41	26 10	09 49	06 59	21 50	27 41	29 33
05 We	12 54 53	06♒35 50	14♒07 16	01 10	17 41	23 15	26 47	09 59	06 58	21 53	27 41	29 31
06 Th	13 52 04	21 36 41	29 03 03	01 01	19 47	23 47	27 23	10 09	06 56	21 55	27 41	29 30
07 Fr	14 49 15	06♓25 29	13♓43 16	00 55	21 53	24 18	27 59	10 19	06 54	21 58	27 41	29 29
08 Sa	15 46 27	20 55 53	28 03 01	00 51	23 57	24 47	28 36	10 29	06 52	22 00	27 40	29 27
09 Su	16 43 39	05♈04 29	12♈00 18	00 49	25 59	25 15	29 12	10 38	06 50	22 02	27 40	29 26
10 Mo	17 40 51	18 50 33	25 35 28	00 48 D	28 00	25 41	29 48	10 48	06 48	22 05	27 40	29 25
11 Tu	18 38 03	02♉15 20	08♉50 29	00 48 R	29 59	26 06	00♍25	10 57	06 46	22 07	27 40	29 23
12 We	19 35 17	15 21 15	21 48 01	00 48	01♌56	26 29	01 01	11 06	06 44	22 09	27 39	29 22
13 Th	20 32 30	28 11 08	04♊30 56	00 45	03 52	26 50	01 38	11 15	06 41	22 11	27 39	29 20
14 Fr	21 29 44	10♊47 42	17 01 45	00 40	05 45	27 10	02 15	11 24	06 39	22 13	27 38	29 19
15 Sa	22 26 59	23 13 18	29 22 34	00 32	07 37	27 28	02 51	11 33	06 37	22 16	27 38	29 18
16 Su	23 24 14	05♋29 44	11♋34 58	00 22	09 27	27 44	03 28	11 42	06 34	22 18	27 37	29 16
17 Mo	24 21 30	17 38 23	23 40 09	00 09	11 14	27 57	04 05	11 50	06 31	22 20	27 37	29 15
18 Tu	25 18 46	29 40 23	05♌39 13	29♈55	13 00	28 09	04 41	11 59	06 28	22 22	27 36	29 13
19 We	26 16 02	11♌36 50	17 33 23	29 42	14 45	28 19	05 18	12 07	06 26	22 24	27 36	29 12
20 Th	27 13 18	23 29 07	29 24 16	29 29	16 27	28 27	05 55	12 15	06 23	22 26	27 35	29 10
21 Fr	28 10 35	05♍19 07	11♍14 02	29 19	18 07	28 32	06 32	12 23	06 20	22 27	27 35	29 09
22 Sa	29 07 52	17 09 23	23 05 37	29 11	19 46	28 35	07 09	12 31	06 17	22 29	27 34	29 08
23 Su	00♌05 10	29 03 13	05♎02 41	29 06	21 22	28 36 R	07 46	12 39	06 13	22 31	27 33	29 06
24 Mo	01 02 27	11♎04 37	17 09 36	29 04	22 57	28 35	08 23	12 47	06 10	22 33	27 33	29 05
25 Tu	01 59 45	23 18 15	29 31 13	29 03	24 30	28 31	09 00	12 54	06 07	22 34	27 32	29 03
26 We	02 57 04	05♏49 08	12♏12 37	29 03	26 01	28 25	09 37	13 01	06 04	22 36	27 31	29 02
27 Th	03 54 23	18 42 14	25 18 31	29 02	27 30	28 16	10 14	13 08	06 00	22 38	27 30	29 00
28 Fr	04 51 42	02♐01 53	08♐52 37	29 00	28 58	28 05	10 51	13 15	05 57	22 39	27 29	28 59
29 Sa	05 49 02	15 50 54	22 56 40	28 56	00♍23	27 52	11 28	13 22	05 53	22 41	27 29	28 58
30 Su	06 46 22	00♑09 42	07♑29 30	28 49	01 46	27 36	12 06	13 29	05 50	22 42	27 28	28 56
31 Mo	07 43 43	14 55 24	22 26 27	28 40	03 08	27 18	12 43	13 36	05 46	22 44	27 27	28 55

Planetary Data

Ingresses

		Day	Time
♂	♍	10	7:40 AM
☿	♌	11	12:10 AM
☉	♌	22	9:50 PM
☿	♍	28	5:31 PM

Stations

	Day	Time
♆R	30	5:06 PM
♀R	22	9:33 PM

Lunar Ingresses & Void Moons

Ingresses

	Day	Time
♏	28	4:56 AM
♐	30	10:59 AM
♑	2	1:19 PM
♒	4	1:30 PM
♓	6	1:33 PM
♈	8	3:19 PM
♉	10	7:56 PM
♊	13	3:26 AM
♋	15	1:13 PM
♌	18	12:40 AM
♍	20	1:13 PM
♎	23	1:55 AM
♏	25	12:56 PM
♐	27	8:23 PM
♑	29	11:45 PM
♒	31	11:58 PM

Void Times

Day	Time	Last Aspect	
30	10:21 AM	⚹	♇
2	9:34 AM	□	♇
4	12:45 PM	☌	♇
6	9:41 AM	☍	♂
8	2:21 PM	⚹	♇
10	7:11 PM	□	☿
13	2:11 AM	△	♇
15	8:36 AM	□	♇
17	11:06 PM	☍	♇
20	10:09 AM	☌	♀
23	12:06 AM	△	♇
25	11:06 AM	□	♇
27	6:36 PM	⚹	♇
29	7:51 PM	△	♀
31	10:12 PM	☌	♇

Phases & Eclipses

Lunar Phases

Day	Time		
3	7:39 AM	○	11♑19
9	9:48 PM	☽	17♈36
17	2:32 PM	●	24♋56
25	6:07 PM	☽	02♏43

Solar Eclipses

Day Time

~ None ~

Lunar Eclipses

Day Time

~ None ~

NOTES

The Moon is in: _____

The Day Ruler is: _____

I AM GRATEFUL FOR

_____

_____

MOOD TRACKER

😠 😟 😐 🙂 😄

SELF - CARE

DAILY AFFIRMATION

_____

_____

DREAM JOURNAL

_____

_____

_____

_____

_____

_____

_____

_____

_____

SCRIPTING

RITUAL TIME   MINDFUL MINUTES

5
10
15
20
25
30

3-6-9 MANIFESTATION

_____ _____ _____

_____ _____ _____

_____ _____ _____

1 THING I DID TO MOVE FORWARD

_____

_____

The Moon is in: _____

The Day Ruler is: _____

I AM GRATEFUL FOR

_____

_____

MOOD TRACKER

SELF - CARE

DAILY AFFIRMATION

_____

_____

DREAM JOURNAL

_____

_____

_____

_____

_____

_____

_____

_____

_____ 5 _____
_____ 10 _____
_____ 15 _____
_____ 20 _____
_____ 25 _____
_____ 30 _____

SCRIPTING

3-6-9 MANIFESTATION

_____ _____ _____

_____ _____ _____

_____ _____ _____

1 THING I DID TO MOVE FORWARD

_____

_____

The Moon is in: _____

The Day Ruler is: _____

I AM GRATEFUL FOR

_____

_____

MOOD TRACKER

SELF - CARE

DAILY AFFIRMATION

_____

_____

DREAM JOURNAL

_____

_____

_____

_____

_____

_____

_____

_____

RITUAL TIME   MINDFUL MINUTES

_____5_____
_____10_____
_____15_____
_____20_____
_____25_____
_____30_____

SCRIPTING

3-6-9 MANIFESTATION

_____ _____ _____

_____ _____ _____

_____ _____ _____

1 THING I DID TO MOVE FORWARD

_____

THIS LUNATION

Full Moon ☐   ☐ New Moon

The Moon is in the sign of _____ and transits my _____ house,

meaning _____

_____ for me.

Build your Moon ritual: _____

_____

_____

_____

_____

_____

_____

_____

CANDLES	CRYSTALS
HERBS	OTHER

Card 1	Card 2	Card 3
___ Deck	___ Deck	___ Deck
___ Card	___ Card	___ Card

Interpretation & Meaning: _____

_____

_____

_____

_____

_____

Intentions for this lunation: _____

_____

_____

_____

_____

_____

_____

_____

The Moon is in: _____
The Day Ruler is: _____

I AM GRATEFUL FOR

_____
_____

MOOD TRACKER

SELF - CARE

DAILY AFFIRMATION

_____
_____

DREAM JOURNAL

_____
_____
_____
_____
_____
_____
_____
_____
_____

RITUAL TIME   MINDFUL MINUTES

_____5_____
_____10_____
_____15_____
_____20_____
_____25_____
_____30_____

SCRIPTING

_____
_____
_____
_____
_____
_____
_____
_____
_____
_____
_____
_____
_____
_____

3-6-9 MANIFESTATION

_____ _____ _____
_____ _____ _____
_____ _____ _____

1 THING I DID TO MOVE FORWARD

_____
_____

The Moon is in: _____

The Day Ruler is: _____

I AM GRATEFUL FOR

_____

_____

MOOD TRACKER

SELF - CARE

DAILY AFFIRMATION

_____

_____

DREAM JOURNAL

_____

_____

_____

_____

_____

_____

_____

_____

_____

_____

_____5_____
_____10_____
_____15_____
_____20_____
_____25_____
_____30_____

SCRIPTING

3-6-9 MANIFESTATION

_____ _____ _____

_____ _____ _____

_____ _____ _____

1 THING I DID TO MOVE FORWARD

_____

_____

The Moon is in: _____

The Day Ruler is: _____

I AM GRATEFUL FOR

_____

_____

MOOD TRACKER

😠 😟 😐 🙂 😃

SELF - CARE

DAILY AFFIRMATION

_____

_____

DREAM JOURNAL

_____

_____

_____

_____

_____

_____

_____

_____

RITUAL TIME   MINDFUL MINUTES

_____5_____
_____10_____
_____15_____
_____20_____
_____25_____
_____30_____

SCRIPTING

3-6-9 MANIFESTATION

_____ _____ _____

_____ _____ _____

_____ _____ _____

1 THING I DID TO MOVE FORWARD

_____

_____

The Moon is in: _____

The Day Ruler is: _____

I AM GRATEFUL FOR

_____

_____

MOOD TRACKER

SELF - CARE

DAILY AFFIRMATION

_____

_____

DREAM JOURNAL

_____

_____

_____

_____

_____

_____

_____

_____

_____

| 5 |
| 10 |
| 15 |
| 20 |
| 25 |
| 30 |

SCRIPTING

3-6-9 MANIFESTATION

_____ _____ _____

_____ _____ _____

_____ _____ _____

1 THING I DID TO MOVE FORWARD

_____

_____

The Moon is in: _____

The Day Ruler is: _____

I AM GRATEFUL FOR

_____

_____

MOOD TRACKER

😠   🙁   😐   🙂   😀

SELF - CARE

DAILY AFFIRMATION

_____

_____

DREAM JOURNAL

_____

_____

_____

_____

_____

_____

_____

_____

SCRIPTING

RITUAL TIME   MINDFUL MINUTES

_____ 5 _____
_____ 10 _____
_____ 15 _____
_____ 20 _____
_____ 25 _____
_____ 30 _____

3-6-9 MANIFESTATION

_____ _____ _____
_____ _____ _____
_____ _____ _____

1 THING I DID TO MOVE FORWARD

_____

_____

The Moon is in: _____

The Day Ruler is: _____

I AM GRATEFUL FOR

_____

_____

MOOD TRACKER

SELF - CARE

DAILY AFFIRMATION

_____

_____

DREAM JOURNAL

_____

_____

_____

_____

_____

_____

_____

_____

_____ 5 _____
_____ 10 _____
_____ 15 _____
_____ 20 _____
_____ 25 _____
_____ 30 _____

SCRIPTING

3-6-9 MANIFESTATION

_____ _____ _____

_____ _____ _____

_____ _____ _____

1 THING I DID TO MOVE FORWARD

_____

_____

The Moon is in: _____
The Day Ruler is: _____

I AM GRATEFUL FOR

_____
_____

MOOD TRACKER

SELF - CARE

DAILY AFFIRMATION

_____
_____

DREAM JOURNAL

_____
_____
_____
_____
_____
_____
_____
_____
_____

RITUAL TIME   MINDFUL MINUTES

_____ 5 _____
_____ 10 _____
_____ 15 _____
_____ 20 _____
_____ 25 _____
_____ 30 _____

SCRIPTING

3-6-9 MANIFESTATION

_____ _____ _____
_____ _____ _____
_____ _____ _____

1 THING I DID TO MOVE FORWARD

_____
_____

The Moon is in: _____
The Day Ruler is: _____

I AM GRATEFUL FOR

_____

_____

MOOD TRACKER

SELF - CARE

DAILY AFFIRMATION

_____

_____

DREAM JOURNAL

_____

_____

_____

_____

_____

_____

_____

_____

_____ 5 _____
_____ 10 _____
_____ 15 _____
_____ 20 _____
_____ 25 _____
_____ 30 _____

SCRIPTING

3-6-9 MANIFESTATION

_____ _____ _____

_____ _____ _____

1 THING I DID TO MOVE FORWARD

_____

_____

The Moon is in:_____
The Day Ruler is:_____

I AM GRATEFUL FOR
_____
_____

MOOD TRACKER
😠 ☹️ 😐 🙂 😃

SELF - CARE

DAILY AFFIRMATION
_____
_____

DREAM JOURNAL
_____
_____
_____
_____
_____
_____
_____
_____

RITUAL TIME   MINDFUL MINUTES
_____5_____
_____10_____
_____15_____
_____20_____
_____25_____
_____30_____

SCRIPTING

3-6-9 MANIFESTATION
_____ _____ _____
_____ _____ _____
_____ _____ _____

1 THING I DID TO MOVE FORWARD
_____
_____

The Moon is in: _____

The Day Ruler is: _____

I AM GRATEFUL FOR

_____

_____

MOOD TRACKER

SELF - CARE

DAILY AFFIRMATION

_____

_____

DREAM JOURNAL

_____

_____

_____

_____

_____

_____

_____

_____

_____

_____ 5 _____
_____ 10 _____
_____ 15 _____
_____ 20 _____
_____ 25 _____
_____ 30 _____

SCRIPTING

3-6-9 MANIFESTATION

_____ _____ _____

_____ _____ _____

_____ _____ _____

1 THING I DID TO MOVE FORWARD

_____

_____

The Moon is in: _____
The Day Ruler is: _____

I AM GRATEFUL FOR

_____
_____

MOOD TRACKER

SELF - CARE

DAILY AFFIRMATION

_____
_____

DREAM JOURNAL

_____
_____
_____
_____
_____
_____
_____
_____

RITUAL TIME   MINDFUL MINUTES

_____5_____
_____10_____
_____15_____
_____20_____
_____25_____
_____30_____

SCRIPTING

3-6-9 MANIFESTATION

_____ _____ _____
_____ _____ _____
_____ _____ _____

1 THING I DID TO MOVE FORWARD

_____
_____

The Moon is in: _____

The Day Ruler is: _____

I AM GRATEFUL FOR

_____

_____

MOOD TRACKER

SELF - CARE

DAILY AFFIRMATION

_____

_____

DREAM JOURNAL

_____

_____

_____

_____

_____

_____

_____

_____

_____

_____ 5 _____
_____ 10 _____
_____ 15 _____
_____ 20 _____
_____ 25 _____
_____ 30 _____

SCRIPTING

3-6-9 MANIFESTATION

_____ _____ _____

_____ _____ _____

_____ _____ _____

1 THING I DID TO MOVE FORWARD

_____

_____

The Moon is in: _____

The Day Ruler is: _____

I AM GRATEFUL FOR

_____

_____

MOOD TRACKER

SELF - CARE

DAILY AFFIRMATION

_____

_____

DREAM JOURNAL

_____

_____

_____

_____

_____

_____

_____

RITUAL TIME   MINDFUL MINUTES

_____5_____
_____10_____
_____15_____
_____20_____
_____25_____
_____30_____

SCRIPTING

3-6-9 MANIFESTATION

_____ _____ _____

_____ _____ _____

_____ _____ _____

1 THING I DID TO MOVE FORWARD

_____

_____

The Moon is in: _____

The Day Ruler is: _____

I AM GRATEFUL FOR

_____

_____

MOOD TRACKER

SELF - CARE

DAILY AFFIRMATION

_____

_____

DREAM JOURNAL

_____

_____

_____

_____

_____

_____

_____

_____

_____

_____ 5 _____
_____ 10 _____
_____ 15 _____
_____ 20 _____
_____ 25 _____
_____ 30 _____

SCRIPTING

3-6-9 MANIFESTATION

_____ _____ _____

_____ _____ _____

_____ _____ _____

_____ _____ _____

1 THING I DID TO MOVE FORWARD

_____

_____

THIS LUNATION

Full Moon ☐   ☐ New Moon

The Moon is in the sign of _____ and transits my _____ house,

meaning _____

_____ for me.

Build your Moon ritual: _____

_____

_____

_____

_____

_____

_____

CANDLES	CRYSTALS
HERBS	OTHER

Card 1	Card 2	Card 3
_____	_____	_____
Deck	Deck	Deck
_____	_____	_____
Card	Card	Card

Interpretation & Meaning: _____

_____

_____

_____

_____

Intentions for this lunation: _____

_____

_____

_____

_____

_____

_____

The Moon is in: _____

The Day Ruler is: _____

I AM GRATEFUL FOR

_____

_____

MOOD TRACKER

SELF - CARE

DAILY AFFIRMATION

_____

_____

DREAM JOURNAL

_____

_____

_____

_____

_____

_____

_____

_____

_____

_____ 5 _____
_____ 10 _____
_____ 15 _____
_____ 20 _____
_____ 25 _____
_____ 30 _____

SCRIPTING

3-6-9 MANIFESTATION

_____ _____ _____

_____ _____ _____

_____ _____ _____

1 THING I DID TO MOVE FORWARD

_____

_____

The Moon is in: _____

The Day Ruler is: _____

I AM GRATEFUL FOR

_____

_____

MOOD TRACKER

😠 😞 😐 🙂 😃

SELF - CARE

DAILY AFFIRMATION

_____

_____

DREAM JOURNAL

_____

_____

_____

_____

_____

_____

_____

_____

RITUAL TIME

MINDFUL MINUTES

_____ 5 _____
_____ 10 _____
_____ 15 _____
_____ 20 _____
_____ 25 _____
_____ 30 _____

SCRIPTING

3-6-9 MANIFESTATION

_____ _____ _____

_____ _____ _____

_____ _____ _____

1 THING I DID TO MOVE FORWARD

_____

_____

The Moon is in: _____

The Day Ruler is: _____

I AM GRATEFUL FOR

_____

_____

MOOD TRACKER

SELF - CARE

DAILY AFFIRMATION

_____

_____

DREAM JOURNAL

_____

_____

_____

_____

_____

_____

_____

_____

_____

_____ 5 _____
_____ 10 _____
_____ 15 _____
_____ 20 _____
_____ 25 _____
_____ 30 _____

SCRIPTING

3-6-9 MANIFESTATION

_____ _____ _____

_____ _____ _____

_____ _____ _____

1 THING I DID TO MOVE FORWARD

_____

_____

The Moon is in:_____
The Day Ruler is:_____

I AM GRATEFUL FOR

_____
_____

MOOD TRACKER

SELF - CARE

DAILY AFFIRMATION

_____
_____

DREAM JOURNAL

_____
_____
_____
_____
_____
_____
_____
_____
_____

RITUAL TIME   MINDFUL MINUTES

_____5_____
_____10_____
_____15_____
_____20_____
_____25_____
_____30_____

SCRIPTING

3-6-9 MANIFESTATION

_____ _____ _____
_____ _____ _____
_____ _____ _____

1 THING I DID TO MOVE FORWARD

_____
_____

The Moon is in: _____

The Day Ruler is: _____

I AM GRATEFUL FOR

_____

_____

MOOD TRACKER

SELF - CARE

DAILY AFFIRMATION

_____

_____

DREAM JOURNAL

_____

_____

_____

_____

_____

_____

_____

_____

_____

_____5_____
_____10_____
_____15_____
_____20_____
_____25_____
_____30_____

SCRIPTING

3-6-9 MANIFESTATION

_____ _____ _____

_____ _____ _____

_____ _____ _____

1 THING I DID TO MOVE FORWARD

_____

_____

The Moon is in: _____

The Day Ruler is: _____

I AM GRATEFUL FOR

_____

_____

MOOD TRACKER

SELF - CARE

DAILY AFFIRMATION

_____

_____

DREAM JOURNAL

_____

_____

_____

_____

_____

_____

_____

_____

RITUAL TIME   MINDFUL MINUTES

_____ 5 _____
_____ 10 _____
_____ 15 _____
_____ 20 _____
_____ 25 _____
_____ 30 _____

SCRIPTING

3-6-9 MANIFESTATION

_____ _____ _____
_____ _____ _____
_____ _____ _____

1 THING I DID TO MOVE FORWARD

_____

_____

The Moon is in: _____

The Day Ruler is: _____

I AM GRATEFUL FOR

_____

_____

MOOD TRACKER

SELF - CARE

DAILY AFFIRMATION

_____

_____

DREAM JOURNAL

_____

_____

_____

_____

_____

_____

_____

_____

_____

_____ 5 _____
_____ 10 _____
_____ 15 _____
_____ 20 _____
_____ 25 _____
_____ 30 _____

SCRIPTING

3-6-9 MANIFESTATION

_____ _____ _____

_____ _____ _____

_____ _____ _____

1 THING I DID TO MOVE FORWARD

_____

_____

The Moon is in: _____

The Day Ruler is: _____

I AM GRATEFUL FOR

_____

_____

MOOD TRACKER

😣 😟 😐 🙂 😀

SELF - CARE

DAILY AFFIRMATION

_____

_____

DREAM JOURNAL

_____

_____

_____

_____

_____

_____

_____

SCRIPTING

_____

_____

_____

_____

_____

_____

_____

_____

_____

_____

_____

_____

_____

RITUAL TIME   MINDFUL MINUTES

_____5_____
_____10_____
_____15_____
_____20_____
_____25_____
_____30_____

3-6-9 MANIFESTATION

_____ _____ _____

_____ _____ _____

_____ _____ _____

1 THING I DID TO MOVE FORWARD

_____

_____

The Moon is in: _____

The Day Ruler is: _____

I AM GRATEFUL FOR

_____

_____

MOOD TRACKER

SELF - CARE

DAILY AFFIRMATION

_____

_____

DREAM JOURNAL

_____

_____

_____

_____

_____

_____

_____

_____

_____

_____ 5 _____
_____ 10 _____
_____ 15 _____
_____ 20 _____
_____ 25 _____
_____ 30 _____

SCRIPTING

3-6-9 MANIFESTATION

_____ _____ _____

_____ _____ _____

_____ _____ _____

1 THING I DID TO MOVE FORWARD

_____

_____

The Moon is in: _____

The Day Ruler is: _____

I AM GRATEFUL FOR

_____

_____

MOOD TRACKER

SELF - CARE

DAILY AFFIRMATION

_____

_____

DREAM JOURNAL

_____

_____

_____

_____

_____

_____

_____

_____

RITUAL TIME   MINDFUL MINUTES

_____ 5 _____
_____ 10 _____
_____ 15 _____
_____ 20 _____
_____ 25 _____
_____ 30 _____

SCRIPTING

_____

3-6-9 MANIFESTATION

_____ _____ _____
_____ _____ _____
_____ _____ _____

1 THING I DID TO MOVE FORWARD

_____

_____

The Moon is in: _____
The Day Ruler is: _____

I AM GRATEFUL FOR

_____

_____

MOOD TRACKER

SELF - CARE

DAILY AFFIRMATION

_____

_____

DREAM JOURNAL

_____
_____
_____
_____
_____
_____
_____
_____
_____

_____5_____
_____10_____
_____15_____
_____20_____
_____25_____
_____30_____

SCRIPTING

3-6-9 MANIFESTATION

_____ _____ _____

_____ _____ _____

_____ _____ _____

1 THING I DID TO MOVE FORWARD

_____

_____

The Moon is in: _____

The Day Ruler is: _____

I AM GRATEFUL FOR

_____

_____

MOOD TRACKER

SELF - CARE

DAILY AFFIRMATION

_____

_____

DREAM JOURNAL

_____

_____

_____

_____

_____

_____

_____

_____

SCRIPTING

3-6-9 MANIFESTATION

_____ _____ _____

_____ _____ _____

_____ _____ _____

1 THING I DID TO MOVE FORWARD

_____

_____

RITUAL TIME   MINDFUL MINUTES

___5___
___10___
___15___
___20___
___25___
___30___

The Moon is in: _____

The Day Ruler is: _____

I AM GRATEFUL FOR

_____

_____

MOOD TRACKER

SELF - CARE

DAILY AFFIRMATION

_____

_____

DREAM JOURNAL

_____

_____

_____

_____

_____

_____

_____

_____

_____

_____5_____
_____10_____
_____15_____
_____20_____
_____25_____
_____30_____

SCRIPTING

3-6-9 MANIFESTATION

_____ _____ _____

_____ _____ _____

_____ _____ _____

1 THING I DID TO MOVE FORWARD

_____

_____

The Moon is in: _____

The Day Ruler is: _____

I AM GRATEFUL FOR

_____

_____

MOOD TRACKER

SELF - CARE

DAILY AFFIRMATION

_____

_____

DREAM JOURNAL

_____

_____

_____

_____

_____

_____

_____

_____

RITUAL TIME   MINDFUL MINUTES

_____ 5 _____
_____ 10 _____
_____ 15 _____
_____ 20 _____
_____ 25 _____
_____ 30 _____

SCRIPTING

_____
_____
_____
_____
_____
_____
_____
_____
_____
_____
_____
_____
_____
_____
_____
_____
_____
_____
_____

3-6-9 MANIFESTATION

_____ _____ _____
_____ _____ _____
_____ _____ _____

1 THING I DID TO MOVE FORWARD

_____
_____

NOTES

AUGUST

SUNDAY	MONDAY	TUESDAY	WEDNESDAY
		1 ○	2
6	7	8 ◑	9
13	14	15	16 ●
20	21	22	23
27	28	29	30 ○

THURSDAY	FRIDAY	SATURDAY	NOTES
3	4	5	
10	11	12	
17	18	19	
24 ◑	25	26	
31			

STURGEON MOON

RITUAL FOCUS:
The sturgeon moon is a time for reflecting on what you've been manifesting and how it is showing up for you. Review your manifestations and intentions for the previous year and recommit if you need to.

ZODIACS:
Leo & Virgo

CRYSTALS:
Peridot, Onyx, Sunstone

COLORS:
Gold, Yellow & Green

ELEMENTS:
Fire & Earth

DEITIES:
Demeter, Ceres, Hathor, Isis, Venus, Vesta, Diana, Ganesha, Nemesis

FLOWERS:
Gladiolus, Poppy & Geranium

ANIMALS:
Lion, Phoenix, Sphinx, Dragon

HERBS:
Chamomile, Angelica, Bay, Fennel, Rue, Rosemary, Jasmine, Lilac, Violet, Calamus

MAGICAL ASSOCIATIONS:
Gratitude, Friendship, Bounty, Peace, Symmetry & Reflection

DIVINATION TRACKER

DATE	PULL	MESSAGE

AUGUST TRANSITS

August 2023

Tropical Midnight Ephemeris Time Zone: **EDT (04:00 East)**

Day	☉	☽	+12 Hr	True☊	☿	♀	♂	♃	♄	♅	♆	♇
01 Tu	08 ♌ 41 05	00 ♒ 01 30	07 ♒ 39 16	28 ♈ 30 R	04 ♍ 27 D	26 ♌ 58 R	13 ♍ 20 D	13 ♉ 42 D	05 ♓ 42 R	22 ♉ 45 D	27 ♓ 26 R	28 ♑ 53 R
02 We	09 38 27	15 18 21	22 57 17	28 20	05 44	26 35	13 58	13 48	05 38	22 47	27 25	28 52
03 Th	10 35 51	00 ♓ 34 40	08 ♓ 09 11	28 10	06 59	26 11	14 35	13 54	05 35	22 48	27 24	28 51
04 Fr	11 33 15	15 39 39	23 05 07	28 03	08 12	25 44	15 12	14 00	05 31	22 49	27 23	28 49
05 Sa	12 30 40	00 ♈ 24 47	07 ♈ 38 08	27 58	09 23	25 15	15 50	14 06	05 27	22 50	27 22	28 48
06 Su	13 28 06	14 44 50	21 44 46	27 56	10 31	24 45	16 27	14 12	05 23	22 51	27 21	28 46
07 Mo	14 25 34	28 37 58	05 ♉ 24 38	27 55 D	11 37	24 13	17 05	14 17	05 19	22 53	27 20	28 45
08 Tu	15 23 03	12 ♉ 05 04	18 39 39	27 55	12 40	23 40	17 43	14 22	05 15	22 54	27 19	28 44
09 We	16 20 33	25 08 48	01 ♊ 33 01	27 55 R	13 41	23 05	18 20	14 27	05 10	22 55	27 18	28 42
10 Th	17 18 05	07 ♊ 52 47	14 08 34	27 53	14 39	22 30	18 58	14 32	05 06	22 56	27 16	28 41
11 Fr	18 15 38	20 20 50	26 30 01	27 49	15 34	21 54	19 36	14 37	05 02	22 56	27 15	28 40
12 Sa	19 13 13	02 ♋ 36 33	08 ♋ 40 47	27 43	16 27	21 17	20 13	14 42	04 58	22 57	27 14	28 38
13 Su	20 10 48	14 43 04	20 43 41	27 34	17 16	20 40	20 51	14 46	04 53	22 58	27 13	28 37
14 Mo	21 08 25	26 42 54	02 ♌ 40 59	27 22	18 01	20 02	21 29	14 50	04 49	22 59	27 12	28 36
15 Tu	22 06 04	08 ♌ 38 07	14 34 31	27 10	18 44	19 25	22 07	14 54	04 45	23 00	27 10	28 34
16 We	23 03 43	20 30 21	26 25 49	26 58	19 22	18 48	22 45	14 58	04 40	23 00	27 09	28 33
17 Th	24 01 24	02 ♍ 21 06	08 ♍ 16 25	26 47	19 57	18 12	23 23	15 02	04 36	23 01	27 08	28 32
18 Fr	24 59 06	14 11 59	20 08 02	26 38	20 27	17 37	24 01	15 05	04 32	23 02	27 06	28 31
19 Sa	25 56 50	26 04 53	02 ♎ 02 51	26 31	20 53	17 03	24 39	15 08	04 27	23 02	27 05	28 29
20 Su	26 54 34	08 ♎ 02 16	14 03 33	26 27	21 15	16 30	25 17	15 11	04 23	23 03	27 04	28 28
21 Mo	27 52 20	20 07 08	26 13 29	26 25	21 32	15 58	25 55	15 14	04 18	23 03	27 02	28 27
22 Tu	28 50 07	02 ♏ 23 08	08 ♏ 36 36	26 25 D	21 43	15 28	26 33	15 17	04 14	23 03	27 01	28 26
23 We	29 47 55	14 54 26	21 17 10	26 26	21 50	15 00	27 12	15 20	04 09	23 04	26 59	28 25
24 Th	00 ♍ 45 44	27 45 22	04 ♐ 19 31	26 27	21 51 R	14 33	27 50	15 22	04 05	23 04	26 58	28 23
25 Fr	01 43 34	11 ♐ 00 03	17 47 21	26 26 R	21 46	14 09	28 28	15 24	04 00	23 04	26 57	28 22
26 Sa	02 41 26	24 41 38	01 ♑ 43 01	26 24	21 35	13 47	29 07	15 26	03 55	23 04	26 55	28 21
27 Su	03 39 19	08 ♑ 51 27	16 06 39	26 20	21 19	13 27	29 45	15 28	03 51	23 04	26 54	28 20
28 Mo	04 37 13	23 28 08	00 ♒ 55 14	26 14	20 56	13 09	00 ♎ 24	15 29	03 46	23 04	26 52	28 19
29 Tu	05 35 09	08 ♒ 27 01	16 02 23	26 07	20 28	12 54	01 02	15 31	03 42	23 05 R	26 51	28 18
30 We	06 33 05	23 40 07	01 ♓ 18 50	25 59	19 53	12 41	01 41	15 32	03 37	23 04	26 49	28 17
31 Th	07 31 04	08 ♓ 57 09	16 33 42	25 53	19 14	12 30	02 19	15 33	03 33	23 04	26 48	28 16

Planetary Data

Ingresses

	Day	Time
☉ ♍	23	5:01 AM
♂ ♎	27	9:19 AM

Stations

	Day	Time
☿ R	23	3:59 PM
♅ R	28	10:39 PM

Lunar Ingresses & Void Moons

Ingresses

	Day	Time
♑	29	11:45 PM
♒	31	11:58 PM
♓	2	11:06 PM
♈	4	11:19 PM
♉	7	2:25 AM
♊	9	9:05 AM
♋	11	6:52 PM
♌	14	6:37 AM
♍	16	7:15 PM
♎	19	7:54 AM
♏	21	7:23 PM
♐	24	4:08 AM
♑	26	9:06 AM
♒	28	10:31 AM
♓	30	9:56 AM

Void Times

Day	Time	Last Aspect	
31	10:12 PM	☌	♇
2	5:15 PM	☍	♀
4	9:20 PM	⚹	♇
7	12:13 AM	□	♇
9	6:39 AM	△	♇
11	1:28 PM	□	♆
14	3:47 AM	☍	♇
16	5:39 AM	☌	☉
19	4:51 AM	△	♇
21	4:31 PM	⚹	☉
24	1:11 AM	⚹	♇
26	7:55 AM	□	♂
28	7:48 AM	☌	♇
29	11:04 PM	□	♅

Phases & Eclipses

Lunar Phases

Day	Time		
1	2:32 PM	○	09 ♒ 16
8	6:29 AM	☽	15 ♉ 39
16	5:39 AM	●	23 ♌ 17
24	5:58 AM	☽	01 ♐ 00
30	9:35 PM	○	07 ♓ 25

Solar Eclipses

Day Time

~ None ~

Lunar Eclipses

Day Time

~ None ~

NOTES

The Moon is in: _____

The Day Ruler is: _____

I AM GRATEFUL FOR

_____

_____

MOOD TRACKER

SELF - CARE

DAILY AFFIRMATION

_____

_____

DREAM JOURNAL

_____

_____

_____

_____

_____

_____

_____

_____

RITUAL TIME   MINDFUL MINUTES

_____ 5 _____
_____ 10 _____
_____ 15 _____
_____ 20 _____
_____ 25 _____
_____ 30 _____

SCRIPTING

3-6-9 MANIFESTATION

_____ _____ _____

_____ _____ _____

_____ _____ _____

1 THING I DID TO MOVE FORWARD

_____

_____

THIS LUNATION

Full Moon ☐   ☐ New Moon

The Moon is in the sign of _____ and transits my _____ house,

meaning _____

_____ for me.

Build your Moon ritual: _____

_____

_____

_____

_____

_____

_____

_____

CANDLES	CRYSTALS
HERBS	OTHER

Card 1	Card 2	Card 3
____ Deck	____ Deck	____ Deck
____ Card	____ Card	____ Card

Interpretation & Meaning: _____

_____

_____

_____

_____

_____

Intentions for this lunation: _____

_____

_____

_____

_____

_____

_____

_____

The Moon is in: _____

The Day Ruler is: _____

I AM GRATEFUL FOR

_____

_____

MOOD TRACKER

😠 😟 😐 🙂 😃

SELF - CARE

DAILY AFFIRMATION

_____

_____

DREAM JOURNAL

_____

_____

_____

_____

_____

_____

_____

_____

RITUAL TIME MINDFUL MINUTES

_____5_____
_____10_____
_____15_____
_____20_____
_____25_____
_____30_____

SCRIPTING

_____
_____
_____
_____
_____
_____
_____
_____
_____
_____
_____
_____
_____
_____
_____
_____
_____
_____
_____
_____

3-6-9 MANIFESTATION

_____ _____ _____
_____ _____ _____
_____ _____ _____

1 THING I DID TO MOVE FORWARD

_____

_____

The Moon is in: _____

The Day Ruler is: _____

I AM GRATEFUL FOR

_____

_____

MOOD TRACKER

SELF - CARE

DAILY AFFIRMATION

_____

_____

DREAM JOURNAL

_____

_____

_____

_____

_____

_____

_____

_____

_____

_____5_____
_____10_____
_____15_____
_____20_____
_____25_____
_____30_____

SCRIPTING

3-6-9 MANIFESTATION

_____ _____ _____

_____ _____ _____

_____ _____ _____

1 THING I DID TO MOVE FORWARD

_____

_____

The Moon is in: _____

The Day Ruler is: _____

I AM GRATEFUL FOR

_____

_____

MOOD TRACKER

SELF - CARE

DAILY AFFIRMATION

_____

_____

DREAM JOURNAL

_____

_____

_____

_____

_____

_____

_____

_____

_____

RITUAL TIME   MINDFUL MINUTES

_____ 5 _____
_____ 10 _____
_____ 15 _____
_____ 20 _____
_____ 25 _____
_____ 30 _____

SCRIPTING

3-6-9 MANIFESTATION

_____ _____ _____
_____ _____ _____
_____ _____ _____

1 THING I DID TO MOVE FORWARD

_____

_____

The Moon is in: _____

The Day Ruler is: _____

I AM GRATEFUL FOR

_____

_____

MOOD TRACKER

SELF - CARE

DAILY AFFIRMATION

_____

_____

DREAM JOURNAL

_____

_____

_____

_____

_____

_____

_____

_____

_____

_____ 5 _____
_____ 10 _____
_____ 15 _____
_____ 20 _____
_____ 25 _____
_____ 30 _____

SCRIPTING

3-6-9 MANIFESTATION

_____ _____ _____

_____ _____ _____

_____ _____ _____

1 THING I DID TO MOVE FORWARD

_____

_____

The Moon is in: _____
The Day Ruler is: _____

I AM GRATEFUL FOR

_____
_____

MOOD TRACKER

😠 😟 😐 🙂 😃

SELF - CARE

DAILY AFFIRMATION

_____
_____

DREAM JOURNAL

_____
_____
_____
_____
_____
_____
_____
_____

RITUAL TIME   MINDFUL MINUTES

_____ 5 _____
_____ 10 _____
_____ 15 _____
_____ 20 _____
_____ 25 _____
_____ 30 _____

SCRIPTING

_____
_____
_____
_____
_____
_____
_____
_____
_____
_____
_____
_____
_____
_____
_____
_____
_____

3-6-9 MANIFESTATION

_____ _____ _____
_____ _____ _____
_____ _____ _____

1 THING I DID TO MOVE FORWARD

_____

The Moon is in: _____

The Day Ruler is: _____

I AM GRATEFUL FOR

_____

_____

MOOD TRACKER

SELF - CARE

DAILY AFFIRMATION

_____

_____

DREAM JOURNAL

_____

_____

_____

_____

_____

_____

_____

_____

_____

```
____5____
___10____
___15____
___20____
___25____
___30____
```

SCRIPTING

3-6-9 MANIFESTATION

_____ _____ _____

_____ _____ _____

_____ _____ _____

1 THING I DID TO MOVE FORWARD

_____

_____

The Moon is in: _____

The Day Ruler is: _____

I AM GRATEFUL FOR

_____
_____

MOOD TRACKER

SELF - CARE

DAILY AFFIRMATION

_____
_____

DREAM JOURNAL

_____
_____
_____
_____
_____
_____
_____
_____
_____

RITUAL TIME MINDFUL MINUTES

_____ 5 _____
_____ 10 _____
_____ 15 _____
_____ 20 _____
_____ 25 _____
_____ 30 _____

SCRIPTING

3-6-9 MANIFESTATION

_____ _____ _____
_____ _____ _____
_____ _____ _____

1 THING I DID TO MOVE FORWARD

_____

The Moon is in: _____

The Day Ruler is: _____

I AM GRATEFUL FOR

_____

_____

MOOD TRACKER

SELF - CARE

DAILY AFFIRMATION

_____

_____

DREAM JOURNAL

_____

_____

_____

_____

_____

_____

_____

_____

_____

_____ 5 _____
_____ 10 _____
_____ 15 _____
_____ 20 _____
_____ 25 _____
_____ 30 _____

SCRIPTING

3-6-9 MANIFESTATION

_____ _____ _____

_____ _____ _____

_____ _____ _____

1 THING I DID TO MOVE FORWARD

_____

_____

The Moon is in: _____

The Day Ruler is: _____

I AM GRATEFUL FOR

_____

_____

MOOD TRACKER

😠 😟 😐 🙂 😃

SELF - CARE

DAILY AFFIRMATION

_____

_____

DREAM JOURNAL

_____

_____

_____

_____

_____

_____

_____

_____

_____

RITUAL TIME   MINDFUL MINUTES

___5___
___10___
___15___
___20___
___25___
___30___

SCRIPTING

_____
_____
_____
_____
_____
_____
_____
_____
_____
_____
_____
_____
_____
_____
_____
_____
_____
_____
_____
_____

3-6-9 MANIFESTATION

_____ _____ _____
_____ _____ _____
_____ _____ _____

1 THING I DID TO MOVE FORWARD

_____

The Moon is in: _____

The Day Ruler is: _____

I AM GRATEFUL FOR

_____

_____

MOOD TRACKER

SELF - CARE

DAILY AFFIRMATION

_____

_____

DREAM JOURNAL

_____

_____

_____

_____

_____

_____

_____

_____

_____

_____5_____
_____10_____
_____15_____
_____20_____
_____25_____
_____30_____

SCRIPTING

3-6-9 MANIFESTATION

_____ _____ _____

_____ _____ _____

_____ _____ _____

1 THING I DID TO MOVE FORWARD

_____

_____

The Moon is in:_____

The Day Ruler is:_____

I AM GRATEFUL FOR

_____

_____

MOOD TRACKER

😠　😟　😐　🙂　😄

SELF - CARE

DAILY AFFIRMATION

_____

_____

DREAM JOURNAL

_____

_____

_____

_____

_____

_____

_____

_____

RITUAL TIME　　MINDFUL MINUTES

_____5_____
_____10_____
_____15_____
_____20_____
_____25_____
_____30_____

SCRIPTING

_____
_____
_____
_____
_____
_____
_____
_____
_____
_____
_____
_____
_____
_____
_____
_____
_____
_____
_____

3-6-9 MANIFESTATION

_____ _____ _____
_____ _____ _____
_____ _____ _____

1 THING I DID TO MOVE FORWARD

_____
_____

The Moon is in: _____

The Day Ruler is: _____

I AM GRATEFUL FOR

_____

_____

MOOD TRACKER

SELF - CARE

DAILY AFFIRMATION

_____

_____

DREAM JOURNAL

_____

_____

_____

_____

_____

_____

_____

_____

_____

_____ 5 _____
_____ 10 _____
_____ 15 _____
_____ 20 _____
_____ 25 _____
_____ 30 _____

SCRIPTING

3-6-9 MANIFESTATION

_____ _____ _____

_____ _____ _____

_____ _____ _____

1 THING I DID TO MOVE FORWARD

_____

_____

The Moon is in: _____

The Day Ruler is: _____

I AM GRATEFUL FOR

_____

_____

MOOD TRACKER

😠   ☹️   😐   🙂   😄

SELF - CARE

DAILY AFFIRMATION

_____

_____

DREAM JOURNAL

_____

_____

_____

_____

_____

_____

_____

_____

RITUAL TIME   MINDFUL MINUTES

_____ 5 _____

_____ 10 _____

_____ 15 _____

_____ 20 _____

_____ 25 _____

_____ 30 _____

SCRIPTING

_____

_____

_____

_____

_____

_____

_____

_____

_____

_____

_____

_____

_____

_____

_____

_____

_____

3-6-9 MANIFESTATION

_____   _____   _____

_____   _____   _____

_____   _____   _____

1 THING I DID TO MOVE FORWARD

_____

_____

The Moon is in: _____

The Day Ruler is: _____

I AM GRATEFUL FOR

_____

_____

MOOD TRACKER

SELF - CARE

DAILY AFFIRMATION

_____

_____

DREAM JOURNAL

_____

_____

_____

_____

_____

_____

_____

_____

_____

_____ 5 _____
_____ 10 _____
_____ 15 _____
_____ 20 _____
_____ 25 _____
_____ 30 _____

SCRIPTING

3-6-9 MANIFESTATION

_____ _____ _____

_____ _____ _____

_____ _____ _____

1 THING I DID TO MOVE FORWARD

_____

_____

The Moon is in: _____

The Day Ruler is: _____

I AM GRATEFUL FOR

_____

_____

MOOD TRACKER

SELF - CARE

DAILY AFFIRMATION

_____

_____

DREAM JOURNAL

_____

_____

_____

_____

_____

_____

_____

_____

RITUAL TIME   MINDFUL MINUTES

_____ 5 _____
_____ 10 _____
_____ 15 _____
_____ 20 _____
_____ 25 _____
_____ 30 _____

SCRIPTING

3-6-9 MANIFESTATION

_____ _____ _____

_____ _____ _____

_____ _____ _____

1 THING I DID TO MOVE FORWARD

_____

_____

THIS LUNATION

Full Moon ☐   ☐ New Moon

The Moon is in the sign of _____ and transits my _____ house,

meaning _____

_____ for me.

Build your Moon ritual: _____

_____

_____

_____

_____

_____

_____

_____

_____

CANDLES	CRYSTALS
HERBS	OTHER

Card 1	Card 2	Card 3
____ Deck	____ Deck	____ Deck
____ Card	____ Card	____ Card

Interpretation & Meaning: _____

_____

_____

_____

_____

_____

_____

Intentions for this lunation: _____

_____

_____

_____

_____

_____

_____

_____

The Moon is in: _____

The Day Ruler is: _____

I AM GRATEFUL FOR

_____

_____

MOOD TRACKER

😠   ☹️   😐   🙂   😄

SELF - CARE

DAILY AFFIRMATION

_____

_____

DREAM JOURNAL

_____

_____

_____

_____

_____

_____

_____

_____

_____

RITUAL TIME   MINDFUL MINUTES

____ 5 ____
____ 10 ____
____ 15 ____
____ 20 ____
____ 25 ____
____ 30 ____

SCRIPTING

_____

_____

_____

_____

_____

_____

_____

_____

_____

_____

_____

_____

_____

3-6-9 MANIFESTATION

_____   _____   _____

_____   _____   _____

_____   _____   _____

1 THING I DID TO MOVE FORWARD

_____

_____

The Moon is in: _____

The Day Ruler is: _____

I AM GRATEFUL FOR

_____

_____

MOOD TRACKER

SELF - CARE

DAILY AFFIRMATION

_____

_____

DREAM JOURNAL

_____

_____

_____

_____

_____

_____

_____

_____

_____

_____ 5 _____
_____ 10 _____
_____ 15 _____
_____ 20 _____
_____ 25 _____
_____ 30 _____
_____ . _____

SCRIPTING

3-6-9 MANIFESTATION

_____ _____ _____

_____ _____ _____

_____ _____ _____

1 THING I DID TO MOVE FORWARD

_____

_____

The Moon is in: _____

The Day Ruler is: _____

I AM GRATEFUL FOR

_____

_____

MOOD TRACKER

SELF - CARE

DAILY AFFIRMATION

_____

_____

DREAM JOURNAL

_____

_____

_____

_____

_____

_____

_____

_____

_____

RITUAL TIME   MINDFUL MINUTES

___5___
___10___
___15___
___20___
___25___
___30___

SCRIPTING

3-6-9 MANIFESTATION

_____ _____ _____

_____ _____ _____

_____ _____ _____

1 THING I DID TO MOVE FORWARD

_____

The Moon is in: _____

The Day Ruler is: _____

I AM GRATEFUL FOR

_____

_____

MOOD TRACKER

SELF - CARE

DAILY AFFIRMATION

_____

_____

DREAM JOURNAL

_____

_____

_____

_____

_____

_____

_____

_____

_____

_____5_____
_____10_____
_____15_____
_____20_____
_____25_____
_____30_____

SCRIPTING

3-6-9 MANIFESTATION

_____ _____ _____

_____ _____ _____

_____ _____ _____

1 THING I DID TO MOVE FORWARD

_____

_____

The Moon is in: _____

The Day Ruler is: _____

I AM GRATEFUL FOR

_____

_____

MOOD TRACKER

SELF - CARE

DAILY AFFIRMATION

_____

_____

DREAM JOURNAL

_____

_____

_____

_____

_____

_____

_____

_____

_____

RITUAL TIME

MINDFUL MINUTES

_____ 5 _____
_____ 10 _____
_____ 15 _____
_____ 20 _____
_____ 25 _____
_____ 30 _____

SCRIPTING

3-6-9 MANIFESTATION

_____ _____ _____

_____ _____ _____

_____ _____ _____

1 THING I DID TO MOVE FORWARD

_____

_____

The Moon is in: _____

The Day Ruler is: _____

I AM GRATEFUL FOR

_____

_____

MOOD TRACKER

SELF - CARE

DAILY AFFIRMATION

_____

_____

DREAM JOURNAL

_____

_____

_____

_____

_____

_____

_____

_____

_____

5
10
15
20
25
30

SCRIPTING

3-6-9 MANIFESTATION

_____ _____ _____

_____ _____ _____

_____ _____ _____

1 THING I DID TO MOVE FORWARD

_____

_____

The Moon is in: _____

The Day Ruler is: _____

I AM GRATEFUL FOR

_____
_____

MOOD TRACKER

SELF - CARE

DAILY AFFIRMATION

_____
_____

DREAM JOURNAL

_____
_____
_____
_____
_____
_____
_____
_____

RITUAL TIME   MINDFUL MINUTES

____5____
____10____
____15____
____20____
____25____
____30____

SCRIPTING

3-6-9 MANIFESTATION

_____ _____ _____
_____ _____ _____
_____ _____ _____

1 THING I DID TO MOVE FORWARD

_____
_____

The Moon is in: _____

The Day Ruler is: _____

I AM GRATEFUL FOR

_____

_____

MOOD TRACKER

SELF - CARE

DAILY AFFIRMATION

_____

_____

DREAM JOURNAL

_____

_____

_____

_____

_____

_____

_____

_____

_____

_____ 5 _____
_____ 10 _____
_____ 15 _____
_____ 20 _____
_____ 25 _____
_____ 30 _____

SCRIPTING

3-6-9 MANIFESTATION

_____ _____ _____

_____ _____ _____

_____ _____ _____

_____ _____ _____

1 THING I DID TO MOVE FORWARD

_____

_____

The Moon is in: _____

The Day Ruler is: _____

I AM GRATEFUL FOR

_____
_____

MOOD TRACKER

SELF - CARE

DAILY AFFIRMATION

_____
_____

DREAM JOURNAL

_____
_____
_____
_____
_____
_____
_____
_____

SCRIPTING

3-6-9 MANIFESTATION

_____ _____ _____
_____ _____ _____
_____ _____ _____

1 THING I DID TO MOVE FORWARD

_____
_____

RITUAL TIME   MINDFUL MINUTES

___5___
___10___
___15___
___20___
___25___
___30___

The Moon is in: _____

The Day Ruler is: _____

I AM GRATEFUL FOR

_____

_____

MOOD TRACKER

SELF - CARE

DAILY AFFIRMATION

_____

_____

DREAM JOURNAL

_____

_____

_____

_____

_____

_____

_____

_____

_____

_____ 5 _____
_____ 10 _____
_____ 15 _____
_____ 20 _____
_____ 25 _____
_____ 30 _____

SCRIPTING

3-6-9 MANIFESTATION

_____ _____ _____

_____ _____ _____

_____ _____ _____

1 THING I DID TO MOVE FORWARD

_____

_____

The Moon is in: _____

The Day Ruler is: _____

I AM GRATEFUL FOR

_____

_____

MOOD TRACKER

SELF - CARE

DAILY AFFIRMATION

_____

_____

DREAM JOURNAL

_____

_____

_____

_____

_____

_____

_____

_____

_____

RITUAL TIME   MINDFUL MINUTES

_____5_____
_____10_____
_____15_____
_____20_____
_____25_____
_____30_____

SCRIPTING

3-6-9 MANIFESTATION

_____ _____ _____

_____ _____ _____

_____ _____ _____

1 THING I DID TO MOVE FORWARD

_____

_____

The Moon is in: _____

The Day Ruler is: _____

I AM GRATEFUL FOR

_____

_____

MOOD TRACKER

SELF - CARE

DAILY AFFIRMATION

_____

_____

DREAM JOURNAL

_____

_____

_____

_____

_____

_____

_____

_____

_____

_____

_____5_____
_____10_____
_____15_____
_____20_____
_____25_____
_____30_____

SCRIPTING

3-6-9 MANIFESTATION

_____ _____ _____

_____ _____ _____

_____ _____ _____

1 THING I DID TO MOVE FORWARD

_____

_____

The Moon is in: _____

The Day Ruler is: _____

I AM GRATEFUL FOR

_____

_____

MOOD TRACKER

SELF - CARE

DAILY AFFIRMATION

_____

_____

DREAM JOURNAL

_____

_____

_____

_____

_____

_____

_____

_____

_____

RITUAL TIME   MINDFUL MINUTES

___5___
___10___
___15___
___20___
___25___
___30___

SCRIPTING

3-6-9 MANIFESTATION

_____ _____ _____

_____ _____ _____

_____ _____ _____

1 THING I DID TO MOVE FORWARD

_____

_____

The Moon is in: _____

The Day Ruler is: _____

I AM GRATEFUL FOR

_____

_____

MOOD TRACKER

SELF - CARE

DAILY AFFIRMATION

_____

_____

DREAM JOURNAL

_____

_____

_____

_____

_____

_____

_____

_____

_____

_____

_____ 5 _____
_____ 10 _____
_____ 15 _____
_____ 20 _____
_____ 25 _____
_____ 30 _____

SCRIPTING

3-6-9 MANIFESTATION

_____ _____ _____

_____ _____ _____

_____ _____ _____

1 THING I DID TO MOVE FORWARD

_____

_____

THIS LUNATION

Full Moon ☐   ☐ New Moon

The Moon is in the sign of _____ and transits my _____ house,

meaning _____

_____ for me.

Build your Moon ritual: _____

_____

_____

_____

_____

_____

_____

_____

CANDLES	CRYSTALS
HERBS	OTHER

Card 1	Card 2	Card 3
_____	_____	_____
Deck	Deck	Deck
_____	_____	_____
Card	Card	Card

Interpretation & Meaning: _____

_____

_____

_____

_____

_____

Intentions for this lunation: _____

_____

_____

_____

_____

_____

_____

The Moon is in: _____

The Day Ruler is: _____

I AM GRATEFUL FOR

_____

_____

MOOD TRACKER

SELF - CARE

DAILY AFFIRMATION

_____

_____

DREAM JOURNAL

_____

_____

_____

_____

_____

_____

_____

_____

_____

_____5_____
_____10_____
_____15_____
_____20_____
_____25_____
_____30_____

SCRIPTING

3-6-9 MANIFESTATION

_____ _____ _____

_____ _____ _____

_____ _____ _____

1 THING I DID TO MOVE FORWARD

_____

_____

SEPTEMBER

SUNDAY	MONDAY	TUESDAY	WEDNESDAY
3	4 Labor Day	5	6 ◑
10	11	12	13
17	18	19	20
24	25	26	27

THURSDAY	FRIDAY	SATURDAY	NOTES
	1	2	
7	8	9	
14 ●	15	16	
21	22 ◗ Native American Day	23 Mabon	
28	29 ○	30	

CORN MOON

RITUAL FOCUS:
The corn moon is a good time to refresh the energy in your home! Evaluate whether or not the things in your home or space are helping you to move forward, or are holding you back.

ZODIACS:
Virgo & Libra

CRYSTALS:
Citrine, Quartz & Aventurine

COLORS:
Brown, Yellow & Amber

ELEMENTS:
Air & Earth

DEITIES:
Demeter, Ceres, Isis, Freyja, Nephthys & Persephone

FLOWERS:
Aster, Morning Glory, Forget-Me-Not

ANIMALS:
Snake & Jackal

HERBS:
Copal, Fennel, Valerian, Rye, Lilac, Mugwort, Rose, Thyme

MAGICAL ASSOCIATIONS:
Gratitude, Abundance, Harvest, Transition, Balance, Home, Earth, Rest & Reflection.

DIVINATION TRACKER

DATE	PULL	MESSAGE

SEPTEMBER TRANSITS

September 2023 Tropical Midnight Ephemeris

Time Zone: **EDT (04:00 East)**

Day	☉	☽	+12 Hr	True☊	☿	♀	♂	♃	♄	♅	♆	♇
01 Fr	08 ♍ 29 03	24 ♓ 07 13	01 ♈ 36 31	25 ♈ 48 R	18 ♍ 29 R	12 ♌ 22 R	02 ♎ 58 D	15 ♉ 34 D	03 ♓ 28 R	23 ♉ 04 R	26 ♓ 46 R	28 ♑ 15 R
02 Sa	09 27 05	09 ♈ 00 39	16 18 51	25 44	17 39	12 16	03 36	15 34	03 24	23 04	26 44	28 14
03 Su	10 25 08	23 30 33	00 ♉ 35 23	25 43	16 46	12 13	04 15	15 35	03 19	23 04	26 43	28 13
04 Mo	11 23 13	07 ♉ 33 12	14 24 01	25 44 D	15 50	12 12 D	04 54	15 35	03 15	23 04	26 41	28 12
05 Tu	12 21 21	21 08 00	27 45 25	25 45	14 53	12 14	05 33	15 35 R	03 10	23 03	26 40	28 11
06 We	13 19 30	04 ♊ 16 39	10 ♊ 42 10	25 46	13 54	12 17	06 11	15 35	03 06	23 03	26 38	28 10
07 Th	14 17 41	17 02 27	23 18 02	25 46 R	12 56	12 23	06 50	15 34	03 01	23 02	26 37	28 09
08 Fr	15 15 55	29 29 26	05 ♋ 37 13	25 45	12 00	12 32	07 29	15 34	02 57	23 02	26 35	28 08
09 Sa	16 14 10	11 ♋ 41 53	17 43 57	25 42	11 08	12 42	08 08	15 33	02 53	23 01	26 33	28 07
10 Su	17 12 28	23 43 54	29 42 09	25 38	10 20	12 55	08 47	15 32	02 48	23 01	26 32	28 07
11 Mo	18 10 47	05 ♌ 39 09	11 ♌ 35 15	25 32	09 37	13 09	09 26	15 31	02 44	23 00	26 30	28 06
12 Tu	19 09 08	17 30 49	23 26 09	25 25	09 01	13 26	10 05	15 29	02 40	23 00	26 28	28 05
13 We	20 07 31	29 21 32	05 ♍ 17 15	25 19	08 33	13 44	10 44	15 28	02 36	22 59	26 27	28 04
14 Th	21 05 57	11 ♍ 13 30	17 10 33	25 13	08 13	14 05	11 24	15 26	02 31	22 58	26 25	28 04
15 Fr	22 04 24	23 08 35	29 07 50	25 08	08 02	14 27	12 03	15 24	02 27	22 57	26 23	28 03
16 Sa	23 02 52	05 ♎ 08 30	11 ♎ 10 49	25 04	08 01 D	14 51	12 42	15 21	02 23	22 56	26 22	28 02
17 Su	24 01 23	17 15 02	23 21 23	25 03	08 08	15 16	13 22	15 19	02 19	22 56	26 20	28 01
18 Mo	24 59 56	29 30 10	05 ♏ 41 39	25 02 D	08 26	15 44	14 01	15 16	02 15	22 55	26 18	28 01
19 Tu	25 58 30	11 ♏ 56 11	18 14 06	25 03	08 52	16 12	14 40	15 14	02 11	22 54	26 17	28 00
20 We	26 57 06	24 35 44	01 ♐ 01 28	25 05	09 28	16 43	15 20	15 11	02 07	22 52	26 15	28 00
21 Th	27 55 44	07 ♐ 31 38	14 06 36	25 07	10 12	17 15	15 59	15 07	02 03	22 51	26 13	27 59
22 Fr	28 54 23	20 46 41	27 32 08	25 08	11 04	17 48	16 39	15 04	01 59	22 50	26 12	27 59
23 Sa	29 53 05	04 ♑ 23 09	11 ♑ 19 52	25 08 R	12 04	18 22	17 18	15 00	01 56	22 49	26 10	27 58
24 Su	00 ♎ 51 48	18 22 16	25 30 14	25 07	13 11	18 58	17 58	14 57	01 52	22 48	26 09	27 58
25 Mo	01 50 32	02 ♒ 43 29	10 ♒ 01 37	25 05	14 25	19 35	18 38	14 53	01 48	22 47	26 07	27 57
26 Tu	02 49 18	17 24 01	24 49 58	25 02	15 44	20 14	19 18	14 49	01 45	22 45	26 05	27 57
27 We	03 48 06	02 ♓ 18 35	09 ♓ 48 50	24 59	17 09	20 53	19 57	14 44	01 41	22 44	26 04	27 56
28 Th	04 46 56	17 19 41	24 50 00	24 57	18 37	21 34	20 37	14 40	01 38	22 43	26 02	27 56
29 Fr	05 45 47	02 ♈ 18 39	09 ♈ 44 35	24 55	20 10	22 16	21 17	14 35	01 35	22 41	26 00	27 56
30 Sa	06 44 41	17 06 49	24 24 29	24 54	21 46	22 58	21 57	14 30	01 31	22 40	25 59	27 55
01 Su	07 43 36	01 ♉ 36 51	08 ♉ 43 22	24 54 D	23 25	23 42	22 37	14 25	01 28	22 38	25 57	27 55

Planetary Data

Ingresses

	Day	Time
☉ ♎	23	2:49 AM

Stations

	Day	Time
♀ D	3	9:20 PM
♃ R	4	10:11 AM
☿ D	15	4:21 PM

Lunar Ingresses & Void Moons

Ingresses

	Day	Time
♓	30	9:56 AM
♈	1	9:24 AM
♉	3	10:59 AM
♊	5	4:07 PM
♋	8	1:00 AM
♌	10	12:35 PM
♍	13	1:18 AM
♎	15	1:45 PM
♏	18	12:59 AM
♐	20	10:05 AM
♑	22	4:21 PM
♒	24	7:29 PM
♓	26	8:18 PM
♈	28	8:18 PM
♉	30	9:18 PM

Void Times

Day	Time	Last Aspect	
1	6:35 AM	⚹	♇
3	7:57 AM	□	♇
5	12:45 PM	△	♇
7	6:22 PM	□	♆
10	8:48 AM	☍	♆
12	11:06 AM	□	♅
15	9:50 AM	△	♇
17	9:07 PM	□	♇
20	6:22 AM	⚹	♇
22	3:32 PM	□	☉
24	4:06 PM	☌	♇
26	8:38 AM	□	♅
28	4:58 PM	⚹	♇
30	5:49 PM	□	♇

Phases & Eclipses

Lunar Phases

Day	Time		
6	6:21 PM	☾	14 ♊ 04
14	9:40 PM	●	21 ♍ 59
22	3:32 PM	☽	29 ♐ 32
29	5:58 AM	○	06 ♈ 00

Solar Eclipses

Day Time

~ None ~

Lunar Eclipses

Day Time

~ None ~

NOTES

The Moon is in: _____

The Day Ruler is: _____

I AM GRATEFUL FOR

_____
_____

MOOD TRACKER

SELF - CARE

DAILY AFFIRMATION

_____
_____

DREAM JOURNAL

_____
_____
_____
_____
_____
_____
_____

RITUAL TIME   MINDFUL MINUTES

_____5_____
_____10_____
_____15_____
_____20_____
_____25_____
_____30_____

SCRIPTING

3-6-9 MANIFESTATION

_____ _____ _____
_____ _____ _____
_____ _____ _____

1 THING I DID TO MOVE FORWARD

_____
_____

The Moon is in: _____

The Day Ruler is: _____

I AM GRATEFUL FOR

_____

_____

MOOD TRACKER

SELF - CARE

DAILY AFFIRMATION

_____

_____

DREAM JOURNAL

_____

_____

_____

_____

_____

_____

_____

_____

_____ 5 _____
_____ 10 _____
_____ 15 _____
_____ 20 _____
_____ 25 _____
_____ 30 _____

SCRIPTING

3-6-9 MANIFESTATION

_____ _____ _____

_____ _____ _____

_____ _____ _____

1 THING I DID TO MOVE FORWARD

_____

_____

The Moon is in: _____

The Day Ruler is: _____

I AM GRATEFUL FOR

_____

_____

MOOD TRACKER

SELF - CARE

DAILY AFFIRMATION

_____

_____

DREAM JOURNAL

_____

_____

_____

_____

_____

_____

_____

_____

RITUAL TIME   MINDFUL MINUTES

_____5_____
_____10_____
_____15_____
_____20_____
_____25_____
_____30_____

SCRIPTING

3-6-9 MANIFESTATION

_____ _____ _____

_____ _____ _____

_____ _____ _____

1 THING I DID TO MOVE FORWARD

_____

_____

The Moon is in: _____

The Day Ruler is: _____

I AM GRATEFUL FOR

_____

_____

MOOD TRACKER

SELF - CARE

DAILY AFFIRMATION

_____

_____

DREAM JOURNAL

_____

_____

_____

_____

_____

_____

_____

_____

_____

_____ 5 _____
_____ 10 _____
_____ 15 _____
_____ 20 _____
_____ 25 _____
_____ 30 _____

SCRIPTING

3-6-9 MANIFESTATION

_____ _____ _____

_____ _____ _____

_____ _____ _____

1 THING I DID TO MOVE FORWARD

_____

_____

The Moon is in: _____

The Day Ruler is: _____

I AM GRATEFUL FOR

_____
_____

MOOD TRACKER

SELF - CARE

DAILY AFFIRMATION

_____
_____

DREAM JOURNAL

_____
_____
_____
_____
_____
_____
_____

RITUAL TIME   MINDFUL MINUTES

_____ 5
_____ 10 _____
_____ 15
_____ 20
_____ 25
_____ 30

SCRIPTING

3-6-9 MANIFESTATION

_____ _____ _____
_____ _____ _____
_____ _____ _____

1 THING I DID TO MOVE FORWARD

_____

The Moon is in: _____

The Day Ruler is: _____

I AM GRATEFUL FOR

_____

_____

MOOD TRACKER

SELF - CARE

DAILY AFFIRMATION

_____

_____

DREAM JOURNAL

_____

_____

_____

_____

_____

_____

_____

_____

_____

_____5_____
_____10_____
_____15_____
_____20_____
_____25_____
_____30_____
_____ _____

SCRIPTING

3-6-9 MANIFESTATION

_____ _____ _____

_____ _____ _____

_____ _____ _____

1 THING I DID TO MOVE FORWARD

_____

_____

The Moon is in: _____

The Day Ruler is: _____

I AM GRATEFUL FOR

_____

_____

MOOD TRACKER

SELF - CARE

DAILY AFFIRMATION

_____

_____

DREAM JOURNAL

_____

_____

_____

_____

_____

_____

_____

_____

_____

SCRIPTING

_____

RITUAL TIME   MINDFUL MINUTES

_____ 5
_____ 10 _____
_____ 15
_____ 20
_____ 25
_____ 30

3-6-9 MANIFESTATION

_____ _____ _____

_____ _____ _____

_____ _____ _____

1 THING I DID TO MOVE FORWARD

_____

_____

The Moon is in: _____

The Day Ruler is: _____

I AM GRATEFUL FOR

_____

_____

MOOD TRACKER

SELF - CARE

DAILY AFFIRMATION

_____

_____

DREAM JOURNAL

_____

_____

_____

_____

_____

_____

_____

_____

_____

_____5_____
_____10_____
_____15_____
_____20_____
_____25_____
_____30_____

SCRIPTING

3-6-9 MANIFESTATION

_____ _____ _____

_____ _____ _____

_____ _____ _____

1 THING I DID TO MOVE FORWARD

_____

_____

The Moon is in: _____

The Day Ruler is: _____

I AM GRATEFUL FOR

_____

_____

MOOD TRACKER

SELF - CARE

DAILY AFFIRMATION

_____

_____

DREAM JOURNAL

_____

_____

_____

_____

_____

_____

_____

_____

RITUAL TIME   MINDFUL MINUTES

_____ 5 _____
_____ 10 _____
_____ 15 _____
_____ 20 _____
_____ 25 _____
_____ 30 _____

SCRIPTING

_____
_____
_____
_____
_____
_____
_____
_____
_____
_____
_____
_____
_____
_____
_____
_____
_____
_____

3-6-9 MANIFESTATION

_____ _____ _____

_____ _____ _____

_____ _____ _____

1 THING I DID TO MOVE FORWARD

_____

The Moon is in: _____

The Day Ruler is: _____

I AM GRATEFUL FOR

_____

_____

MOOD TRACKER

SELF - CARE

DAILY AFFIRMATION

_____

_____

DREAM JOURNAL

_____

_____

_____

_____

_____

_____

_____

_____

_____

_____5_____
_____10_____
_____15_____
_____20_____
_____25_____
_____30_____
_____

SCRIPTING

3-6-9 MANIFESTATION

_____ _____ _____

_____ _____ _____

_____ _____ _____

1 THING I DID TO MOVE FORWARD

_____

_____

The Moon is in: _____

The Day Ruler is: _____

I AM GRATEFUL FOR

_____

_____

MOOD TRACKER

SELF - CARE

DAILY AFFIRMATION

_____

_____

DREAM JOURNAL

_____

_____

_____

_____

_____

_____

_____

_____

_____

RITUAL TIME   MINDFUL MINUTES

_____ 5 _____
_____ 10 _____
_____ 15 _____
_____ 20 _____
_____ 25 _____
_____ 30 _____

SCRIPTING

3-6-9 MANIFESTATION

_____ _____ _____

_____ _____ _____

_____ _____ _____

1 THING I DID TO MOVE FORWARD

_____

_____

The Moon is in: _____

The Day Ruler is: _____

I AM GRATEFUL FOR

_____

_____

MOOD TRACKER

SELF - CARE

DAILY AFFIRMATION

_____

_____

DREAM JOURNAL

_____

_____

_____

_____

_____

_____

_____

_____

_____

_____5_____
_____10_____
_____15_____
_____20_____
_____25_____
_____30_____

SCRIPTING

3-6-9 MANIFESTATION

_____ _____ _____

_____ _____ _____

_____ _____ _____

1 THING I DID TO MOVE FORWARD

_____

_____

The Moon is in: _____

The Day Ruler is: _____

I AM GRATEFUL FOR

_____

_____

MOOD TRACKER

SELF - CARE

DAILY AFFIRMATION

_____

_____

DREAM JOURNAL

_____

_____

_____

_____

_____

_____

_____

_____

SCRIPTING

RITUAL TIME   MINDFUL MINUTES

5
10
15
20
25
30

3-6-9 MANIFESTATION

_____ _____ _____

_____ _____ _____

_____ _____ _____

1 THING I DID TO MOVE FORWARD

_____

_____

The Moon is in: _____

The Day Ruler is: _____

I AM GRATEFUL FOR

_____

_____

MOOD TRACKER

SELF - CARE

DAILY AFFIRMATION

_____

_____

DREAM JOURNAL

_____

_____

_____

_____

_____

_____

_____

_____

_____

5
10
15
20
25
30

SCRIPTING

3-6-9 MANIFESTATION

_____ _____ _____

_____ _____ _____

_____ _____ _____

1 THING I DID TO MOVE FORWARD

_____

_____

THIS LUNATION

Full Moon ☐   ☐ New Moon

The Moon is in the sign of _____ and transits my _____ house,

meaning _____

_____ for me.

Build your Moon ritual: _____

_____
_____
_____
_____
_____
_____
_____
_____

CANDLES	CRYSTALS
HERBS	OTHER

Card 1	Card 2	Card 3
___ Deck	___ Deck	___ Deck
___ Card	___ Card	___ Card

Interpretation & Meaning: _____

_____
_____
_____
_____
_____

Intentions for this lunation: _____

_____
_____
_____
_____
_____
_____
_____

The Moon is in: _____
The Day Ruler is: _____

I AM GRATEFUL FOR

_____
_____

MOOD TRACKER

SELF - CARE

DAILY AFFIRMATION

_____
_____

DREAM JOURNAL

_____
_____
_____
_____
_____
_____
_____
_____
_____

_____ 5 _____
_____ 10 _____
_____ 15 _____
_____ 20 _____
_____ 25 _____
_____ 30 _____

SCRIPTING

3-6-9 MANIFESTATION

_____ _____ _____
_____ _____ _____
_____ _____ _____

1 THING I DID TO MOVE FORWARD

_____
_____

The Moon is in: _____

The Day Ruler is: _____

I AM GRATEFUL FOR

_____

_____

MOOD TRACKER

SELF - CARE

DAILY AFFIRMATION

_____

_____

DREAM JOURNAL

_____

_____

_____

_____

_____

_____

_____

_____

_____

_____

SCRIPTING

RITUAL TIME   MINDFUL MINUTES

_____ 5 _____
_____ 10 _____
_____ 15 _____
_____ 20 _____
_____ 25 _____
_____ 30 _____

3-6-9 MANIFESTATION

_____ _____ _____

_____ _____ _____

_____ _____ _____

1 THING I DID TO MOVE FORWARD

_____

_____

The Moon is in: _____

The Day Ruler is: _____

I AM GRATEFUL FOR

_____

_____

MOOD TRACKER

SELF - CARE

DAILY AFFIRMATION

_____

_____

DREAM JOURNAL

_____

_____

_____

_____

_____

_____

_____

_____

_____

_____ 5 _____
_____ 10 _____
_____ 15 _____
_____ 20 _____
_____ 25 _____
_____ 30 _____

SCRIPTING

3-6-9 MANIFESTATION

_____ _____ _____

_____ _____ _____

_____ _____ _____

1 THING I DID TO MOVE FORWARD

_____

_____

The Moon is in: _____

The Day Ruler is: _____

I AM GRATEFUL FOR

_____

_____

MOOD TRACKER

SELF - CARE

DAILY AFFIRMATION

_____

_____

DREAM JOURNAL

_____

_____

_____

_____

_____

_____

_____

_____

RITUAL TIME   MINDFUL MINUTES

5
10
15
20
25
30

SCRIPTING

_____
_____
_____
_____
_____
_____
_____
_____
_____
_____
_____
_____
_____
_____
_____
_____
_____
_____
_____

3-6-9 MANIFESTATION

_____ _____ _____

_____ _____ _____

_____ _____ _____

1 THING I DID TO MOVE FORWARD

_____

_____

The Moon is in: _____

The Day Ruler is: _____

I AM GRATEFUL FOR

_____

_____

MOOD TRACKER

SELF - CARE

DAILY AFFIRMATION

_____

_____

DREAM JOURNAL

_____

_____

_____

_____

_____

_____

_____

_____

_____

5
10
15
20
25
30

SCRIPTING

3-6-9 MANIFESTATION

_____ _____ _____

_____ _____ _____

_____ _____ _____

1 THING I DID TO MOVE FORWARD

_____

_____

The Moon is in: _____

The Day Ruler is: _____

I AM GRATEFUL FOR

_____

_____

MOOD TRACKER

SELF - CARE

DAILY AFFIRMATION

_____

_____

DREAM JOURNAL

_____

_____

_____

_____

_____

_____

_____

_____

RITUAL TIME   MINDFUL MINUTES

___ 5 ___
___ 10 ___
___ 15 ___
___ 20 ___
___ 25 ___
___ 30 ___

SCRIPTING

3-6-9 MANIFESTATION

_____ _____ _____

_____ _____ _____

_____ _____ _____

1 THING I DID TO MOVE FORWARD

_____

_____

The Moon is in: _____

The Day Ruler is: _____

I AM GRATEFUL FOR

_____

_____

MOOD TRACKER

SELF - CARE

DAILY AFFIRMATION

_____

_____

DREAM JOURNAL

_____

_____

_____

_____

_____

_____

_____

_____

_____

_____

_____5_____
_____10_____
_____15_____
_____20_____
_____25_____
_____30_____

SCRIPTING

3-6-9 MANIFESTATION

_____ _____ _____

_____ _____ _____

_____ _____ _____

1 THING I DID TO MOVE FORWARD

_____

_____

The Moon is in: _____

The Day Ruler is: _____

I AM GRATEFUL FOR

_____

_____

MOOD TRACKER

SELF - CARE

DAILY AFFIRMATION

_____

_____

DREAM JOURNAL

_____

_____

_____

_____

_____

_____

_____

_____

_____

RITUAL TIME   MINDFUL MINUTES

___5___
___10___
___15___
___20___
___25___
___30___

SCRIPTING

3-6-9 MANIFESTATION

_____ _____ _____

_____ _____ _____

_____ _____ _____

1 THING I DID TO MOVE FORWARD

_____

_____

The Moon is in: _____

The Day Ruler is: _____

I AM GRATEFUL FOR

_____

_____

MOOD TRACKER

SELF - CARE

DAILY AFFIRMATION

_____

_____

DREAM JOURNAL

_____

_____

_____

_____

_____

_____

_____

_____

_____

_____5_____
_____10_____
_____15_____
_____20_____
_____25_____
_____30_____

SCRIPTING

3-6-9 MANIFESTATION

_____ _____ _____

_____ _____ _____

_____ _____ _____

1 THING I DID TO MOVE FORWARD

_____

_____

The Moon is in: _____

The Day Ruler is: _____

I AM GRATEFUL FOR

_____

_____

MOOD TRACKER

😠 😟 😐 🙂 😃

SELF - CARE

DAILY AFFIRMATION

_____

_____

DREAM JOURNAL

_____

_____

_____

_____

_____

_____

_____

_____

_____

RITUAL TIME   MINDFUL MINUTES

_____ 5 _____
_____ 10 _____
_____ 15 _____
_____ 20 _____
_____ 25 _____
_____ 30 _____

SCRIPTING

_____

_____

_____

_____

_____

_____

_____

_____

_____

_____

_____

_____

_____

_____

_____

_____

_____

_____

_____

3-6-9 MANIFESTATION

_____ _____ _____

_____ _____ _____

_____ _____ _____

1 THING I DID TO MOVE FORWARD

_____

_____

The Moon is in: _____

The Day Ruler is: _____

I AM GRATEFUL FOR

_____

_____

MOOD TRACKER

☹ ☹ 😐 🙂 😃

SELF - CARE

DAILY AFFIRMATION

_____

_____

DREAM JOURNAL

_____

_____

_____

_____

_____

_____

_____

_____

_____ 5 _____
_____ 10 _____
_____ 15 _____
_____ 20 _____
_____ 25 _____
_____ 30 _____

SCRIPTING

3-6-9 MANIFESTATION

_____ _____ _____

_____ _____ _____

_____ _____ _____

1 THING I DID TO MOVE FORWARD

_____

_____

The Moon is in: _____

The Day Ruler is: _____

I AM GRATEFUL FOR

_____

_____

MOOD TRACKER

SELF - CARE

DAILY AFFIRMATION

_____

_____

DREAM JOURNAL

_____

_____

_____

_____

_____

_____

_____

_____

_____

_____

RITUAL TIME   MINDFUL MINUTES

_____ 5 _____
_____ 10 _____
_____ 15 _____
_____ 20 _____
_____ 25 _____
_____ 30 _____

SCRIPTING

3-6-9 MANIFESTATION

_____ _____ _____

_____ _____ _____

_____ _____ _____

1 THING I DID TO MOVE FORWARD

_____

_____

The Moon is in: _____

The Day Ruler is: _____

I AM GRATEFUL FOR

_____

_____

MOOD TRACKER

😠 😦 😐 🙂 😀

SELF - CARE

DAILY AFFIRMATION

_____

_____

DREAM JOURNAL

_____

_____

_____

_____

_____

_____

_____

_____

_____

_____

_____5_____
_____10_____
_____15_____
_____20_____
_____25_____
_____30_____

SCRIPTING

3-6-9 MANIFESTATION

_____ _____ _____

_____ _____ _____

_____ _____ _____

1 THING I DID TO MOVE FORWARD

_____

_____

The Moon is in: _____

The Day Ruler is: _____

I AM GRATEFUL FOR

_____

_____

MOOD TRACKER

SELF - CARE

DAILY AFFIRMATION

_____

_____

DREAM JOURNAL

_____

_____

_____

_____

_____

_____

_____

_____

_____

RITUAL TIME   MINDFUL MINUTES

_____ 5 _____
_____ 10 _____
_____ 15 _____
_____ 20 _____
_____ 25 _____
_____ 30 _____

SCRIPTING

3-6-9 MANIFESTATION

_____ _____ _____
_____ _____ _____
_____ _____ _____

1 THING I DID TO MOVE FORWARD

_____

_____

The Moon is in: _____

The Day Ruler is: _____

I AM GRATEFUL FOR

_____

_____

MOOD TRACKER

SELF - CARE

DAILY AFFIRMATION

_____

_____

DREAM JOURNAL

_____

_____

_____

_____

_____

_____

_____

_____

_____

_____ 5 _____
_____ 10 _____
_____ 15 _____
_____ 20 _____
_____ 25 _____
_____ 30 _____

SCRIPTING

3-6-9 MANIFESTATION

_____ _____ _____

_____ _____ _____

_____ _____ _____

1 THING I DID TO MOVE FORWARD

_____

_____

THIS LUNATION

Full Moon ☐   ☐ New Moon

The Moon is in the sign of _____ and transits my _____ house,

meaning _____

_____ for me.

Build your Moon ritual: _____

_____

_____

_____

_____

_____

_____

CANDLES	CRYSTALS
HERBS	OTHER

Card 1	Card 2	Card 3
___	___	___
Deck	Deck	Deck
___	___	___
Card	Card	Card

Interpretation & Meaning: _____

_____

_____

_____

_____

_____

Intentions for this lunation: _____

_____

_____

_____

_____

_____

_____

The Moon is in: _____

The Day Ruler is: _____

I AM GRATEFUL FOR

_____

_____

MOOD TRACKER

SELF - CARE

DAILY AFFIRMATION

_____

_____

DREAM JOURNAL

_____

_____

_____

_____

_____

_____

_____

_____

_____

_____

_____5_____
_____10_____
_____15_____
_____20_____
_____25_____
_____30_____

SCRIPTING

3-6-9 MANIFESTATION

_____ _____ _____

_____ _____ _____

_____ _____ _____

1 THING I DID TO MOVE FORWARD

_____

_____

OCTOBER

SUNDAY	MONDAY	TUESDAY	WEDNESDAY
1	2	3	4
8	9 Columbus Day	10	11
15	16	17	18
22	23	24	25
29	30	31 Halloween/Samhain	

THURSDAY	FRIDAY	SATURDAY	NOTES
5	6 ◑	7	
12	13	14 ● Annular Solar Eclipse	
19	20	21 ◐	
26	27	28 ○ Partial Lunar Eclipse	

HUNTER MOON

RITUAL FOCUS:
The season for deep internal work and journaling or working in your grimoire, Look into the darkness and figure out what it wants to show you about who you are!

ZODIACS:
Libra & Scorpio

CRYSTALS:
Amethyst, Obsidian & Tourmaline

COLORS:
Red, Purple, Black & Navy

ELEMENTS:
Air & Water

DEITIES:
Hecate, Hermes, Anubis, Shiva & Azreal

FLOWERS:
Dahlia & Pennyroal

ANIMALS:
Stag, Elephant, Scorpion, Ram & Wolf

HERBS:
Rosemary, Sage, Catnip, Thyme, Burdock & Ginger

MAGICAL ASSOCIATIONS:
Protection magic & Deep meditation

DIVINATION TRACKER

DATE	PULL	MESSAGE

October 2023 — Tropical Midnight Ephemeris — Time Zone: EDT (04:00 East)

Day	☉	☽	+12 Hr	True☊	☿	♀	♂	♃	♄	♅	♆	♇
01 Su	07♎43₃₆	01♉36₅₁	08♉43₂₂	24♈54 D	23♍25 D	23♌42 D	22♎37 D	14♉25 ℞	01♓28 ℞	22♉38 ℞	25♓57 ℞	27♑55 ℞
02 Mo	08 42₃₄	15 43₃₉	22 37₂₇	24 55	25 05	24 27	23 17	14 20	01 25	22 36	25 55	27 55
03 Tu	09 41₃₄	29 24₄₂	06♊05₂₇	24 56	26 48	25 13	23 57	14 15	01 22	22 35	25 54	27 54
04 We	10 40₃₇	12♊39₅₅	19 08₂₁	24 57	28 32	26 00	24 37	14 09	01 19	22 33	25 52	27 54
05 Th	11 39₄₂	25 31₁₀	01♋48₄₇	24 58	00♎17	26 47	25 17	14 04	01 16	22 32	25 51	27 54
06 Fr	12 38₄₉	08♋01₄₃	14 10₃₀	24 58	02 03	27 36	25 58	13 58	01 13	22 30	25 49	27 54
07 Sa	13 37₅₈	20 15₄₀	26 17₄₉	24 58 ℞	03 49	28 25	26 38	13 52	01 10	22 28	25 48	27 54
08 Su	14 37₁₀	02♌17₂₉	08♌15₁₅	24 58	05 35	29 15	27 18	13 46	01 08	22 26	25 46	27 54
09 Mo	15 36₂₃	14 11₃₉	20 07₁₂	24 57	07 22	00♍06	27 58	13 39	01 05	22 25	25 44	27 54
10 Tu	16 35₄₀	26 02₂₃	01♍57₄₂	24 56	09 08	00 58	28 39	13 33	01 03	22 23	25 43	27 54
11 We	17 34₅₈	07♍53₃₂	13 50₁₉	24 55	10 54	01 50	29 19	13 26	01 00	22 21	25 41	27 54 D
12 Th	18 34₁₈	19 48₂₄	25 48₀₇	24 54	12 40	02 43	29 59	13 20	00 58	22 19	25 40	27 54
13 Fr	19 33₄₁	01♎49₄₃	07♎53₃₀	24 53	14 25	03 37	00♏40	13 13	00 56	22 17	25 38	27 54
14 Sa	20 33₀₆	13 59₄₀	20 08₂₆	24 53	16 10	04 31	01 21	13 06	00 53	22 15	25 37	27 54
15 Su	21 32₃₃	26 19₅₅	02♏34₁₉	24 52 D	17 55	05 26	02 02	12 59	00 51	22 13	25 35	27 54
16 Mo	22 32₀₂	08♏51₄₃	15 12₁₆	24 53	19 38	06 21	02 42	12 52	00 49	22 11	25 34	27 54
17 Tu	23 31₃₃	21 36₀₁	28 03₀₆	24 53	21 22	07 17	03 23	12 45	00 48	22 09	25 33	27 54
18 We	24 31₀₆	04♐33₃₄	11♐07₃₀	24 53	23 04	08 14	04 04	12 37	00 46	22 07	25 31	27 54
19 Th	25 30₄₀	17 44₅₉	24 26₀₄	24 53 ℞	24 46	09 11	04 45	12 30	00 44	22 04	25 30	27 54
20 Fr	26 30₁₇	01♑10₄₇	07♑59₁₁	24 53	26 27	10 09	05 26	12 22	00 43	22 02	25 28	27 55
21 Sa	27 29₅₅	14 51₁₅	21 46₅₉	24 53	28 08	11 07	06 07	12 15	00 41	22 00	25 27	27 55
22 Su	28 29₃₅	28 46₁₇	05♒49₀₂	24 52 D	29 48	12 06	06 48	12 07	00 40	21 58	25 26	27 55
23 Mo	29 29₁₇	12♒55₀₄	20 04₀₇	24 53	01♏28	13 05	07 29	11 59	00 38	21 56	25 25	27 56
24 Tu	00♏29₀₀	27 15₅₁	04♓29₅₂	24 53	03 07	14 04	08 10	11 51	00 37	21 53	25 23	27 56
25 We	01 28₄₅	11♓45₄₁	19 02₄₃	24 53	04 45	15 04	08 51	11 44	00 36	21 51	25 22	27 56
26 Th	02 28₃₂	26 20₂₀	03♈37₅₂	24 54	06 23	16 05	09 32	11 36	00 35	21 49	25 21	27 57
27 Fr	03 28₂₀	10♈54₃₅	18 09₄₄	24 55	08 00	17 06	10 13	11 28	00 34	21 47	25 19	27 57
28 Sa	04 28₁₀	25 22₃₅	02♉32₂₆	24 55 ℞	09 37	18 07	10 55	11 20	00 33	21 44	25 18	27 58
29 Su	05 28₀₃	09♉38₃₇	16 40₃₃	24 55	11 13	19 09	11 36	11 12	00 33	21 42	25 17	27 58
30 Mo	06 27₅₇	23 37₄₆	00♊29₅₀	24 54	12 48	20 11	12 18	11 03	00 32	21 39	25 16	27 59
31 Tu	07 27₅₃	07♊16₃₀	13 57₃₆	24 52	14 23	21 13	12 59	10 55	00 32	21 37	25 15	27 59

Planetary Data

Ingresses

		Day	Time
☿	♎	4	8:08 PM
♀	♍	8	9:10 PM
♂	♏	12	12:03 AM
☿	♏	22	2:48 AM
☉	♏	23	12:20 PM

Stations

	Day	Time
♇ D	10	9:10 PM

Lunar Ingresses & Void Moons

Ingresses

	Day	Time
♈	28	8:18 PM
♉	30	9:18 PM
♊	3	1:02 AM
♋	5	8:32 AM
♌	7	7:25 PM
♍	10	8:02 AM
♎	12	8:22 PM
♏	15	7:04 AM
♐	17	3:37 PM
♑	19	9:54 PM
♒	22	2:05 AM
♓	24	4:32 AM
♈	26	6:01 AM
♉	28	7:45 AM
♊	30	11:08 AM

Void Times

Day	Time	Last Aspect	
30	5:49 PM	□	♇
2	9:20 PM	△	♇
5	2:34 AM	✶	♀
7	3:12 PM	☍	♇
10	5:37 AM	✶	♂
12	4:11 PM	△	♇
15	3:02 AM	□	♇
17	11:44 AM	✶	♇
19	3:02 PM	✶	☉
22	2:00 AM	□	☿
23	3:05 PM	□	♅
26	2:39 AM	✶	♇
28	4:20 AM	□	♇
30	7:35 AM	△	♇

Phases & Eclipses

Lunar Phases

Day	Time		
6	9:48 AM	☽	13♋03
14	1:55 PM	●	21♎08
21	11:30 PM	☽	28♑28
28	4:24 PM	○	05♉09

Solar Eclipses

Day	Time		
14	1:59 PM	A	5'17

Lunar Eclipses

Day	Time		
28	4:14 PM	P	.2f

386

NOTES

The Moon is in: _____

The Day Ruler is: _____

I AM GRATEFUL FOR

_____

_____

MOOD TRACKER

😠 😟 😐 🙂 😀

SELF - CARE

DAILY AFFIRMATION

_____

_____

DREAM JOURNAL

_____

_____

_____

_____

_____

_____

_____

_____

RITUAL TIME   MINDFUL MINUTES

_____ 5 _____
_____ 10 _____
_____ 15 _____
_____ 20 _____
_____ 25 _____
_____ 30 _____

SCRIPTING

_____
_____
_____
_____
_____
_____
_____
_____
_____
_____
_____
_____
_____
_____
_____
_____
_____
_____
_____

3-6-9 MANIFESTATION

_____ _____ _____
_____ _____ _____
_____ _____ _____

1 THING I DID TO MOVE FORWARD

_____
_____

The Moon is in: _____

The Day Ruler is: _____

I AM GRATEFUL FOR

_____

_____

MOOD TRACKER

SELF - CARE

DAILY AFFIRMATION

_____

_____

DREAM JOURNAL

_____

_____

_____

_____

_____

_____

_____

_____

_____ 5 _____
_____ 10 _____
_____ 15 _____
_____ 20 _____
_____ 25 _____
_____ 30 _____

SCRIPTING

3-6-9 MANIFESTATION

_____ _____ _____

_____ _____ _____

_____ _____ _____

1 THING I DID TO MOVE FORWARD

_____

_____

The Moon is in: _____

The Day Ruler is: _____

I AM GRATEFUL FOR

_____

_____

MOOD TRACKER

SELF - CARE

DAILY AFFIRMATION

_____

_____

DREAM JOURNAL

_____

_____

_____

_____

_____

_____

_____

_____

_____

RITUAL TIME   MINDFUL MINUTES

_____5_____
_____10_____
_____15_____
_____20_____
_____25_____
_____30_____

SCRIPTING

_____
_____
_____
_____
_____
_____
_____
_____
_____
_____
_____
_____
_____
_____
_____
_____
_____
_____

3-6-9 MANIFESTATION

_____ _____ _____
_____ _____ _____
_____ _____ _____

1 THING I DID TO MOVE FORWARD

_____

_____

The Moon is in: _____

The Day Ruler is: _____

I AM GRATEFUL FOR

_____

_____

MOOD TRACKER

SELF - CARE

DAILY AFFIRMATION

_____

_____

DREAM JOURNAL

_____

_____

_____

_____

_____

_____

_____

_____

_____

_____5_____
_____10_____
_____15_____
_____20_____
_____25_____
_____30_____
_____

SCRIPTING

3-6-9 MANIFESTATION

_____ _____ _____

_____ _____ _____

_____ _____ _____

1 THING I DID TO MOVE FORWARD

_____

_____

The Moon is in: _____

The Day Ruler is: _____

I AM GRATEFUL FOR

_____

_____

MOOD TRACKER

😠   🙁   😐   🙂   😄

SELF - CARE

DAILY AFFIRMATION

_____

_____

DREAM JOURNAL

_____

_____

_____

_____

_____

_____

_____

_____

_____

RITUAL TIME   MINDFUL MINUTES

_____ 5 _____
_____ 10 _____
_____ 15 _____
_____ 20 _____
_____ 25 _____
_____ 30 _____

SCRIPTING

3-6-9 MANIFESTATION

_____   _____   _____

_____   _____   _____

_____   _____   _____

1 THING I DID TO MOVE FORWARD

_____

_____

The Moon is in: _____

The Day Ruler is: _____

I AM GRATEFUL FOR

_____

_____

MOOD TRACKER

SELF - CARE

DAILY AFFIRMATION

_____

_____

DREAM JOURNAL

_____

_____

_____

_____

_____

_____

_____

_____

_____

_____5_____
_____10_____
_____15_____
_____20_____
_____25_____
_____30_____

SCRIPTING

3-6-9 MANIFESTATION

_____ _____ _____

_____ _____ _____

_____ _____ _____

1 THING I DID TO MOVE FORWARD

_____

_____

The Moon is in: _____

The Day Ruler is: _____

I AM GRATEFUL FOR

_____

_____

MOOD TRACKER

SELF - CARE

DAILY AFFIRMATION

_____

_____

DREAM JOURNAL

_____

_____

_____

_____

_____

_____

_____

_____

SCRIPTING

RITUAL TIME   MINDFUL MINUTES

5
10
15
20
25
30

3-6-9 MANIFESTATION

_____ _____ _____

_____ _____ _____

_____ _____ _____

1 THING I DID TO MOVE FORWARD

_____

_____

The Moon is in: _____

The Day Ruler is: _____

I AM GRATEFUL FOR

_____

_____

MOOD TRACKER

SELF - CARE

DAILY AFFIRMATION

_____

_____

DREAM JOURNAL

_____

_____

_____

_____

_____

_____

_____

_____

_____

_____ 5 _____
_____ 10 _____
_____ 15 _____
_____ 20 _____
_____ 25 _____
_____ 30 _____

SCRIPTING

3-6-9 MANIFESTATION

_____ _____ _____

_____ _____ _____

_____ _____ _____

1 THING I DID TO MOVE FORWARD

_____

_____

The Moon is in:_____
The Day Ruler is:_____

I AM GRATEFUL FOR

_____
_____

MOOD TRACKER

SELF - CARE

DAILY AFFIRMATION

_____
_____

DREAM JOURNAL

_____
_____
_____
_____
_____
_____
_____
_____

RITUAL TIME   MINDFUL MINUTES

_____5
_____10_____
_____15_____
_____20_____
_____25_____
_____30_____

SCRIPTING

3-6-9 MANIFESTATION

_____ _____ _____
_____ _____ _____
_____ _____ _____

1 THING I DID TO MOVE FORWARD

_____
_____

The Moon is in: _____

The Day Ruler is: _____

I AM GRATEFUL FOR

_____

_____

MOOD TRACKER

SELF - CARE

DAILY AFFIRMATION

_____

_____

DREAM JOURNAL

_____

_____

_____

_____

_____

_____

_____

_____

_____

_____ 5 _____
_____ 10 _____
_____ 15 _____
_____ 20 _____
_____ 25 _____
_____ 30 _____

SCRIPTING

3-6-9 MANIFESTATION

_____ _____ _____

_____ _____ _____

_____ _____ _____

1 THING I DID TO MOVE FORWARD

_____

_____

The Moon is in: _____

The Day Ruler is: _____

I AM GRATEFUL FOR

_____

_____

MOOD TRACKER

SELF - CARE

DAILY AFFIRMATION

_____

_____

DREAM JOURNAL

_____

_____

_____

_____

_____

_____

_____

_____

_____

RITUAL TIME   MINDFUL MINUTES

_____ 5 _____
_____ 10 _____
_____ 15 _____
_____ 20 _____
_____ 25 _____
_____ 30 _____

SCRIPTING

3-6-9 MANIFESTATION

_____ _____ _____

_____ _____ _____

_____ _____ _____

1 THING I DID TO MOVE FORWARD

_____

_____

The Moon is in: _____

The Day Ruler is: _____

I AM GRATEFUL FOR

_____

_____

MOOD TRACKER

SELF - CARE

DAILY AFFIRMATION

_____

_____

DREAM JOURNAL

_____

_____

_____

_____

_____

_____

_____

_____

_____

_____ 5 _____
_____ 10 _____
_____ 15 _____
_____ 20 _____
_____ 25 _____
_____ 30 _____

SCRIPTING

3-6-9 MANIFESTATION

_____ _____ _____

_____ _____ _____

_____ _____ _____

1 THING I DID TO MOVE FORWARD

_____

_____

The Moon is in: _____

The Day Ruler is: _____

I AM GRATEFUL FOR

_____

_____

MOOD TRACKER

SELF - CARE

DAILY AFFIRMATION

_____

_____

DREAM JOURNAL

_____

_____

_____

_____

_____

_____

_____

_____

RITUAL TIME   MINDFUL MINUTES

___5___
___10___
___15___
___20___
___25___
___30___

SCRIPTING

3-6-9 MANIFESTATION

_____ _____ _____

_____ _____ _____

_____ _____ _____

1 THING I DID TO MOVE FORWARD

_____

_____

The Moon is in: _____

The Day Ruler is: _____

I AM GRATEFUL FOR

_____

_____

MOOD TRACKER

SELF - CARE

DAILY AFFIRMATION

_____

_____

DREAM JOURNAL

_____

_____

_____

_____

_____

_____

_____

_____

_____

_____ 5 _____
_____ 10 _____
_____ 15 _____
_____ 20 _____
_____ 25 _____
_____ 30 _____

SCRIPTING

3-6-9 MANIFESTATION

_____ _____ _____

_____ _____ _____

_____ _____ _____

1 THING I DID TO MOVE FORWARD

_____

_____

THIS LUNATION

Full Moon ☐   ☐ New Moon

The Moon is in the sign of _____ and transits my _____ house,

meaning _____

_____ for me.

Build your Moon ritual: _____

_____

_____

_____

_____

_____

_____

_____

CANDLES	CRYSTALS
HERBS	OTHER

Card 1	Card 2	Card 3
_____	_____	_____
Deck	Deck	Deck
_____	_____	_____
Card	Card	Card

Interpretation & Meaning: _____

_____

_____

_____

_____

_____

Intentions for this lunation: _____

_____

_____

_____

_____

_____

_____

The Moon is in: _____

The Day Ruler is: _____

I AM GRATEFUL FOR

_____

_____

MOOD TRACKER

SELF - CARE

DAILY AFFIRMATION

_____

_____

DREAM JOURNAL

_____

_____

_____

_____

_____

_____

_____

_____

_____

_____ 5 _____
_____ 10 _____
_____ 15 _____
_____ 20 _____
_____ 25 _____
_____ 30 _____

SCRIPTING

3-6-9 MANIFESTATION

_____ _____ _____

_____ _____ _____

_____ _____ _____

1 THING I DID TO MOVE FORWARD

_____

_____

The Moon is in:_____

The Day Ruler is:_____

I AM GRATEFUL FOR

_____

_____

MOOD TRACKER

SELF - CARE

DAILY AFFIRMATION

_____

_____

DREAM JOURNAL

_____

_____

_____

_____

_____

_____

_____

_____

_____

SCRIPTING

RITUAL TIME   MINDFUL MINUTES

_____5_____
_____10_____
_____15_____
_____20_____
_____25_____
_____30_____

3-6-9 MANIFESTATION

_____ _____ _____

_____ _____ _____

_____ _____ _____

1 THING I DID TO MOVE FORWARD

_____

_____

The Moon is in: _____

The Day Ruler is: _____

I AM GRATEFUL FOR

_____

_____

MOOD TRACKER

SELF - CARE

DAILY AFFIRMATION

_____

_____

DREAM JOURNAL

_____

_____

_____

_____

_____

_____

_____

_____

_____

_____

_____5_____
_____10_____
_____15_____
_____20_____
_____25_____
_____30_____

SCRIPTING

_____
_____
_____
_____
_____
_____
_____
_____
_____
_____
_____
_____
_____
_____
_____
_____
_____
_____

3-6-9 MANIFESTATION

_____ _____ _____

_____ _____ _____

_____ _____ _____

1 THING I DID TO MOVE FORWARD

_____

_____

DAILY *10/18*

The Moon is in: _____
The Day Ruler is: _____

I AM GRATEFUL FOR
_____
_____

MOOD TRACKER
😠 😟 😐 🙂 😀

SELF - CARE

DAILY AFFIRMATION
_____
_____

DREAM JOURNAL
_____
_____
_____
_____
_____
_____
_____
_____

RITUAL TIME   MINDFUL MINUTES

___5___
___10___
___15___
___20___
___25___
___30___

SCRIPTING

3-6-9 MANIFESTATION
_____ _____ _____
_____ _____ _____
_____ _____ _____

1 THING I DID TO MOVE FORWARD
_____
_____

The Moon is in: _____

The Day Ruler is: _____

I AM GRATEFUL FOR

_____

_____

MOOD TRACKER

😠 😦 😐 🙂 😀

SELF - CARE

DAILY AFFIRMATION

_____

_____

DREAM JOURNAL

_____

_____

_____

_____

_____

_____

_____

_____

_____

_____ 5 _____
_____ 10 _____
_____ 15 _____
_____ 20 _____
_____ 25 _____
_____ 30 _____

SCRIPTING

3-6-9 MANIFESTATION

_____ _____ _____

_____ _____ _____

_____ _____ _____

1 THING I DID TO MOVE FORWARD

_____

_____

The Moon is in: _____

The Day Ruler is: _____

I AM GRATEFUL FOR

_____

_____

MOOD TRACKER

SELF - CARE

DAILY AFFIRMATION

_____

_____

DREAM JOURNAL

_____

_____

_____

_____

_____

_____

_____

_____

_____

RITUAL TIME   MINDFUL MINUTES

_____ 5 _____
_____ 10 _____
_____ 15 _____
_____ 20 _____
_____ 25 _____
_____ 30 _____

SCRIPTING

_____

_____

_____

_____

_____

_____

_____

_____

_____

_____

_____

_____

_____

_____

_____

_____

_____

_____

_____

3-6-9 MANIFESTATION

_____ _____ _____

_____ _____ _____

_____ _____ _____

1 THING I DID TO MOVE FORWARD

_____

_____

The Moon is in: _____

The Day Ruler is: _____

I AM GRATEFUL FOR

_____

_____

MOOD TRACKER

SELF - CARE

DAILY AFFIRMATION

_____

_____

DREAM JOURNAL

_____

_____

_____

_____

_____

_____

_____

_____

_____

_____5_____
_____10_____
_____15_____
_____20_____
_____25_____
_____30_____

SCRIPTING

3-6-9 MANIFESTATION

_____ _____ _____

_____ _____ _____

_____ _____ _____

1 THING I DID TO MOVE FORWARD

_____

_____

The Moon is in:_____

The Day Ruler is:_____

I AM GRATEFUL FOR

_____

_____

MOOD TRACKER

SELF - CARE

DAILY AFFIRMATION

_____

_____

DREAM JOURNAL

_____

_____

_____

_____

_____

_____

_____

_____

RITUAL TIME

MINDFUL MINUTES

___5___
___10___
___15___
___20___
___25___
___30___

SCRIPTING

3-6-9 MANIFESTATION

_____ _____ _____

_____ _____ _____

_____ _____ _____

1 THING I DID TO MOVE FORWARD

_____

_____

The Moon is in: _____

The Day Ruler is: _____

I AM GRATEFUL FOR

_____

_____

MOOD TRACKER

SELF - CARE

DAILY AFFIRMATION

_____

_____

DREAM JOURNAL

_____

_____

_____

_____

_____

_____

_____

_____

_____

_____ 5 _____
_____ 10 _____
_____ 15 _____
_____ 20 _____
_____ 25 _____
_____ 30 _____

SCRIPTING

3-6-9 MANIFESTATION

_____ _____ _____

_____ _____ _____

_____ _____ _____

1 THING I DID TO MOVE FORWARD

_____

_____

The Moon is in:_____

The Day Ruler is:_____

I AM GRATEFUL FOR

_____

_____

MOOD TRACKER

SELF - CARE

DAILY AFFIRMATION

_____

_____

DREAM JOURNAL

_____

_____

_____

_____

_____

_____

_____

_____

_____

RITUAL TIME   MINDFUL MINUTES

5
10
15
20
25
30

SCRIPTING

3-6-9 MANIFESTATION

____ ____ ____

____ ____ ____

____ ____ ____

1 THING I DID TO MOVE FORWARD

_____

_____

412

The Moon is in: _____

The Day Ruler is: _____

I AM GRATEFUL FOR

_____

_____

MOOD TRACKER

SELF - CARE

DAILY AFFIRMATION

_____

_____

DREAM JOURNAL

_____

_____

_____

_____

_____

_____

_____

_____

_____

_____

_____ 5 _____
_____ 10 _____
_____ 15 _____
_____ 20 _____
_____ 25 _____
_____ 30 _____

SCRIPTING

3-6-9 MANIFESTATION

_____ _____ _____

_____ _____ _____

_____ _____ _____

1 THING I DID TO MOVE FORWARD

_____

_____

The Moon is in: _____

The Day Ruler is: _____

I AM GRATEFUL FOR

_____

_____

MOOD TRACKER

SELF - CARE

DAILY AFFIRMATION

_____

_____

DREAM JOURNAL

_____

_____

_____

_____

_____

_____

_____

_____

_____

RITUAL TIME   MINDFUL MINUTES

_____5_____
_____10_____
_____15_____
_____20_____
_____25_____
_____30_____

SCRIPTING

3-6-9 MANIFESTATION

_____ _____ _____

_____ _____ _____

_____ _____ _____

1 THING I DID TO MOVE FORWARD

_____

_____

The Moon is in: _____

The Day Ruler is: _____

I AM GRATEFUL FOR

_____

_____

MOOD TRACKER

SELF - CARE

DAILY AFFIRMATION

_____

_____

DREAM JOURNAL

_____

_____

_____

_____

_____

_____

_____

_____

_____

_____5_____
_____10_____
_____15_____
_____20_____
_____25_____
_____30_____

SCRIPTING

3-6-9 MANIFESTATION

_____ _____ _____

_____ _____ _____

_____ _____ _____

1 THING I DID TO MOVE FORWARD

_____

_____

The Moon is in: _____

The Day Ruler is: _____

I AM GRATEFUL FOR

_____

_____

MOOD TRACKER

😠 😟 😐 🙂 😀

SELF - CARE

DAILY AFFIRMATION

_____

_____

DREAM JOURNAL

_____

_____

_____

_____

_____

_____

_____

_____

RITUAL TIME   MINDFUL MINUTES

_____ 5 _____
_____ 10 _____
_____ 15 _____
_____ 20 _____
_____ 25 _____
_____ 30 _____

SCRIPTING

_____
_____
_____
_____
_____
_____
_____
_____
_____
_____
_____
_____
_____
_____
_____
_____
_____
_____
_____
_____

3-6-9 MANIFESTATION

_____ _____ _____
_____ _____ _____
_____ _____ _____

1 THING I DID TO MOVE FORWARD

_____

_____

THIS LUNATION

Full Moon ☐   ☐ New Moon

The Moon is in the sign of _____ and transits my _____ house,

meaning _____

_____ for me.

Build your Moon ritual: _____

_____

_____

_____

_____

_____

_____

_____

CANDLES	CRYSTALS
HERBS	OTHER

Card 1	Card 2	Card 3
___ Deck	___ Deck	___ Deck
___ Card	___ Card	___ Card

Interpretation & Meaning: _____

_____

_____

_____

_____

_____

Intentions for this lunation: _____

_____

_____

_____

_____

_____

_____

_____

The Moon is in:_____

The Day Ruler is:_____

I AM GRATEFUL FOR

_____

_____

MOOD TRACKER

SELF - CARE

DAILY AFFIRMATION

_____

_____

DREAM JOURNAL

_____

_____

_____

_____

_____

_____

_____

_____

RITUAL TIME   MINDFUL MINUTES

_____5_____
_____10_____
_____15_____
_____20_____
_____25_____
_____30_____

SCRIPTING

3-6-9 MANIFESTATION

_____ _____ _____
_____ _____ _____
_____ _____ _____

1 THING I DID TO MOVE FORWARD

_____

_____

The Moon is in: _____

The Day Ruler is: _____

I AM GRATEFUL FOR

_____

_____

MOOD TRACKER

SELF - CARE

DAILY AFFIRMATION

_____

_____

DREAM JOURNAL

_____

_____

_____

_____

_____

_____

_____

_____

_____

_____5_____
_____10_____
_____15_____
_____20_____
_____25_____
_____30_____

SCRIPTING

3-6-9 MANIFESTATION

_____ _____ _____

_____ _____ _____

_____ _____ _____

1 THING I DID TO MOVE FORWARD

_____

_____

The Moon is in: _____

The Day Ruler is: _____

I AM GRATEFUL FOR

_____

_____

MOOD TRACKER

SELF - CARE

DAILY AFFIRMATION

_____

_____

DREAM JOURNAL

_____

_____

_____

_____

_____

_____

_____

_____

_____

RITUAL TIME MINDFUL MINUTES

_____5_____
_____10_____
_____15_____
_____20_____
_____25_____
_____30_____

SCRIPTING

3-6-9 MANIFESTATION

_____ _____ _____

_____ _____ _____

_____ _____ _____

1 THING I DID TO MOVE FORWARD

_____

_____

NOTES

NOVEMBER

SUNDAY	MONDAY	TUESDAY	WEDNESDAY
			1
5 ◑ Daylight Savings	6	7	8
12	13 ●	14	15
19	20 ◐	21	22
26	27 ○	28	29

2023

THURSDAY	FRIDAY	SATURDAY	NOTES
2	3	4	
9	10	11 Veteran's Day	
16	17	18	
23 Thanksgiving	24	25	
30			

BEAVER MOON

RITUAL FOCUS:
The beaver moon is a time for connecting with your need to release toxic habits, focus on empathy, and transformation.

ZODIACS:
Scorpio & Sagittarius

CRYSTALS:
Topaz, Citrine & Labradorite

COLORS:
Dark Blue, Dark Purple & Black

ELEMENTS:
Water & Fire

DEITIES:
Astarte, Circe, Hel, Holda, Kali, Bast, Osiris & Sarasvati

FLOWERS:
White Lily, Dahlia & Chrysanthemum

ANIMALS:
Scorpion & Centaur

HERBS:
Mugwort, Ginger, Wormwood, Hyssop, Patchouli, Sage & Nutmeg

MAGICAL ASSOCIATIONS:
Release, Protection Magic & Divine Connection

DIVINATION TRACKER

DATE	PULL	MESSAGE

NOVEMBER TRANSITS

November 2023 Tropical Midnight Ephemeris

Time Zone: **EST (05:00 East)**

Day	☉	☽	+12 Hr	True ☊	☿	♀	♂	♃	♄	♅	♆	♇
01 We	08 ♏ 30 21	21 ♊ 05 48	27 ♊ 35 16	24 ♈ 50 ℞	16 ♏ 02 D	22 ♍ 19 D	13 ♏ 42 D	10 ♉ 47 ℞	00 ♓ 31 ℞	21 ♉ 35 ℞	25 ♓ 14 ℞	28 ♑ 00 D
02 Th	09 30 22	03 ♋ 59 23	10 ♋ 18 24	24 48	17 36	23 22	14 24	10 39	00 31	21 32	25 13	28 01
03 Fr	10 30 24	16 32 41	22 42 39	24 47	19 10	24 25	15 05	10 31	00 31	21 30	25 11	28 01
04 Sa	11 30 29	28 48 48	04 ♌ 51 38	24 45	20 43	25 29	15 47	10 22	00 31	21 27	25 10	28 02
05 Su	12 30 36	10 ♌ 51 44	16 49 42	24 45	22 16	26 33	16 29	10 14	00 31 D	21 25	25 09	28 03
06 Mo	13 30 45	22 46 07	28 41 37	24 45 D	23 49	27 38	17 10	10 06	00 31	21 22	25 08	28 04
07 Tu	14 30 55	04 ♍ 36 47	10 ♍ 32 13	24 46	25 21	28 43	17 52	09 58	00 31	21 20	25 07	28 04
08 We	15 31 08	16 28 31	22 26 14	24 48	26 52	29 48	18 34	09 50	00 32	21 17	25 07	28 05
09 Th	16 31 23	28 25 52	04 ♎ 27 55	24 49	28 24	00 ♎ 53	19 16	09 42	00 32	21 15	25 06	28 06
10 Fr	17 31 40	10 ♎ 32 48	16 40 55	24 51	29 55	01 59	19 58	09 34	00 33	21 13	25 05	28 07
11 Sa	18 31 59	22 52 35	29 08 03	24 51	01 ♐ 25	03 05	20 40	09 26	00 33	21 10	25 04	28 08
12 Su	19 32 19	05 ♏ 27 32	11 ♏ 51 08	24 51 ℞	02 55	04 11	21 22	09 18	00 34	21 08	25 03	28 09
13 Mo	20 32 42	18 18 55	24 50 51	24 49	04 25	05 17	22 04	09 10	00 35	21 05	25 02	28 09
14 Tu	21 33 06	01 ♐ 26 51	08 ♐ 06 46	24 46	05 55	06 24	22 46	09 02	00 36	21 03	25 02	28 10
15 We	22 33 32	14 50 24	21 37 28	24 42	07 24	07 31	23 29	08 54	00 37	21 00	25 01	28 11
16 Th	23 33 59	28 27 41	05 ♑ 20 45	24 37	08 53	08 38	24 11	08 47	00 38	20 58	25 00	28 12
17 Fr	24 34 28	12 ♑ 16 19	19 14 03	24 33	10 21	09 45	24 53	08 39	00 40	20 55	25 00	28 13
18 Sa	25 34 58	26 13 37	03 ♒ 14 44	24 29	11 48	10 53	25 35	08 32	00 41	20 53	24 59	28 15
19 Su	26 35 29	10 ♒ 17 06	17 20 27	24 27	13 16	12 01	26 18	08 24	00 42	20 50	24 58	28 16
20 Mo	27 36 02	24 24 33	01 ♓ 29 09	24 25	14 42	13 09	27 00	08 17	00 44	20 48	24 58	28 17
21 Tu	28 36 35	08 ♓ 34 05	15 39 06	24 26 D	16 08	14 17	27 43	08 10	00 46	20 45	24 57	28 18
22 We	29 37 10	22 44 01	29 48 37	24 27	17 34	15 25	28 25	08 03	00 48	20 43	24 57	28 19
23 Th	00 ♐ 37 46	06 ♈ 52 39	13 ♈ 55 51	24 29	18 58	16 34	29 08	07 56	00 49	20 40	24 56	28 20
24 Fr	01 38 23	20 57 56	27 58 34	24 29	20 22	17 43	29 51	07 49	00 51	20 38	24 56	28 21
25 Sa	02 39 02	04 ♉ 57 23	11 ♉ 54 01	24 29 ℞	21 45	18 52	00 ♐ 33	07 42	00 54	20 35	24 55	28 23
26 Su	03 39 41	18 48 05	25 39 12	24 27	23 06	20 01	01 16	07 36	00 56	20 33	24 55	28 24
27 Mo	04 40 22	02 ♊ 26 58	09 ♊ 11 05	24 22	24 27	21 10	01 59	07 29	00 58	20 31	24 55	28 25
28 Tu	05 41 05	15 51 14	22 27 09	24 16	25 46	22 19	02 42	07 23	01 00	20 28	24 54	28 27
29 We	06 41 49	28 58 43	05 ♋ 25 47	24 09	27 03	23 29	03 25	07 17	01 03	20 26	24 54	28 28
30 Th	07 42 34	11 ♋ 48 23	18 06 35	24 01	28 18	24 39	04 08	07 11	01 06	20 23	24 54	28 29
01 Fr	08 43 20	24 20 33	00 ♌ 30 32	23 53	29 32	25 49	04 51	07 05	01 08	20 21	24 54	28 31

Planetary Data

Ingresses

		Day	Time
♀	♎	8	4:30 AM
☿	♐	10	1:24 AM
☉	♐	22	9:02 AM
♂	♐	24	5:14 AM
☿	♑	1	9:31 AM

Stations

	Day	Time
♄ D	4	2:03 AM

Lunar Ingresses & Void Moons

Ingresses

	Day	Time
♊	30	10:08 AM
♋	1	4:31 PM
♌	4	2:21 AM
♍	6	2:39 PM
♎	9	3:08 AM
♏	11	1:39 PM
♐	13	9:23 PM
♑	16	2:42 AM
♒	18	6:28 AM
♓	20	9:29 AM
♈	22	12:19 PM
♉	24	3:29 PM
♊	26	7:40 PM
♋	29	1:53 AM
♌	1	11:00 AM

Void Times

Day	Time	Last Aspect	
1	7:37 AM	□	♇
3	10:28 PM	☍	♇
6	2:26 AM	□	☿
8	11:56 PM	⚹	☿
11	10:06 AM	□	♇
13	6:03 PM	⚹	♇
15	5:56 PM	□	♆
18	3:27 AM	☌	♇
20	5:50 AM	□	☉
22	10:09 AM	△	♂
24	12:41 PM	□	♇
26	4:52 PM	△	♇
28	8:04 PM	☍	☿
1	8:07 AM	☍	♇

Phases & Eclipses

Lunar Phases

Day	Time		
5	3:37 AM	☽	12♌40
13	4:28 AM	●	20♏44
20	5:50 AM	☽	27♒51
27	4:17 AM	○	04♊51

Solar Eclipses

Day Time

~ None ~

Lunar Eclipses

Day Time

~ None ~

NOTES

The Moon is in: _____

The Day Ruler is: _____

I AM GRATEFUL FOR

_____

_____

MOOD TRACKER

SELF - CARE

DAILY AFFIRMATION

_____

_____

DREAM JOURNAL

_____

_____

_____

_____

_____

_____

_____

_____

RITUAL TIME   MINDFUL MINUTES

_____ 5 _____
_____ 10 _____
_____ 15 _____
_____ 20 _____
_____ 25 _____
_____ 30 _____

SCRIPTING

3-6-9 MANIFESTATION

_____ _____ _____

_____ _____ _____

_____ _____ _____

1 THING I DID TO MOVE FORWARD

_____

_____

The Moon is in: _____

The Day Ruler is: _____

I AM GRATEFUL FOR

_____

_____

MOOD TRACKER

SELF - CARE

DAILY AFFIRMATION

_____

_____

DREAM JOURNAL

_____

_____

_____

_____

_____

_____

_____

_____

_____

_____ 5 _____
_____ 10 _____
_____ 15 _____
_____ 20 _____
_____ 25 _____
_____ 30 _____

SCRIPTING

3-6-9 MANIFESTATION

_____ _____ _____

_____ _____ _____

_____ _____ _____

1 THING I DID TO MOVE FORWARD

_____

_____

The Moon is in:_____

The Day Ruler is:_____

I AM GRATEFUL FOR

_____

_____

MOOD TRACKER

SELF - CARE

DAILY AFFIRMATION

_____

_____

DREAM JOURNAL

_____

_____

_____

_____

_____

_____

_____

_____

_____

RITUAL TIME   MINDFUL MINUTES

5
10
15
20
25
30

SCRIPTING

3-6-9 MANIFESTATION

_____ _____ _____

_____ _____ _____

_____ _____ _____

1 THING I DID TO MOVE FORWARD

_____

_____

The Moon is in: _____

The Day Ruler is: _____

I AM GRATEFUL FOR

_____

_____

MOOD TRACKER

SELF - CARE

DAILY AFFIRMATION

_____

_____

DREAM JOURNAL

_____

_____

_____

_____

_____

_____

_____

_____

_____

_____

_____5_____
_____10_____
_____15_____
_____20_____
_____25_____
_____30_____

SCRIPTING

3-6-9 MANIFESTATION

_____ _____ _____

_____ _____ _____

_____ _____ _____

1 THING I DID TO MOVE FORWARD

_____

_____

The Moon is in: _____

The Day Ruler is: _____

I AM GRATEFUL FOR

_____

_____

MOOD TRACKER

SELF - CARE

DAILY AFFIRMATION

_____

_____

DREAM JOURNAL

_____

_____

_____

_____

_____

_____

_____

_____

RITUAL TIME   MINDFUL MINUTES

_____ 5 _____
_____ 10 _____
_____ 15 _____
_____ 20 _____
_____ 25 _____
_____ 30 _____

SCRIPTING

_____

_____

_____

_____

_____

_____

_____

_____

_____

_____

_____

_____

_____

_____

_____

_____

_____

_____

_____

3-6-9 MANIFESTATION

_____ _____ _____

_____ _____ _____

_____ _____ _____

1 THING I DID TO MOVE FORWARD

_____

_____

The Moon is in: _____

The Day Ruler is: _____

I AM GRATEFUL FOR

_____

_____

MOOD TRACKER

😠   🙁   😐   🙂   😃

SELF - CARE

DAILY AFFIRMATION

_____

_____

DREAM JOURNAL

_____

_____

_____

_____

_____

_____

_____

_____

_____

_____

_____5_____
_____10_____
_____15_____
_____20_____
_____25_____
_____30_____

SCRIPTING

_____

_____

_____

_____

_____

_____

_____

_____

_____

_____

_____

_____

_____

_____

_____

_____

_____

_____

3-6-9 MANIFESTATION

_____ _____ _____

_____ _____ _____

_____ _____ _____

1 THING I DID TO MOVE FORWARD

_____

_____

The Moon is in: _____

The Day Ruler is: _____

I AM GRATEFUL FOR

_____

_____

MOOD TRACKER

SELF - CARE

DAILY AFFIRMATION

_____

_____

DREAM JOURNAL

_____

_____

_____

_____

_____

_____

_____

_____

RITUAL TIME   MINDFUL MINUTES

_____5_____
_____10_____
_____15_____
_____20_____
_____25_____
_____30_____

SCRIPTING

3-6-9 MANIFESTATION

_____ _____ _____

_____ _____ _____

_____ _____ _____

1 THING I DID TO MOVE FORWARD

_____

_____

The Moon is in: _____

The Day Ruler is: _____

I AM GRATEFUL FOR

_____

_____

MOOD TRACKER

SELF - CARE

DAILY AFFIRMATION

_____

_____

DREAM JOURNAL

_____

_____

_____

_____

_____

_____

_____

_____

_____

_____5_____
_____10_____
_____15_____
_____20_____
_____25_____
_____30_____

SCRIPTING

3-6-9 MANIFESTATION

_____ _____ _____

_____ _____ _____

_____ _____ _____

1 THING I DID TO MOVE FORWARD

_____

_____

The Moon is in: _____
The Day Ruler is: _____

I AM GRATEFUL FOR

_____
_____

MOOD TRACKER

SELF - CARE

DAILY AFFIRMATION

_____
_____

DREAM JOURNAL

_____
_____
_____
_____
_____
_____
_____
_____

RITUAL TIME   MINDFUL MINUTES

_____ 5 _____
_____ 10 _____
_____ 15 _____
_____ 20 _____
_____ 25 _____
_____ 30 _____

SCRIPTING

3-6-9 MANIFESTATION

_____ _____ _____
_____ _____ _____
_____ _____ _____

1 THING I DID TO MOVE FORWARD

_____
_____

The Moon is in: _____

The Day Ruler is: _____

I AM GRATEFUL FOR

_____

_____

MOOD TRACKER

SELF - CARE

DAILY AFFIRMATION

_____

_____

DREAM JOURNAL

_____

_____

_____

_____

_____

_____

_____

_____

_____

_____

_____ 5 _____
_____ 10 _____
_____ 15 _____
_____ 20 _____
_____ 25 _____
_____ 30 _____

SCRIPTING

3-6-9 MANIFESTATION

_____ _____ _____

_____ _____ _____

_____ _____ _____

1 THING I DID TO MOVE FORWARD

_____

_____

The Moon is in: _____

The Day Ruler is: _____

I AM GRATEFUL FOR

_____

_____

MOOD TRACKER

😠 😟 😐 🙂 😄

SELF - CARE

DAILY AFFIRMATION

_____

_____

DREAM JOURNAL

_____

_____

_____

_____

_____

_____

_____

_____

RITUAL TIME   MINDFUL MINUTES

_____ 5 _____
_____ 10 _____
_____ 15 _____
_____ 20 _____
_____ 25 _____
_____ 30 _____

SCRIPTING

3-6-9 MANIFESTATION

_____ _____ _____
_____ _____ _____
_____ _____ _____

1 THING I DID TO MOVE FORWARD

_____

_____

The Moon is in: _____

The Day Ruler is: _____

I AM GRATEFUL FOR

_____

_____

MOOD TRACKER

SELF - CARE

DAILY AFFIRMATION

_____

_____

DREAM JOURNAL

_____

_____

_____

_____

_____

_____

_____

_____

_____

_____ 5 _____
_____ 10 _____
_____ 15 _____
_____ 20 _____
_____ 25 _____
_____ 30 _____

SCRIPTING

3-6-9 MANIFESTATION

_____ _____ _____

_____ _____ _____

_____ _____ _____

1 THING I DID TO MOVE FORWARD

_____

_____

The Moon is in: _____

The Day Ruler is: _____

I AM GRATEFUL FOR

_____

_____

MOOD TRACKER

SELF - CARE

DAILY AFFIRMATION

_____

_____

DREAM JOURNAL

_____

_____

_____

_____

_____

_____

_____

_____

RITUAL TIME   MINDFUL MINUTES

_____ 5 _____
_____ 10 _____
_____ 15 _____
_____ 20 _____
_____ 25 _____
_____ 30 _____

SCRIPTING

3-6-9 MANIFESTATION

_____ _____ _____

_____ _____ _____

_____ _____ _____

1 THING I DID TO MOVE FORWARD

_____

THIS LUNATION

Full Moon ☐   ☐ New Moon

The Moon is in the sign of _____ and transits my _____ house,

meaning _____

_____ for me.

Build your Moon ritual: _____

_____ | CANDLES | CRYSTALS |
_____ | HERBS | OTHER |
_____
_____
_____
_____
_____
_____

Card 1	Card 2	Card 3
Deck	Deck	Deck
Card	Card	Card

Interpretation & Meaning: _____

_____

_____

_____

_____

_____

Intentions for this lunation: _____

_____

_____

_____

_____

_____

_____

_____

The Moon is in:_____

The Day Ruler is:_____

I AM GRATEFUL FOR

_____

_____

MOOD TRACKER

😠　😕　😐　🙂　😁

SELF - CARE

DAILY AFFIRMATION

_____

_____

DREAM JOURNAL

_____

_____

_____

_____

_____

_____

_____

_____

_____

RITUAL TIME   MINDFUL MINUTES

_____5_____
_____10_____
_____15_____
_____20_____
_____25_____
_____30_____

SCRIPTING

_____

_____

_____

_____

_____

_____

_____

_____

_____

_____

_____

_____

_____

_____

_____

_____

_____

3-6-9 MANIFESTATION

_____ _____ _____

_____ _____ _____

_____ _____ _____

1 THING I DID TO MOVE FORWARD

_____

_____

The Moon is in: _____

The Day Ruler is: _____

I AM GRATEFUL FOR

_____

_____

MOOD TRACKER

SELF - CARE

DAILY AFFIRMATION

_____

_____

DREAM JOURNAL

_____

_____

_____

_____

_____

_____

_____

_____

_____

_____

_____ 5 _____
_____ 10 _____
_____ 15 _____
_____ 20 _____
_____ 25 _____
_____ 30 _____

SCRIPTING

3-6-9 MANIFESTATION

_____ _____ _____

_____ _____ _____

_____ _____ _____

1 THING I DID TO MOVE FORWARD

_____

_____

The Moon is in:_____

The Day Ruler is:_____

I AM GRATEFUL FOR

_____

_____

MOOD TRACKER

SELF - CARE

DAILY AFFIRMATION

_____

_____

DREAM JOURNAL

_____

_____

_____

_____

_____

_____

_____

_____

SCRIPTING

RITUAL TIME   MINDFUL MINUTES

5
10
15
20
25
30

3-6-9 MANIFESTATION

_____ _____ _____

_____ _____ _____

_____ _____ _____

1 THING I DID TO MOVE FORWARD

_____

_____

The Moon is in: _____
The Day Ruler is: _____

I AM GRATEFUL FOR

_____
_____

MOOD TRACKER

😠   🙁   😐   🙂   😃

SELF - CARE

DAILY AFFIRMATION

_____
_____

DREAM JOURNAL

_____
_____
_____
_____
_____
_____
_____
_____
_____

```
____5____
___10____
___15____
___20____
___25____
___30____
```

SCRIPTING

3-6-9 MANIFESTATION

_____ _____ _____
_____ _____ _____
_____ _____ _____

1 THING I DID TO MOVE FORWARD

_____
_____

The Moon is in: _____

The Day Ruler is: _____

I AM GRATEFUL FOR

_____

_____

MOOD TRACKER

SELF - CARE

DAILY AFFIRMATION

_____

_____

DREAM JOURNAL

_____

_____

_____

_____

_____

_____

_____

_____

RITUAL TIME   MINDFUL MINUTES

_____5_____
_____10_____
_____15_____
_____20_____
_____25_____
_____30_____

SCRIPTING

_____

3-6-9 MANIFESTATION

_____ _____ _____
_____ _____ _____
_____ _____ _____

1 THING I DID TO MOVE FORWARD

_____

_____

The Moon is in: _____

The Day Ruler is: _____

I AM GRATEFUL FOR

_____

_____

MOOD TRACKER

SELF - CARE

DAILY AFFIRMATION

_____

_____

DREAM JOURNAL

_____

_____

_____

_____

_____

_____

_____

_____

_____

_____5_____
_____10_____
_____15_____
_____20_____
_____25_____
_____30_____

SCRIPTING

3-6-9 MANIFESTATION

_____ _____ _____

_____ _____ _____

_____ _____ _____

1 THING I DID TO MOVE FORWARD

_____

_____

The Moon is in: _____

The Day Ruler is: _____

I AM GRATEFUL FOR

_____

_____

MOOD TRACKER

SELF - CARE

DAILY AFFIRMATION

_____

_____

DREAM JOURNAL

_____

_____

_____

_____

_____

_____

_____

_____

_____

RITUAL TIME   MINDFUL MINUTES

_____5_____
_____10_____
_____15_____
_____20_____
_____25_____
_____30_____

SCRIPTING

3-6-9 MANIFESTATION

_____ _____ _____

_____ _____ _____

_____ _____ _____

1 THING I DID TO MOVE FORWARD

_____

_____

The Moon is in: _____

The Day Ruler is: _____

I AM GRATEFUL FOR

_____

_____

MOOD TRACKER

SELF - CARE

DAILY AFFIRMATION

_____

_____

DREAM JOURNAL

_____

_____

_____

_____

_____

_____

_____

_____

_____

_____5_____
_____10_____
_____15_____
_____20_____
_____25_____
_____30_____

SCRIPTING

3-6-9 MANIFESTATION

_____ _____ _____

_____ _____ _____

_____ _____ _____

1 THING I DID TO MOVE FORWARD

_____

_____

The Moon is in: _____

The Day Ruler is: _____

I AM GRATEFUL FOR

_____

_____

MOOD TRACKER

SELF - CARE

DAILY AFFIRMATION

_____

_____

DREAM JOURNAL

_____

_____

_____

_____

_____

_____

_____

_____

RITUAL TIME   MINDFUL MINUTES

_____5_____
_____10_____
_____15_____
_____20_____
_____25_____
_____30_____

SCRIPTING

3-6-9 MANIFESTATION

_____ _____ _____

_____ _____ _____

_____ _____ _____

1 THING I DID TO MOVE FORWARD

_____

_____

The Moon is in: _____

The Day Ruler is: _____

I AM GRATEFUL FOR

_____

_____

MOOD TRACKER

SELF - CARE

DAILY AFFIRMATION

_____

_____

DREAM JOURNAL

_____

_____

_____

_____

_____

_____

_____

_____

_____

_____

_____5_____
_____10_____
_____15_____
_____20_____
_____25_____
_____30_____

SCRIPTING

3-6-9 MANIFESTATION

_____ _____ _____

_____ _____ _____

_____ _____ _____

1 THING I DID TO MOVE FORWARD

_____

_____

The Moon is in: _____

The Day Ruler is: _____

I AM GRATEFUL FOR

_____

_____

MOOD TRACKER

SELF - CARE

DAILY AFFIRMATION

_____

_____

DREAM JOURNAL

_____

_____

_____

_____

_____

_____

_____

_____

_____

RITUAL TIME

MINDFUL MINUTES

```
___5___
___10___
___15___
___20___
___25___
___30___
```

SCRIPTING

3-6-9 MANIFESTATION

_____ _____ _____

_____ _____ _____

_____ _____ _____

1 THING I DID TO MOVE FORWARD

_____

_____

The Moon is in: _____

The Day Ruler is: _____

I AM GRATEFUL FOR

_____
_____

MOOD TRACKER

SELF - CARE

DAILY AFFIRMATION

_____
_____

DREAM JOURNAL

_____
_____
_____
_____
_____
_____
_____
_____
_____

_____5_____
_____10_____
_____15_____
_____20_____
_____25_____
_____30_____

SCRIPTING

3-6-9 MANIFESTATION

_____ _____ _____
_____ _____ _____

1 THING I DID TO MOVE FORWARD

_____
_____

The Moon is in: _____

The Day Ruler is: _____

I AM GRATEFUL FOR

_____

_____

MOOD TRACKER

SELF - CARE

DAILY AFFIRMATION

_____

_____

DREAM JOURNAL

_____

_____

_____

_____

_____

_____

_____

_____

_____

RITUAL TIME   MINDFUL MINUTES

_____ 5 _____
_____ 10 _____
_____ 15 _____
_____ 20 _____
_____ 25 _____
_____ 30 _____

SCRIPTING

3-6-9 MANIFESTATION

_____ _____ _____

_____ _____ _____

_____ _____ _____

1 THING I DID TO MOVE FORWARD

_____

_____

The Moon is in: _____

The Day Ruler is: _____

I AM GRATEFUL FOR

_____

_____

MOOD TRACKER

SELF - CARE

DAILY AFFIRMATION

_____

_____

DREAM JOURNAL

_____

_____

_____

_____

_____

_____

_____

_____

_____

_____ 5 _____
_____ 10 _____
_____ 15 _____
_____ 20 _____
_____ 25 _____
_____ 30 _____

SCRIPTING

3-6-9 MANIFESTATION

_____ _____ _____

_____ _____ _____

_____ _____ _____

1 THING I DID TO MOVE FORWARD

_____

_____

THIS LUNATION

Full Moon ☐   ☐ New Moon

The Moon is in the sign of _____ and transits my _____ house,

meaning _____

_____ for me.

Build your Moon ritual: _____

_____

_____

_____

_____

_____

_____

CANDLES	CRYSTALS
HERBS	OTHER

Card 1	Card 2	Card 3
___ Deck	___ Deck	___ Deck
___ Card	___ Card	___ Card

Interpretation & Meaning: _____

_____

_____

_____

_____

_____

Intentions for this lunation: _____

_____

_____

_____

_____

_____

_____

The Moon is in: _____

The Day Ruler is: _____

I AM GRATEFUL FOR

_____

_____

MOOD TRACKER

SELF - CARE

DAILY AFFIRMATION

_____

_____

DREAM JOURNAL

_____

_____

_____

_____

_____

_____

_____

_____

_____

_____5_____
_____10_____
_____15_____
_____20_____
_____25_____
_____30_____

SCRIPTING

3-6-9 MANIFESTATION

_____ _____ _____

_____ _____ _____

_____ _____ _____

1 THING I DID TO MOVE FORWARD

_____

_____

The Moon is in: _____

The Day Ruler is: _____

I AM GRATEFUL FOR

_____

_____

MOOD TRACKER

SELF - CARE

DAILY AFFIRMATION

_____

_____

DREAM JOURNAL

_____

_____

_____

_____

_____

_____

_____

_____

RITUAL TIME   MINDFUL MINUTES

_____5_____
_____10_____
_____15_____
_____20_____
_____25_____
_____30_____

SCRIPTING

3-6-9 MANIFESTATION

_____ _____ _____

_____ _____ _____

_____ _____ _____

1 THING I DID TO MOVE FORWARD

_____

_____

The Moon is in: _____

The Day Ruler is: _____

I AM GRATEFUL FOR

_____

_____

MOOD TRACKER

SELF - CARE

DAILY AFFIRMATION

_____

_____

DREAM JOURNAL

_____

_____

_____

_____

_____

_____

_____

_____

_____

_____

_____ 5 _____
_____ 10 _____
_____ 15 _____
_____ 20 _____
_____ 25 _____
_____ 30 _____

SCRIPTING

3-6-9 MANIFESTATION

_____ _____ _____

_____ _____ _____

_____ _____ _____

1 THING I DID TO MOVE FORWARD

_____

_____

DECEMBER

SUNDAY	MONDAY	TUESDAY	WEDNESDAY
3	4 ◑	5	6
10	11	12 ●	13
17	18	19 ◐	20
24 Christmas Eve	25 Christmas Day	26 ○	27
31 New Year's Eve			

2023

THURSDAY	FRIDAY	SATURDAY	NOTES
	1	2	
7	8	9	
14	15	16	
21	22	23	
28 Yule	29	30	

COLD MOON

RITUAL FOCUS:
The cold moon is a time for connecting with the need for reflection, development, change; focus on peace, growth, and reawakening.

ZODIACS:
Sagittarius & Capricorn

CRYSTALS:
Serpentine, Lapis Lazuli & Garnet

COLORS:
White, Black, Silver & Green

ELEMENTS:
Fire & Water

DEITIES:
Juno, Hera, Isis, Neith, Green Man & Cerridwen

FLOWERS:
Mistletoe, Juniper & Daffodil

ANIMALS:
Wolves, Foxes, Coyotes, Blue Jay, Pheasants

HERBS:
Holly, English Ivy, Fir, Cedar, Sage & Narcissus

MAGICAL ASSOCIATIONS:
Transitions, Long-term Projects, Ancestral Work & Inner Renewal

DIVINATION TRACKER

DATE	PULL	MESSAGE

December 2023 Tropical Midnight Ephemeris

Time Zone: **EST (05:00 East)**

Day	☉	☽	+12 Hr	True☊	☿	♀	♂	♃	♄	♅	♆	♇
01 Fr	08 ♐ 43 20	24 ♋ 20 33	00 ♌ 30 32	23 ♈ 53 ℞	29 ♐ 32 D	25 ♎ 49 D	04 ♐ 51 D	07 ♉ 05 ℞	01 ♓ 08 D	20 ♉ 21 ℞	24 ♓ 54 ℞	28 ♑ 31 D
02 Sa	09 44 08	06 ♌ 36 52	12 39 56	23 46	00 ♑ 42	26 59	05 34	06 59	01 11	20 19	24 54	28 32
03 Su	10 44 57	18 40 14	24 38 14	23 42	01 50	28 09	06 17	06 54	01 14	20 17	24 53	28 33
04 Mo	11 45 48	00 ♍ 34 33	06 ♍ 29 47	23 39	02 55	29 19	07 00	06 48	01 17	20 14	24 53	28 35
05 Tu	12 46 40	12 24 33	18 19 31	23 38	03 56	00 ♏ 30	07 43	06 43	01 20	20 12	24 53	28 36
06 We	13 47 33	24 15 21	00 ♎ 12 43	23 39 D	04 53	01 40	08 26	06 38	01 23	20 10	24 53	28 38
07 Th	14 48 28	06 ♎ 12 17	12 14 40	23 40	05 44	02 51	09 10	06 33	01 26	20 08	24 53 D	28 39
08 Fr	15 49 23	18 20 30	24 30 19	23 41	06 30	04 02	09 53	06 29	01 30	20 05	24 53	28 41
09 Sa	16 50 20	00 ♏ 44 38	07 ♏ 03 53	23 41 ℞	07 10	05 13	10 36	06 24	01 33	20 03	24 53	28 42
10 Su	17 51 19	13 28 23	19 58 25	23 39	07 43	06 24	11 20	06 20	01 37	20 01	24 54	28 44
11 Mo	18 52 18	26 34 04	03 ♐ 15 20	23 34	08 07	07 36	12 03	06 16	01 40	19 59	24 54	28 45
12 Tu	19 53 19	10 ♐ 02 07	16 54 08	23 27	08 23	08 47	12 47	06 12	01 44	19 57	24 54	28 47
13 We	20 54 20	23 50 58	00 ♑ 52 08	23 18	08 29	09 58	13 31	06 08	01 48	19 55	24 54	28 49
14 Th	21 55 22	07 ♑ 56 59	15 04 50	23 08	08 25 ℞	11 10	14 14	06 04	01 52	19 53	24 54	28 50
15 Fr	22 56 25	22 14 56	29 26 32	22 58	08 09	12 22	14 58	06 01	01 56	19 51	24 55	28 52
16 Sa	23 57 29	06 ♒ 38 53	13 ♒ 51 16	22 49	07 42	13 33	15 42	05 58	02 00	19 49	24 55	28 53
17 Su	24 58 32	21 03 03	28 13 42	22 42	07 04	14 45	16 25	05 55	02 04	19 47	24 55	28 55
18 Mo	25 59 37	05 ♓ 22 46	12 ♓ 29 54	22 38	06 14	15 57	17 09	05 52	02 08	19 45	24 56	28 57
19 Tu	27 00 41	19 34 51	26 37 28	22 36	05 13	17 09	17 53	05 50	02 13	19 43	24 56	28 59
20 We	28 01 46	03 ♈ 37 39	10 ♈ 35 23	22 36 D	04 04	18 21	18 37	05 47	02 17	19 41	24 57	29 00
21 Th	29 02 51	17 30 40	24 23 31	22 37	02 48	19 33	19 21	05 45	02 21	19 40	24 57	29 02
22 Fr	00 ♑ 03 56	01 ♉ 13 59	08 ♉ 02 05	22 36 ℞	01 27	20 46	20 05	05 43	02 26	19 38	24 58	29 04
23 Sa	01 05 02	14 47 50	21 31 11	22 34	00 04	21 58	20 49	05 41	02 31	19 36	24 58	29 05
24 Su	02 06 08	28 12 06	04 ♊ 50 29	22 30	28 ♐ 43	23 10	21 33	05 40	02 35	19 35	24 59	29 07
25 Mo	03 07 14	11 ♊ 26 14	17 59 12	22 22	27 24	24 23	22 17	05 38	02 40	19 33	24 59	29 09
26 Tu	04 08 20	24 29 15	00 ♋ 56 14	22 11	26 12	25 35	23 02	05 37	02 45	19 31	25 00	29 11
27 We	05 09 27	07 ♋ 20 03	13 40 36	21 59	25 08	26 48	23 46	05 36	02 50	19 30	25 01	29 13
28 Th	06 10 34	19 57 48	26 11 39	21 45	24 12	28 01	24 30	05 36	02 55	19 28	25 01	29 14
29 Fr	07 11 41	02 ♌ 22 13	08 ♌ 29 37	21 32	23 27	29 13	25 14	05 35	03 00	19 27	25 02	29 16
30 Sa	08 12 49	14 34 00	20 35 38	21 20	22 53	00 ♐ 26	25 59	05 35	03 05	19 25	25 03	29 18
31 Su	09 13 57	26 34 51	02 ♍ 32 02	21 10	22 29	01 39	26 43	05 35 D	03 10	19 24	25 04	29 20

Planetary Data

Ingresses

		Day	Time
☿	♑	1	9:31 AM
♀	♏	4	1:50 PM
☉	♑	21	10:27 PM
☿	♐	23	1:17 AM
♀	♐	29	3:23 PM

Stations

	Day	Time
♆ D	6	8:22 AM
☿ ℞	13	2:09 AM
♃ D	30	9:40 PM

Lunar Ingresses & Void Moons

Ingresses

	Day	Time
♋	29	1:53 AM
♌	1	11:00 AM
♍	3	10:51 PM
♎	6	11:35 AM
♏	8	10:35 PM
♐	11	6:10 AM
♑	13	10:31 AM
♒	15	12:55 PM
♓	17	2:58 PM
♈	19	5:47 PM
♉	21	9:50 PM
♊	24	3:15 AM
♋	26	10:16 AM
♌	28	7:23 PM
♍	31	6:54 AM

Void Times

Day	Time	Last Aspect	
1	8:07 AM	☍	♇
3	9:12 PM	⚹	♀
6	8:51 AM	△	♇
8	8:06 PM	□	♇
11	3:57 AM	⚹	♇
13	1:49 AM	□	♆
15	11:04 AM	☌	♇
17	7:03 AM	⚹	☉
19	4:04 PM	⚹	♇
21	9:47 PM	△	☉
24	1:39 AM	△	♇
26	2:56 AM	☍	☿
28	5:58 PM	☍	♇
31	12:19 AM	△	♂

Phases & Eclipses

Lunar Phases

Day	Time		
5	12:50 AM	☽	12♍49
12	6:32 PM	●	20♐40
19	1:40 PM	☽	27♓35
26	7:34 PM	○	04♋58

Solar Eclipses

Day Time

~ None ~

Lunar Eclipses

Day Time

~ None ~

NOTES

The Moon is in: _____

The Day Ruler is: _____

I AM GRATEFUL FOR

_____

_____

MOOD TRACKER

SELF - CARE

DAILY AFFIRMATION

_____

_____

DREAM JOURNAL

_____

_____

_____

_____

_____

_____

_____

_____

RITUAL TIME   MINDFUL MINUTES

_____5_____
_____10_____
_____15_____
_____20_____
_____25_____
_____30_____

SCRIPTING

3-6-9 MANIFESTATION

_____ _____ _____

_____ _____ _____

_____ _____ _____

1 THING I DID TO MOVE FORWARD

_____

_____

The Moon is in: _____

The Day Ruler is: _____

I AM GRATEFUL FOR

_____

_____

MOOD TRACKER

SELF - CARE

DAILY AFFIRMATION

_____

_____

DREAM JOURNAL

_____

_____

_____

_____

_____

_____

_____

_____

_____

_____

_____ 5 _____
_____ 10 _____
_____ 15 _____
_____ 20 _____
_____ 25 _____
_____ 30 _____

SCRIPTING

3-6-9 MANIFESTATION

_____   _____   _____

_____   _____   _____

_____   _____   _____

1 THING I DID TO MOVE FORWARD

_____

_____

The Moon is in: _____

The Day Ruler is: _____

I AM GRATEFUL FOR

_____

_____

MOOD TRACKER

😠 😟 😐 🙂 😄

SELF - CARE

DAILY AFFIRMATION

_____

_____

DREAM JOURNAL

_____

_____

_____

_____

_____

_____

_____

_____

_____

RITUAL TIME   MINDFUL MINUTES

___5___
___10___
___15___
___20___
___25___
___30___

SCRIPTING

_____

_____

_____

_____

_____

_____

_____

_____

_____

_____

_____

_____

_____

_____

_____

_____

_____

_____

_____

3-6-9 MANIFESTATION

_____ _____ _____

_____ _____ _____

_____ _____ _____

1 THING I DID TO MOVE FORWARD

_____

_____

The Moon is in: _____
The Day Ruler is: _____

I AM GRATEFUL FOR
_____
_____

MOOD TRACKER

SELF - CARE

DAILY AFFIRMATION
_____
_____

DREAM JOURNAL
_____
_____
_____
_____
_____
_____
_____
_____
_____

5
10
15
20
25
30

SCRIPTING

3-6-9 MANIFESTATION
_____ _____ _____
_____ _____ _____

1 THING I DID TO MOVE FORWARD
_____
_____

The Moon is in: _____

The Day Ruler is: _____

I AM GRATEFUL FOR

_____

_____

MOOD TRACKER

SELF - CARE

DAILY AFFIRMATION

_____

_____

DREAM JOURNAL

_____

_____

_____

_____

_____

_____

_____

_____

RITUAL TIME   MINDFUL MINUTES

5
10
15
20
25
30

SCRIPTING

3-6-9 MANIFESTATION

_____ _____ _____

_____ _____ _____

_____ _____ _____

1 THING I DID TO MOVE FORWARD

_____

_____

The Moon is in: _____

The Day Ruler is: _____

I AM GRATEFUL FOR

_____

_____

MOOD TRACKER

SELF - CARE

DAILY AFFIRMATION

_____

_____

DREAM JOURNAL

_____

_____

_____

_____

_____

_____

_____

_____

_____

_____

_____ 5 _____
_____ 10 _____
_____ 15 _____
_____ 20 _____
_____ 25 _____
_____ 30 _____

SCRIPTING

3-6-9 MANIFESTATION

_____ _____ _____

_____ _____ _____

_____ _____ _____

1 THING I DID TO MOVE FORWARD

_____

_____

The Moon is in:_____

The Day Ruler is:_____

I AM GRATEFUL FOR

_____

_____

MOOD TRACKER

😠 😟 😐 🙂 😀

SELF - CARE

DAILY AFFIRMATION

_____

_____

DREAM JOURNAL

_____

_____

_____

_____

_____

_____

_____

_____

_____

_____

RITUAL TIME   MINDFUL MINUTES

___5___
___10___
___15___
___20___
___25___
___30___

SCRIPTING

3-6-9 MANIFESTATION

_____ _____ _____
_____ _____ _____
_____ _____ _____

1 THING I DID TO MOVE FORWARD

_____

_____

The Moon is in: _____

The Day Ruler is: _____

I AM GRATEFUL FOR

_____

_____

MOOD TRACKER

😠 😦 😐 🙂 😄

SELF - CARE

DAILY AFFIRMATION

_____

_____

DREAM JOURNAL

_____

_____

_____

_____

_____

_____

_____

_____

_____

_____

_____ 5 _____
_____ 10 _____
_____ 15 _____
_____ 20 _____
_____ 25 _____
_____ 30 _____

SCRIPTING

3-6-9 MANIFESTATION

_____ _____ _____

_____ _____ _____

_____ _____ _____

1 THING I DID TO MOVE FORWARD

_____

_____

The Moon is in: _____

The Day Ruler is: _____

I AM GRATEFUL FOR

_____

_____

MOOD TRACKER

SELF - CARE

DAILY AFFIRMATION

_____

_____

DREAM JOURNAL

_____

_____

_____

_____

_____

_____

_____

_____

_____

RITUAL TIME   MINDFUL MINUTES

5
10
15
20
25
30

SCRIPTING

3-6-9 MANIFESTATION

_____ _____ _____

_____ _____ _____

_____ _____ _____

1 THING I DID TO MOVE FORWARD

_____

_____

The Moon is in: _____

The Day Ruler is: _____

I AM GRATEFUL FOR

_____

_____

MOOD TRACKER

SELF - CARE

DAILY AFFIRMATION

_____

_____

DREAM JOURNAL

_____

_____

_____

_____

_____

_____

_____

_____

_____

_____

_____5_____
_____10_____
_____15_____
_____20_____
_____25_____
_____30_____

SCRIPTING

3-6-9 MANIFESTATION

_____ _____ _____

_____ _____ _____

_____ _____ _____

1 THING I DID TO MOVE FORWARD

_____

_____

The Moon is in: _____

The Day Ruler is: _____

I AM GRATEFUL FOR

_____

_____

MOOD TRACKER

😠 😦 😐 🙂 😀

SELF - CARE

DAILY AFFIRMATION

_____

_____

DREAM JOURNAL

_____

_____

_____

_____

_____

_____

_____

_____

RITUAL TIME   MINDFUL MINUTES

___5___
___10___
___15___
___20___
___25___
___30___

SCRIPTING

3-6-9 MANIFESTATION

_____ _____ _____

_____ _____ _____

_____ _____ _____

1 THING I DID TO MOVE FORWARD

_____

_____

The Moon is in: _____

The Day Ruler is: _____

I AM GRATEFUL FOR

_____

_____

MOOD TRACKER

SELF - CARE

DAILY AFFIRMATION

_____

_____

DREAM JOURNAL

_____

_____

_____

_____

_____

_____

_____

_____

_____

_____ 5 _____
_____ 10 _____
_____ 15 _____
_____ 20 _____
_____ 25 _____
_____ 30 _____

SCRIPTING

3-6-9 MANIFESTATION

_____ _____ _____

_____ _____ _____

_____ _____ _____

1 THING I DID TO MOVE FORWARD

_____

_____

THIS LUNATION

Full Moon ☐   ☐ New Moon

The Moon is in the sign of _____ and transits my _____ house,

meaning _____

_____ for me.

Build your Moon ritual: _____

_____

_____

_____

_____

_____

_____

CANDLES	CRYSTALS
HERBS	OTHER

Card 1	Card 2	Card 3
_____ Deck	_____ Deck	_____ Deck
_____ Card	_____ Card	_____ Card

Interpretation & Meaning: _____

_____

_____

_____

_____

_____

Intentions for this lunation: _____

_____

_____

_____

_____

_____

_____

The Moon is in: _____

The Day Ruler is: _____

I AM GRATEFUL FOR

_____

_____

MOOD TRACKER

SELF - CARE

DAILY AFFIRMATION

_____

_____

DREAM JOURNAL

_____

_____

_____

_____

_____

_____

_____

_____

_____

_____5_____
_____10_____
_____15_____
_____20_____
_____25_____
_____30_____

SCRIPTING

3-6-9 MANIFESTATION

_____ _____ _____

_____ _____ _____

_____ _____ _____

1 THING I DID TO MOVE FORWARD

_____

_____

The Moon is in: _____

The Day Ruler is: _____

I AM GRATEFUL FOR

_____

_____

MOOD TRACKER

SELF - CARE

DAILY AFFIRMATION

_____

_____

DREAM JOURNAL

_____

_____

_____

_____

_____

_____

_____

_____

_____

RITUAL TIME   MINDFUL MINUTES

_____ 5 _____
_____ 10 _____
_____ 15 _____
_____ 20 _____
_____ 25 _____
_____ 30 _____

SCRIPTING

3-6-9 MANIFESTATION

_____ _____ _____

_____ _____ _____

1 THING I DID TO MOVE FORWARD

_____

_____

The Moon is in: _____
The Day Ruler is: _____

I AM GRATEFUL FOR

_____
_____

MOOD TRACKER

SELF - CARE

DAILY AFFIRMATION

_____
_____

DREAM JOURNAL

_____
_____
_____
_____
_____
_____
_____
_____

_____ 5 _____
_____ 10 _____
_____ 15 _____
_____ 20 _____
_____ 25 _____
_____ 30 _____

SCRIPTING

3-6-9 MANIFESTATION

_____ _____ _____
_____ _____ _____
_____ _____ _____

1 THING I DID TO MOVE FORWARD

_____
_____

The Moon is in:_____

The Day Ruler is:_____

I AM GRATEFUL FOR

_____
_____

MOOD TRACKER

SELF - CARE

DAILY AFFIRMATION

_____
_____

DREAM JOURNAL

_____
_____
_____
_____
_____
_____
_____
_____
_____

RITUAL TIME   MINDFUL MINUTES

5
10
15
20
25
30

SCRIPTING

3-6-9 MANIFESTATION

_____ _____ _____
_____ _____ _____
_____ _____ _____

1 THING I DID TO MOVE FORWARD

_____
_____

The Moon is in: _____

The Day Ruler is: _____

I AM GRATEFUL FOR

_____

_____

MOOD TRACKER

SELF - CARE

DAILY AFFIRMATION

_____

_____

DREAM JOURNAL

_____

_____

_____

_____

_____

_____

_____

_____

_____

_____5_____
_____10_____
_____15_____
_____20_____
_____25_____
_____30_____

SCRIPTING

3-6-9 MANIFESTATION

_____ _____ _____

_____ _____ _____

1 THING I DID TO MOVE FORWARD

_____

_____

The Moon is in: _____

The Day Ruler is: _____

I AM GRATEFUL FOR

_____

_____

MOOD TRACKER

SELF - CARE

DAILY AFFIRMATION

_____

_____

DREAM JOURNAL

_____

_____

_____

_____

_____

_____

_____

_____

_____

RITUAL TIME   MINDFUL MINUTES

5
10
15
20
25
30

SCRIPTING

3-6-9 MANIFESTATION

_____ _____ _____

_____ _____ _____

_____ _____

1 THING I DID TO MOVE FORWARD

_____

_____

The Moon is in: _____

The Day Ruler is: _____

I AM GRATEFUL FOR

_____

_____

MOOD TRACKER

SELF - CARE

DAILY AFFIRMATION

_____

_____

DREAM JOURNAL

_____

_____

_____

_____

_____

_____

_____

_____

_____

_____ 5 _____
_____ 10 _____
_____ 15 _____
_____ 20 _____
_____ 25 _____
_____ 30 _____

SCRIPTING

3-6-9 MANIFESTATION

_____ _____ _____

_____ _____ _____

_____ _____ _____

1 THING I DID TO MOVE FORWARD

_____

_____

The Moon is in: _____

The Day Ruler is: _____

I AM GRATEFUL FOR

_____

_____

MOOD TRACKER

SELF - CARE

DAILY AFFIRMATION

_____

_____

DREAM JOURNAL

_____

_____

_____

_____

_____

_____

_____

_____

_____

_____

RITUAL TIME   MINDFUL MINUTES

_____5_____
_____10_____
_____15_____
_____20_____
_____25_____
_____30_____

SCRIPTING

3-6-9 MANIFESTATION

_____ _____ _____

_____ _____ _____

1 THING I DID TO MOVE FORWARD

_____

_____

DAILY

The Moon is in: _____

The Day Ruler is: _____

I AM GRATEFUL FOR

_____

_____

MOOD TRACKER

SELF - CARE

DAILY AFFIRMATION

_____

_____

DREAM JOURNAL

_____

_____

_____

_____

_____

_____

_____

_____

_____

_____5_____
_____10_____
_____15_____
_____20_____
_____25_____
_____30_____

SCRIPTING

3-6-9 MANIFESTATION

_____ _____ _____

_____ _____ _____

1 THING I DID TO MOVE FORWARD

_____

_____

The Moon is in: _____

The Day Ruler is: _____

I AM GRATEFUL FOR

_____

_____

MOOD TRACKER

SELF - CARE

DAILY AFFIRMATION

_____

_____

DREAM JOURNAL

_____

_____

_____

_____

_____

_____

_____

_____

_____

_____

RITUAL TIME   MINDFUL MINUTES

_____5_____
_____10_____
_____15_____
_____20_____
_____25_____
_____30_____

SCRIPTING

3-6-9 MANIFESTATION

_____ _____ _____

_____ _____ _____

1 THING I DID TO MOVE FORWARD

_____

_____

The Moon is in: _____

The Day Ruler is: _____

I AM GRATEFUL FOR

_____

_____

MOOD TRACKER

SELF - CARE

DAILY AFFIRMATION

_____

_____

DREAM JOURNAL

_____

_____

_____

_____

_____

_____

_____

_____

_____

_____5_____
_____10_____
_____15_____
_____20_____
_____25_____
_____30_____

SCRIPTING

3-6-9 MANIFESTATION

_____ _____ _____

_____ _____ _____

_____ _____ _____

1 THING I DID TO MOVE FORWARD

_____

_____

The Moon is in:_____

The Day Ruler is:_____

I AM GRATEFUL FOR

_____
_____

MOOD TRACKER

SELF - CARE

DAILY AFFIRMATION

_____
_____

DREAM JOURNAL

_____
_____
_____
_____
_____
_____
_____
_____
_____
_____

RITUAL TIME   MINDFUL MINUTES

_____5_____
_____10_____
_____15_____
_____20_____
_____25_____
_____30_____

SCRIPTING

3-6-9 MANIFESTATION

_____ _____ _____
_____ _____ _____
_____ _____ _____

1 THING I DID TO MOVE FORWARD

_____
_____

The Moon is in: _____

The Day Ruler is: _____

I AM GRATEFUL FOR

_____

_____

MOOD TRACKER

☹️ 🙁 😐 🙂 😃

SELF - CARE

DAILY AFFIRMATION

_____

_____

DREAM JOURNAL

_____

_____

_____

_____

_____

_____

_____

_____

_____

_____ 5 _____
_____ 10 _____
_____ 15 _____
_____ 20 _____
_____ 25 _____
_____ 30 _____

SCRIPTING

3-6-9 MANIFESTATION

_____ _____ _____

_____ _____ _____

_____ _____ _____

1 THING I DID TO MOVE FORWARD

_____

_____

491

The Moon is in: _____

The Day Ruler is: _____

I AM GRATEFUL FOR

_____

_____

MOOD TRACKER

SELF - CARE

DAILY AFFIRMATION

_____

_____

DREAM JOURNAL

_____

_____

_____

_____

_____

_____

_____

_____

_____

RITUAL TIME   MINDFUL MINUTES

_____ 5 _____
_____ 10 _____
_____ 15 _____
_____ 20 _____
_____ 25 _____
_____ 30 _____

SCRIPTING

3-6-9 MANIFESTATION

_____ _____ _____

_____ _____ _____

_____ _____ _____

1 THING I DID TO MOVE FORWARD

_____

_____

THIS LUNATION

Full Moon ☐   ☐ New Moon

The Moon is in the sign of _____ and transits my _____ house,

meaning _____

_____ for me.

Build your Moon ritual: _____

_____

_____

_____

_____

_____

_____

_____

CANDLES	CRYSTALS
HERBS	OTHER

Card 1	Card 2	Card 3
_____ Deck	_____ Deck	_____ Deck
_____ Card	_____ Card	_____ Card

Interpretation & Meaning: _____

_____

_____

_____

_____

_____

Intentions for this lunation: _____

_____

_____

_____

_____

_____

_____

The Moon is in:_____

The Day Ruler is:_____

I AM GRATEFUL FOR

_____

_____

MOOD TRACKER

SELF - CARE

DAILY AFFIRMATION

_____

_____

DREAM JOURNAL

_____

_____

_____

_____

_____

_____

_____

_____

_____

RITUAL TIME   MINDFUL MINUTES

_____5_____
_____10_____
_____15_____
_____20_____
_____25_____
_____30_____

SCRIPTING

3-6-9 MANIFESTATION

_____ _____ _____

_____ _____ _____

_____ _____ _____

1 THING I DID TO MOVE FORWARD

_____

_____

The Moon is in: _____

The Day Ruler is: _____

I AM GRATEFUL FOR

_____

_____

MOOD TRACKER

SELF - CARE

DAILY AFFIRMATION

_____

_____

DREAM JOURNAL

_____

_____

_____

_____

_____

_____

_____

_____

_____

_____

_____

5

10

15

20

25

30

SCRIPTING

3-6-9 MANIFESTATION

_____ _____ _____

_____ _____ _____

_____ _____ _____

1 THING I DID TO MOVE FORWARD

_____

_____

The Moon is in: _____

The Day Ruler is: _____

I AM GRATEFUL FOR

_____

_____

MOOD TRACKER

SELF - CARE

DAILY AFFIRMATION

_____

_____

DREAM JOURNAL

_____

_____

_____

_____

_____

_____

_____

_____

_____

RITUAL TIME   MINDFUL MINUTES

_____5_____
_____10_____
_____15_____
_____20_____
_____25_____
_____30_____

SCRIPTING

3-6-9 MANIFESTATION

_____ _____ _____

_____ _____ _____

1 THING I DID TO MOVE FORWARD

_____

_____

The Moon is in: _____

The Day Ruler is: _____

I AM GRATEFUL FOR

_____

_____

MOOD TRACKER

SELF - CARE

DAILY AFFIRMATION

_____

_____

DREAM JOURNAL

_____

_____

_____

_____

_____

_____

_____

_____

_____

_____5_____
_____10_____
_____15_____
_____20_____
_____25_____
_____30_____

SCRIPTING

_____

_____

_____

_____

_____

_____

_____

_____

_____

_____

_____

_____

_____

_____

_____

_____

_____

_____

3-6-9 MANIFESTATION

_____ _____ _____

_____ _____ _____

_____ _____ _____

1 THING I DID TO MOVE FORWARD

_____

_____

The Moon is in:_____

The Day Ruler is:_____

I AM GRATEFUL FOR

_____

_____

MOOD TRACKER

SELF - CARE

DAILY AFFIRMATION

_____

_____

DREAM JOURNAL

_____

_____

_____

_____

_____

_____

_____

_____

_____

RITUAL TIME   MINDFUL MINUTES

_____5_____
_____10_____
_____15_____
_____20_____
_____25_____
_____30_____

SCRIPTING

3-6-9 MANIFESTATION

_____ _____ _____

_____ _____ _____

_____ _____ _____

1 THING I DID TO MOVE FORWARD

_____

_____

NOTES

NOTES

CPSIA information can be obtained
at www.ICGtesting.com
Printed in the USA
JSHW031822220922
30721JS00003B/3

9 798765 230329